Images and Shadows
Part of a Life

Iris Origo's childhood was divided between three different worlds: that of her American grandparents, the Bayard Cuttings, in one of the massive brownstone houses of old New York or at Westbrook, their Long Island estate; that of her Anglo-Irish grandparents, Lord and Lady Desart, in their more relaxed environment in County Kerry; and that of her mother's villa in Fiesole, the Villa Medici, to which gravitated the cosmopolitan, intellectual society of Florence.

Leading the life of an only child, cared for by nurses and governesses, she turned to books for companionship and discovered the joys of learning which became an important part of her life.

Her marriage to Antonio Origo in 1924 brought the deliberate choice of an entirely different life, in the setting of their farm at La Foce, in Tuscany. There she shared her husband's responsibilities in bringing back prosperity to the barren land and the impoverished people of the Val d'Orcia. When the war came she worked for the Italian Red Cross and then turned her attention to sheltering refugee children, feeding Italian partisans and hiding and guiding Allied prisoners-of-war during the German occupation.

This delightful and evocative memoir was originally published in 1970 to enthusiastic acclaim and has given pleasure to all those who have read it ever since.

Iris Origo was the author of many books including *The Last Attachment*, *War in Val d'Orcia* and *The Merchant of Prato*.

Front cover photograph: Iris Origo in the 1930s
Back cover photograph: La Foce, The Castelluccio

Images and Shadows

Part of a Life

IRIS ORIGO

With a Foreword by Gian Giacomo Migone

JOHN MURRAY
Albemarle Street, London

TO ANTONIO

Contents

Illustrations

(*between pages 150 and 151*)

Westbrook
A pond in the grounds
Justine and Bayard Cutting at the South Side Club, 1888
My grandmother and Aunt Olivia in 'the electric'
Travel at the beginning of the century:
    The W. Bayard Cuttings in Switzerland, 1902
    In Pompeii, 1909
The Golden Wedding of my great-grandparents, Bronson Murray
    and Ann E. Peyton, celebrated at Westbrook on October 1, 1898.
    Olivia Cutting at the head of the table
Desart Court
Lord and Lady Desart, 1904
My father and myself in California, 1904
The *dahabeah* on the Nile near Assuan
My mother and myself, 1906
Lady Wenlock and her daughter, Irene, *c.* 1896
The Villa Medici
The *sala degli uccelli* in the Villa Medici
Antonio at the time of our engagement
Gianni and myself, 1930. *Photo: Marcus Adams*
La Foce: boulders in uncultivated land
Threshing
A ruined farmhouse at La Foce
A new farmhouse
La Foce: the house and garden. *Photo: Otso Pietinen*
La Foce: The Castelluccio. *Photo: Otso Pietinen*
La Foce from the valley. *Photo: Otso Pietinen*
In our library in Rome. *Photo: Bosio, Rome*
Antonio at La Foce
The Val d'Orcia and Monte Amiata. *Photo: Otso Pietinen*
La Foce: looking out from the chapel. *Photo: Otso Pietinen*

Foreword

by Gian Giacomo Migone

'If you wish to see a person you must not
start by seeing through him.'   IRIS ORIGO

'**W**ERE YOU MUCH afraid?' This was the question Iris
used to be asked most frequently by people who
had read *War in Val d'Orcia*. Her answer was,
'No, except for one single moment of panic. This is odd for
I have generally been quite easily frightened.'

Anyone who has 'eaten and drunk and lived in social
intercourse' with her – a necessary condition according to
Dr Johnson for describing a person's life – would not hesitate to ascribe to her among many virtues that of courage, in
all its forms. She did not baulk at ridding a Caribbean hotel
room of a tropical insect, repulsive to most people, or
braving roads full of German occupying troops, or compelling a group of Wall Street bankers to open their pocket-
books in order to allow Florentine artisans to return to their
shops after the great flood. One of the bankers observed to
me later: 'Your mother-in-law [for that is what Iris was for
me at the time] possesses real *Schrecklichkeit*'. I never
reported the compliment to her because I was afraid she
might not take it as such, but also because, at that time, it
seemed incongruous.

It was only after several years of very close association
and occasional periods of life together that I came to realize
how true this was. Let me be clear. Iris did not like conflicts
and never raised her voice. At most she would mumble a bit
and retreat slightly from her original position. She never
seemed to defend her territory to the utmost (and it was
vast, as were her passions, both public and private); even less
would she attack her opponent's.

vii

Resilience was her weapon, especially in disagreements with the opposite sex, whose weak points she knew well. A great friend of hers, the publisher Helen Wolff, once explained to me how she reduced her famous authors, most of them quite egocentric, to compliance: 'I just use the tone you men are used to: wash your hands before dinner, it's time you took a bath, cut the third chapter . . .' Iris belonged to the same school.

To give in or desist from her long-cherished projects was out of the question. As a woman of her generation, she knew when to hold her tongue without necessarily changing her mind. I think too that twenty years of fascism – when her position as a foreigner in her husband's 'fatherland' was delicate – forced her to keep a long and painful silence, though she never yielded an ounce of her firmly rooted convictions. Nor did she limit her choice of friends, especially the Italian ones (Gaetano Salvemini and Ignazio Silone, for instance, as she describes in her volume of essays, *A Need to Testify*), or her search for opportunities where she could act according to her beliefs.

It would indeed be ironical if Iris were to be remembered as a *grande dame* of letters – a definition that would have mortified her – or as an *insigne studiosa* (eminent scholar), as a famous Italian historian once called her, provoking her to giggles (one giggled a lot with Iris). Should I ever attempt an overall definition of her – and Iris as a biographer and scholar would probably have disapproved of such a thing – I would describe her as a woman of thought and action, continually striving to bring the two together. It was thus that she worked with Antonio, her husband, in the development of the Val d'Orcia, and in facing the perils of the war, which were possibly the happiest days of their life, as this book also suggests. She was always ready to accept any challenge: hiding partisans, helping Allied prisoners to escape, taking in refugee children or, later, in times of peace, children devastated by an orphanage, before either restoring them to their families or finding them new ones if necessary. She was always ready, too, to come to the rescue in a family crisis, real or imaginary, sometimes perhaps even more actively than was required.

Foreword

No reader of *Images and Shadows* will be unaware of the complex relationship between Iris and her mother. I have said that Iris knew how to keep silence. I must add that, in life as in her books, her silences or her reticence could be extraordinarily eloquent. One only needs to read the words, never hostile, that she dedicates to her mother, or the very few (and very beautiful) ones with which she describes Antonio and their son Gianni. The total silence which surrounds her two daughters Benedetta and Donata has a different origin. She once said to me: 'When *Images and Shadows* appears, I don't want to receive a telegram like the one another writer received from her daughter, after she had read her mother's autobiography: "Shame on you, Mother!"'

Iris was quite used to playing down her scholarly writing (work which was remarkably scholarly bearing in mind that she was never given the opportunity to go to Oxford University as she had wished): 'Antonio likes and is proud of my books, but only when they are published, not while I am writing them.' She would never put her work before a meeting with a daughter or grandchild, if possible *tête-à-tête*, or any 'real conversation' (her words), which she always preferred to social or in some way collective situations.

Iris did not lack either courage or tenacity, as I have mentioned, nor was she wanting in planning ability. Her difficulty lay rather in making odd ends meet, in reconciling the multiple aims that sprang from her public and private passions, and, if absolutely necessary, in choosing her priorities. In peace as in war, as she wrote in her diary, her problem 'arose from a continual necessity to weigh in the balance not courage and cowardice, or right and wrong, but conflicting duties and responsibilities equally urgent . . . At the end of each day prudence inquired, "Have I done too much?" and enthusiasm or compassion, "Might I not, perhaps, have done more?"'

Needless to say, both then and later, enthusiasm or compassion would always prevail over prudence. Thought and action; but impulse too, as I think Antonio would have added with a smile.

Gian Giacomo Migone

Behold! human beings living in an underground den which has a mouth open towards the light . . . here they, have been from their childhood, and have their legs and necks chained so that they cannot move, and can only see before them, being prevented by the chains from turning their heads. Above and behind them a fire is blazing at a distance, and between the fire and the prisoners there is a raised way; and you will see, if you look, a low wall built along the way, like the screen which marionette players have in front of them, over which they show the puppets.

I see.

And do you see, I said, men passing along the wall carrying all sorts of vessels, and statues and figures of animals made of wood and stone and various materials, which appear over the wall? . . .

You have shown me a strange image, and they are strange prisoners.

Like ourselves, I replied; and they see only their own shadows, or the shadows of one another, which the fire throws on the opposite wall of the cave.

True, he said . . .

To them, I said, the truth would be literally nothing but the shadows of the images . . .

And now look again, and see what will naturally follow, if the prisoners are released . . .

At first when any of them is liberated and compelled suddenly to stand up. . . . When he approaches the light his eyes will be dazzled . . . he will require to grow accustomed to the sight of the upper world. At first he will see shadows best, next the reflections of men and other objects in the water, and then the objects themselves; then he will gaze upon the light of the moon and the stars and the spangled heaven . . .

Last of all he will be able to see the sun.

PLATO: *The Republic*, VII, 3rd edn. (1888)
trs. Benjamin Jowett

Introduction

De temps à autre, on est soi, un instant.

PÈRE BOULOGNE

IT HAS SOMETIMES been pointed out to me that I have had a very varied and interesting life, have lived in some extremely beautiful places and have met some remarkable people. I suppose it is true, but now that I have reached 'the end game', I do not find myself dwelling upon these pieces on the board. The figures that still stand out there now are the people to whom, in different ways and in different degrees, I have been bound by affection. Not only are they the people whom I most vividly remember, but I realise that it is only through them that I have learned anything about life at all. The brilliant talk I heard at I Tatti in my youth, in Bloomsbury in the thirties, in New York and Rome in later years, has lost some of its glitter. I was tipped, as Desmond MacCarthy once remarked about Santayana's writings, 'with fairy gold'. All that is left to me of my past life that has not faded into mist has passed through the filter, not of my mind, but of my affections. What was not warmed by them is now for me as if it had never been.

One consequence of this is that—since the people who have touched my heart have belonged to different countries, as well as to very different backgrounds—I have been able to participate vicariously in some aspects of life beyond the field of my own personal experience: to catch a glimpse, as it were, of worlds seen through the peep-hole of someone else's stage. But equally many other worlds have remained closed to me. Because, for instance, I never happened to have in my youth an intimate friend in France or Germany—not even a French or German governess to whom I was particularly attached—I know no more about those countries than what has been told me by books or by my eyes. On the other hand my affection for the gentle, courageous woman who was my first Italian teacher, Signora Signorini, and later on, for the fiery genial *professore* with whom I first read Homer and Virgil, acquainted me once for all and from within with the life of the educated Tuscan *borghesia*—a world whose values, at the time of my childhood, were still those of De Amicis' *Cuore*. And equally it was my love for my grandfather, Lord Desart, which bestowed on me the flavour of life as it used to be in the Irish country-house in which I spent my summer holidays—a world of blue distances and infinite leisure and ease, flavoured with the scent of sweet peas and the crisp clear taste of red currants, in which the doors were always open to children, dogs, and neighbours, and I would jog on my pony with my grandfather from cottage to farm, or down the green rides in the beech woods, where one might see, in the early morning, a vixen and her cubs slinking away through the tall grass.

Why then am I writing this book at all, and what sort of book would I like it to be? Desmond MacCarthy once remarked, at Mr. Asquith's breakfast table, that there are only three motives for writing an autobiography: St. Augustine's, Casanova's or Rousseau's—"either because a man thinks he has found 'The Way', or to tell what a splendid time he has had, and enjoy it again by describing it, or to show—well, that he was a much better fellow than the world supposed." "I'm glad to hear you say that," said Mr. Asquith, who was cutting himself a slice of ham. "That is just what I am trying to do."

Few books, in point of fact, could less resemble Rousseau's *Confessions* than Asquith's *Memories and Reflections*, and this leads one to wonder whether anyone who sets down his reminiscences ends up by producing quite the book he had in mind. In my case, I must humbly disclaim all three motives. I have no wish (even if I had the matter) to convert, to reveal or to confess. I am only trying to set down a fragmentary account of what it has been like to live in three totally distinct periods of civilisation: first briefly, and partly through hearsay, in the pre-war world of 1914; then in the world between two wars; and finally in the present time, which is so rapidly taking on new shapes both intellectually and materially, that I have found myself unwillingly becoming, in some aspects at least, a spectator rather than a participator. This record will not try to be complete or even chronological; it is merely an attempt to describe certain past ways of living, and a few phases of my own life, taking as my starting point the various houses I have lived in: the country houses of my grand-parents both in the United States and Ireland, and the life which they led there long before I was born, and which later on I shared with them; then my mother's house in Fiesole, where I spent my childhood; and finally the Tuscan villa and farm, La Foce, which—after so many years in other people's houses and atmo-spheres—has been, for the forty-six years since my marriage, my own home.

During those years, there were also many aspects of my life not centred upon La Foce, which I have not dwelled on here. There were long periods spent by me in England or America, and a few vital personal relationships irrelevant to the course of this story; and there were also many long journeys with my husband—to Mexico and Yucatan, to Guatemala and the Carib-bean, to Egypt and Greece, to Southern India, Thailand and Angkor—all delightful and exciting to us, but, by the standards of present-day travel, which has left no South Sea island un-explored, no primitive tribe unphotographed, very small beer.

One advantage of all these changes of scene, or perhaps merely of my own temperament, is that I have never in my life found a day too long. "I am blessed," the much-loved Bostonian writer and editor, Mark Howe, was heard to mutter in his old age, "blessed and *bored*"—but this, as yet at least, I have never known. On the other hand, I have also never known the unquestioning security of background of my grandparents' generation, and this perhaps has also contributed, as for many others of my genera-tion, to the difficulty of holding to a stable faith. Too much has been put before us, too much! Too much destruction and change, too many trends in spiritual leadership, too many new fields of discovery and awareness.

Most of these experiences I share, of course, with many others, and I certainly do not think that the things that have happened to me are important, except to myself. But also I believe that *every* life, irrespective of its events and setting, holds something of unique value, which it should be possible to communicate, if only one can first see one's experiences honestly and then set them down without too much dressing-up. This is, I suppose, what is meant by the conventional remark about first novels, that all men have at least one book in them. I myself was never tempted to write that book in my youth, chiefly owing to a lack of self-confidence, and it may have been for a similar reason that, when I first began to write for publication, the field I chose was that of biography. It is safer to write about other people than about oneself, and easier (or so I then thought) to shape their lives into a harmonious, consistent pattern. It was only when I began to examine my subjects more closely that I realised that the process was somewhat more complex than I had thought, that it was nearly as difficult to set down the truth about other people as about oneself, and very tempting to rely upon the biographers and critics who had preceded one. It was only after a good many years that I began to wish, and dare, to speak for myself. I then became aware of how much in my earlier books—except for *War in Val d'Orcia* which was not originally written for publication—had been, not insincere, but second-hand. This book is an attempt, very late in the day, to do something different: to record a few of the things that have happened to myself and to speak, at the risk of speaking flatly, in my own voice: to speak, at last, my mind.

But not my whole mind—not even if I could. There are, of course, dangers familiar to every biographer, that arise as soon as one begins to select, difficulties of which I once spoke in a lecture entitled, *Biography—True and False*. I called them 'the seductive tricks of the trade . . . the smoothing-out and the touching-up. In the end a portrait is built up: slick, vivid, convincing—and false.' And even greater temptations confront the painter of a self-portrait. Not only is it difficult not to distort by framing a perspective or gilding a picture, but also to prevent self-awareness from turning into self-consciousness. Sir Herbert Read once rightly said in a review of Rilke's *Letters* that one is never sure that one is listening to 'the true voice', whereas no such doubt ever crosses one's mind, for instance, in reading those of Keats.

Nevertheless, selection is necessary. '*Le secret d'ennuyer est celui de tout dire.*' There are also considerations of reticence and taste, and most of all, a realisation that every human life is at once so complex and so simple, so perplexing and so clear, so superficial and so profound, that any attempt to present it as a unified, consistent whole, to enclose it within a rigid frame, inevitably tempts one to cheat or to falsify. 'I am always astounded to see',

4

wrote Pasternak in an unpublished letter, 'that what is laid down, ordered, factual, is never enough to embrace the whole truth, that life always brims over the rim of every vessel.' It is partly for this reason and also because no part of one's life is more complex, as well as more private, than one's family life and the emotions it arouses that I have written so little in this book about either my marriage or my children. Tolstoy's famous sentence is far too great a simplification: not only unhappy but happy families are serene or troubled not in one, but in innumerable different ways. I am always amazed when I hear people talking about other people's marriages: "This was *his* fault, that was *her* fault." How can they think they know? Have they never considered their own marriages and how much, in even the happiest unions, remains unknown to each of us about the other? We are all not islands but icebergs, more than half under water. What husbands and wives do know, after many years of living together, is surely not acquired through any process of the mind, but rather through a kind of symbiosis, a slow assimilation of one nature into another, so that, as in the tale of Philemon and Baucis, the branches of two plants, however different their original roots, become slowly, inextricably intertwined to form a single tree.

As to one's children and grandchildren, someone once remarked to me that over every nursery door should be written: 'This too will pass.' These words do not apply only to measles and mumps, to tantrums and growing-pains, but also, unfortunately, to that idyllic stage of early childhood in which wonder and trust are the first windows opening upon the world, in which the kindness and wisdom of one's parents are as boundless as the universe, in which one knows absolute joy and absolute security. When the reaction comes and (swiftly or gradually, according to individual character and circumstances) the umbilical cord is cut, the suffering of the child—since it is accompanied by the adventure of discovery and the acquisition of freedom—is inevitably less than that of the parent. This has been true in all periods; not, as each generation of parents likes to think, only in its own. 'Love is presently out of Breath', wrote Lord Halifax, 'when it has to go up Hill, from the Children to the Parents.' The Japanese, according to C. P. Snow, have an especial name for describing this stage of a parent's love: they call it 'a darkness of the heart'.

Then, as the children grow up to find partners and have children of their own, new complexities creep in; not only the impact of another family, another nucleus, of different traditions and divided loyalties, but also, inevitably, new standards and values and the rejection of the old. Yet there may also sometimes be, for the fortunate, a new drawing together, in an understanding that does not need to be expressed: the mutual enjoyment of a child's remark, the eye caught across the table in the presence of strangers, the tacit understanding and trust (in spite of waves of worry, irritation or claustrophobia). And another change, too, sometimes takes place: whereas in childhood (how long ago!) it was the parents' judgement that mattered to the child, later on the situation becomes reversed: it is then that the opinions of one's grown-up children become what matters, as well as their kindness.

At the time of the marriage of one of my daughters I drew up for myself a 'Decalogue for Mothers-in-law':

Don't ask all the questions.
Don't know all the answers.
Don't hurry.
Don't worry.
Don't probe.
Don't pry.
Don't linger.
Don't interfere.
Don't compare—or at least don't complain.
Don't try too hard.

These precepts, of which the last is the most important, were not, I need hardly say, all kept.

Yet what a strange thing it is, this family bond, with its tugs and withdrawals, its irritations and comprehensions, its ebbs and flows, an affection constantly changing, sometimes fading, never wholly destroyed. With grandchildren, it is all easier. Here the bond, however dear, is at one remove and so can be an almost unmixed, if cooler, joy. In this I have been singularly fortunate, both in the closeness of my own friendship as a child with my English grandfather, in particular, and now with some of my grandchildren, who have bestowed upon me the happiest hours of my old age. With them I have sometimes had a sense of turning back the leaves and living over again my relationship with my own grandfather: a similar frictionless ease, due to the absence of final responsibility, a similar leap over a gulf of sixty years and, for myself at least, a similar enrichment.

I am aware that this book appears to show a considerable detachment from public affairs, but this is partly due to my disinclination to write about the long years of Fascism, during which I learned to hold my tongue and preserve my own convictions, especially during the last few years before the entry of Italy into what Churchill himself, in retrospect, called 'The Unnecessary War'. Just as I do not think that one is likely to write a good biography unless one feels some sympathy with its subject, so I doubt whether much is to be gained by dwelling on those periods of one's life of which the dominant flavour, in recollection, is distaste. Times of grief, hardship or danger may all be fruitful, but not a reluctant acceptance of events in which one could play no part.

By this I do not mean to suggest that from the first I realised to the full the implications of the rise of Fascism. During the growth of the new regime which followed upon the years of isolation in my mother's ivory tower at the top of the Fiesole hill, and coincided with the time of my own engagement and marriage, my adaptation to an entirely new way of life upon our Tuscan farm, and the birth and death of my first child—I was as self-absorbed as many another ill-informed young woman, taken up wholly by my own personal life and insulated to a degree which now seems to me very odd from what was happening outside it. I felt an instinctive dislike for a few external aspects of the new order which I could hardly fail to observe: the truculent manners and boastful speech inculcated into a naturally courteous and moderate people, and the cult of rhetoric and violence. But —having as yet no political opinions of my own and being still very conscious of my foreign origins—I did not feel justified in criticising events of which I did not fully understand the cause, and I therefore took refuge in the blank vagueness of a young woman uninterested in public affairs—an attitude which was considered quite natural.

Even when the evidence of both my eyes and ears gradually

made me begin to realise what was happening, I was still isolated, by the circumstances of my daily life, from much direct contact with the political life of our time, and I do not think that there is much value in second-hand accounts of events in which one was not either a direct participant or a very acute observer. Both my husband's life and my own were centred upon our Tuscan farm, La Foce, where our work—as I shall describe—brought us into contact with one of the most constructive aspects of Fascism and with some of its most sincere adherents, but otherwise we remained cut off from the main course of Italian political life. (In this independence, of course, we were singularly fortunate.)

I realise, as I said at the beginning, that I have had a very varied and full life. But I am also aware, with a discomfort which increases as I get older, how much it has been a life of privilege, in all the ways which had already caused distress to my uncle Bronson Cutting some seventy years ago: unfair advantages of birth, education, money, environment, and opportunity. I must be honest and admit that some of these advantages have, at times, been highly enjoyable; but, like everything else, there is a price to be paid for them. One cannot have it all ways. These privileges have cut me off (both when I was younger and unaware of it, and now that I am, partly in consequence of the changing world around me, very well aware) from many people whom I would have liked to have as my friends, both because of the differences in our ways of life, and because of an invisible but unsurmountable barrier on *their* side. (It could be surmounted, of course, but at a price which I have not had the courage to pay: 'sell all that you have and follow Me'.) I also feel very strongly, now, that over the years I could and should have made more use of my 'privileges', spent more of my money and used more of my energy and imagination for the relief of poverty and suffering. That I did not do so was partly due to ignorance, partly to having scattered my interests, friendships and experiments, too wide; but this is not really an excuse.

All this was brought home to me when I was working after the Florentine flood of 1966 with a small committee of people of very varied ages, professions and political opinions, in an attempt to bring a measure of relief to some of the small craftsmen and tradesmen of Florence. We all managed to work together harmoniously, in spite of these differences, and I have remained with a warm memory of these months as well as some new friends, but I fully realised how much better work was done, in the sense of forming a real contact with the people we were trying to get back upon their feet, by those of us who were not separated from them by artificial barriers of wealth and class, whose knowledge of their needs sprang from a similar (or not too widely dissimilar) way of life, and who could therefore offer real understanding, not only material help. The well-worn analogy of the camel and the needle's eye, which in youth I had always considered unfair, then took on a real significance.

Besides, in this particular period of history, I realise that this barrier of privilege—added to that of age, which continues to exist even for those older people who most genuinely attempt to embrace the new ideologies of the young—has the effect, as Stephen Spender once remarked, of rendering one 'almost invisible, as blacks were supposed to be in America'.

Well, there are advantages in invisibility. They give one a chance to watch more carefully the reflections upon the wall, and perhaps gradually to let one's eyes become accustomed to 'the sight of the upper world'. All I can relate now, is the little I have seen so far. I can only say: this, at sixty-eight, is what I have to tell.

IRIS ORIGO
La Foce, 1970

Part One

1
Westbrook

ON A SPRING DAY IN 1748, a young Englishman of twenty-three, Leonard Cutting, of Great Yarmouth in Norfolk, was sitting in a coffee-house, thinking that, in spite of his education at Eton and Cambridge, his prospects in life were 'very low', when a Virginia sea-captain suddenly came in, exclaiming in a loud voice, "Who's for America?" Cutting at once rose and replied that he was. He paid for his passage by becoming a 'Redemptioner' (that is, by binding himself to the captain for a certain number of years of service after arrival), worked first on a plantation in Virginia and then on an estate in New Jersey, became a classical tutor in New York at what was then called King's College and is now Columbia University; and finally, having taken orders, became the Rector of St. George's Church in Hempstead, Long Island. He was, on the Cutting side, my first American ancestor.

My first awareness of being, not myself alone, but the last and smallest acorn of a big tree, came to me when I was very young, in my American grandmother's house on a Sunday morning after church, when she told me to climb up on to a chair and showed me, on the front page of the family Bible, which lay open upon a tall lectern in the hall, a pattern of names—and at the end of them, in fresher ink, my own. At the same moment, the grandfather clock which stood at the other end of the wide panelled hall, and which is now in the entrance hall of my own house in Rome, began to chime; and sometimes to this day, when I come out of the Roman sunlight and climb up the cool dark staircase to the sound of the same chimes, I am taken back to that moment, and to my grandmother's voice saying: "That's where you come in, dear."

Further explanations, however, proved a little confusing. After telling me that through my grandfather's mother we descended from a cadet branch, which had settled in Flanders, of the Bayard family, rendered illustrious by the *Chevalier sans peur et sans*

13

reproche, she then went back a little too far and tried to hold my interest by telling me the story of the legendary horse Bayard, presented by Charlemagne to the four sons of Aymon, who possessed the magic gift of being able to stretch himself out to carry all his four masters at once, and who may still sometimes be heard neighing on midsummer days in the forest of Ardennes. My imagination was indeed stirred, but the impression left upon my mind, and confirmed by the animal on the family crest, was that we were all descended from a magic horse.

On another occasion, I was shown the portraits of our ancestors in the well-bound, gilt-edged family history which my grandmother had caused to be compiled, but these I did not find attractive. Those stern-faced men and women in stiff white ruffs (Dutch Huguenots, as I now know, Bayards and Stuyvesants), those Scottish lairds in ruffles or stocks (Murrays and Livingstones), those white-banded, black-gowned clergymen, and, later on, those portly, prosperous merchants with whiskers and gold watch-chains, and wives with smooth bandeaux and thin lips— they all looked to me very strange, formidable and dull. Like most of the self-appointed little aristocracy of 'Old New York', my grandparents came, on both sides, of good respectable middle-class stock, which, as Edith Wharton was to observe about her own relatives, 'does not often produce eagles'. If I felt a slight interest in any of my grandfather's more remote kin, it was perhaps in Robert Livingstone of Roxburghshire, who, having set sail for the New World in 1673 and settled in Albany, at the time when New Amsterdam was being handed over by Holland to the English and renamed New York, changed his crest from *Si je puis* to *Spero meliora*, and purchased from the Indians some 2,000 acres on the East bank of the Hudson, on payment of 300 guilders, plus some paint, a few blankets, coats, shirts and stockings, six guns and gunpowder, and a small assortment of axes, tobacco, and pipes, three kegs of rum, and one barrel of strong beer— a transaction to which he later on referred as 'vast charges and expenses'. He then obtained from the Governor of New York the right to call this land 'A Lordship or Manor', acquired the rights of patronage over any churches built there, and subsequently increased his estate to such effect that by 1714 it consisted of more than 160,000 acres, of which he sold 6,000 to the government for the resettlement of some 3,000 German refugees (called 'Palatines'), whose lands at home had been invaded by the French, providing them for six months with wine and beer. He also, on behalf of the British government, took part in 'the suppression of piracy', fitting out for this purpose a privateer called the *Adventure*, appointing to its command notorious Captain William Kidd, who soon afterwards hoisted the black flag himself to attack merchant vessels bound for the East. He was captured, tried at the Old Bailey and hanged at Execution Dock on May 23, 1701. Kidd's trial was plainly not a fair one; he had no proper counsel for his defence and it now appears he was condemned unjustly. Livingstone, we are told, felt the matter keenly.

I also feel a mild curiosity about some of my Bayard ancestors, in particular a somewhat formidable lady, Mrs. Samuel Bayard of Amsterdam, who, having been left a widow in her youth, set off in 1647 with four small children for the New World. She was described as being 'of imposing appearance, highly educated, alert in business and imperious in manner'—and she also apparently had a strong sense of justice, since it was through her intercession with her brother Peter Stuyvesant, the governor of New Amsterdam, that a Quaker, Robert Hodgson, was freed from imprisonment on account of his faith. Her son, too, Colonel Nicholas Bayard, seems to have been a man of some independence of spirit, since he incurred a sentence of imprisonment in 1664 for sponsoring a petition pleading for freedom of religion and exemption from bearing arms against the Dutch, and also, some thirty years later, narrowly escaped being executed for High Treason as 'a leader of sedition' and a Jacobite. But his chief interest for me lies in his marriage in 1668 to the only one of my American ancestors whose story I should really like to know, a young woman called Judith Verleth, whose life before her marriage is described in a single sentence: 'She was imprisoned in 1662 as a witch by the Puritans of Hartford.' How had the accusation come about, I used to wonder; how had she escaped death, how had Colonel Bayard come to marry her? Her only other appearance in our family records is some years later, when her husband had bought an estate on the west side of the Bowery, close to a hill then called Bayard's Mount and later on Bunkers Hill. She was then seen walking down Broadway on a fine spring morning on her way to church, wearing 'a head-dress of rows of muslin stuffed with wire', a dress of purple and gold 'cut away to show her black velvet petticoat with silver orrices', green silk stockings and fine embroidered shoes. 'Her hair was powdered and her handkerchief scented with rose-water.' I should still like to know more about this lady.

*   *   *   *   *

Back—back—how far back should one go? My own inheritance is an extremely mixed one, since, in addition to the English, French, Dutch, and Scottish blood on my American side, I can lay claim to both an Anglo-Irish, a purely English, and a Scottish strain through my mother, Lady Sybil Cuffe, who was married in London to William Bayard Cutting Jr.—then the private secretary of the American Ambassador to England, Joseph Choate— on April 19, 1901.

When the young couple first announced their intention of becoming engaged, my English grandfather, Lord Desart— always reluctant to intrude upon another person's privacy, even that of his own children, and inclined to believe that everyone else was as serenely ruled by reason as he was himself—felt obliged to ask his daughter whether she had weighed *all* the consequences of changing her nationality and living in a foreign country. Being much in love and never having seen anything of the world beyond her own family circle, she naturally answered that she had.

Twenty-two years later, when I told my grandfather that I, in my turn, was engaged to an Italian, Antonio Origo, he asked me, with equal tentativeness, the same question, and received a similar reply.

Both my mother and I, in our sincere but totally uninformed replies, gave not a moment's thought to the persons whom our decision would affect most closely: our future children.

As far as I am concerned, the consequent double strain in my inheritance has undoubtedly enriched my life; but it was also responsible for a sense of rootlessness and insecurity during my youth. Extremely adaptable on the surface (though this was largely misleading), I found no difficulty in 'fitting in', as I passed from my mother's Tuscan villa at Fiesole to the country-house on Long Island which was my American home or to Desart Court in County Kilkenny. Indeed the trouble was that—up to a point —I fitted in so completely, was so conscious of the distinctive flavour of each house and its inhabitants, that whenever a change had to be made, the uprooting was followed by a re-adjustment of my manners and, to some extent, of my values. It was not only a question of leaving a familiar place and people I had come to love, but of becoming each time, as one was moved on, a slightly different person. Even a child could then hardly fail to ask herself, "But which, then, is me?"

And now, in my children—of even more mixed blood, since to the American and Anglo-Irish strain on my side has been added an Italian-Russian-Spanish inheritance from their Italian father (who had a Russian grandmother, Paolina Polyectoff, on one side, and a grandfather of Spanish descent, Paolo Tarsis, on the other) —I see the pattern repeated or rather the small piece of the pattern that is known to me. Should I try, I wonder, to find out more?

Some part of my family history I have, of course, been told. Turning to my mother's side of the family, I know that my Anglo-Irish grandfather's house in Ireland, Desart Court, came to him through his ancestor, Joseph Cuffe, who served in Ireland under Cromwell and was awarded some lands in County Kilkenny which were called Cuffe's Desert. I know too that the ancestry of my grandfather's mother (who was Lady Elizabeth Campbell, daughter of the first Earl of Cawdor) goes back to Lady Mary Bruce, the sister of Robert Bruce, King of Scotland—thus providing an admirable excuse for edifying us, as children, with the story of Bruce and the Spider, though we were not then told about the more recent and less creditable incident of the massacre of Glencoe (for these ancestors, alas, were the 'Black Campbells' of Breadalbane). We can also claim kinship, I believe, with various Plantagenets, while on the side of my English grandmother, Lady Margaret Lascelles—whose parents were the 4th Earl of Harewood and a daughter of the Marquess of Clanricarde—the Clanricarde ancestry goes back to Ulick Bourke, Lord Clanricarde, whose wife Honora was the daughter of Connor O'Brien, one of the legendary kings of Ireland. Clearly, however, I lack a genealogical mind, for—even at my present age, when many people, perhaps because they expect fairly soon to leave this world, develop an interest in their kinsmen who left it long ago—I find it difficult to feel much concern for these traditions, except perhaps in our connection with 'great-aunt Harriet Clanricarde', who married a great-grandson of Stafford Canning, and thus transmitted to me an agreeable possession: an exquisitely set necklace, brooch and earrings, known as 'the Canning emeralds', which I have now handed on to my eldest daughter. In general, though, I feel no more personal connection with the people mentioned in the 'ancestral tablets' so carefully compiled by my mother's sister, Joan Verney, than with any other name read in a history book—perhaps because I know so little about them, that they have remained nothing more than names. But I do feel (and already felt in childhood) a great interest in the life of my four grandparents on both sides of the Atlantic, whom I both knew and loved, and a wish to set down what I have learned about them, and this wish has been strengthened by realising that the life they led has already become as irrevocably remote, as completely a 'period piece', as if they had lived many centuries ago. I will try to set down, in the first two chapters of this book, what has been told me about it, and what I myself remember.

*   *   *   *   *

The family Bible in which my name was inscribed lay in the hall of my American grandparents' house, Westbrook, on the South Shore of Long Island, beside the river named Connetquot, from the Indian tribe which had lived on its banks in the seventeenth century. It was there that my grandparents, with much imagination and enterprise, had transformed a spit of sandy, mosquito-haunted land and marsh into a wild garden and park of great beauty, and had built, in 1886, the house which became their home. Although constructed in the period in which the monumental country houses of their friends were still rising in Newport along Ocean Drive, it had the great merit of not attempting to be either a French chateau, an Elizabethan manor-house or a Florentine villa; its material was the unpretentious indigenous shingle, and its design that of an English cottage, if a somewhat overgrown one. Any architectural infelicities, however, such as gabled windows and an occasional turret, were soon softened by the luxuriant creepers on the walls and by the planting of shrubs and trees, and indoors the house certainly had a remarkable degree of Victorian spaciousness and comfort: large rooms cool in summer and glowing with heat in winter, a panelled library filled not only with the well-bound sets of an orthodox 'gentleman's library', but also with first editions of Stevenson, Conrad, and Oscar Wilde; a dining-room and breakfast-room in which the old English silver was as fine as the Canton and Lowestoft china, and upstairs, in the bedrooms, every device to enhance a guest's comfort that the imagination could conceive. A 'play-room' in an annexe, joined to the main buildings by a wide arch, provided a billiard table and ping-pong table, and even, in my father's time, a small electric organ, and, on the edge of the lawn, a wide 'piazza'—enclosed in a wire netting like a meat-safe against the ferocious Long Island mosquitoes (which both the inhabitants of the North and the South Shore declared to be far worse on the *other* side of the island)—looked out over a velvety expanse of green, shaded by a few great trees, to the wide river flowing down to the Great South Bay. It was here, out of doors, that the real charm of Westbrook began, with the tall English oaks beside the house, the shrubs and ferns bordering the mossy paths that led into the woods, and the three ponds edged with tall trees and shrubs which reflected, in the autumn, the brilliant reds and pinks of swamp maple and dogwood, and in the spring, massed banks of azaleas and hybrid rhododendrons. Best of all, to my mind, was the shaded, winding path along the river's brink, leading to the stretch of natural, unplanted woodland and marsh, where one might see a sudden flight of startled wild fowl and smell the faint acrid odour of rotting leaves and fallen boughs, and watch the still, melancholy expanse of water turn to copper in the sunset light.

Here, in their childhood, my father, his brother and sisters and their friends canoed and fished and ran wild in the woods during their holidays, here my grandparents gave tennis and croquet-parties and dinner-parties for Long Island neighbours in the 80's and 90's and entertained friends from New York for the week-end, with much fishing and driving and some sailing in the bay, visits to the model farm with its herd of Jersey cows, and, for the more energetic, the exercise of blazing new trails with a hatchet through the woods—thus satisfying the nostalgia for 'the primitive life' which afflicts the well-to-do, while also acquiring an appetite for the excellent dinner to follow.* Every week-day morning, my grandfather would drive his tandem to the little station at Islip to take the two-hour journey to his work in New York, so it was really only at week-ends that he and his wife were able to plan the improvements to the farm and garden, or to the landscape planting of the rest of the grounds. The pinetum, indeed, gradually became one of the finest collections of exotic trees in the United States, containing rare specimens from China and Japan, from Europe and Africa and Asia Minor—among them a towering blue cedar from Mount Atlas, an eighty-foot Cilician fir from Asia Minor, a dawn redwood from Western China and a stone pine from Siberia. Strangely enough, the hot, damp climate and sandy soil of Long Island appeared to suit them all.

The other chief feature of the place in those days was the stables, to which family and guests (since of course no horse was allowed to work on Sundays) all paid a formal visit on Sunday afternoons. "We would find the carriage house decorated," my aunt Justine has told me, "with bright coloured sands, red, blue, yellow and green, and braided straw. The passage behind the horses' stalls was decorated in like manner. It must have taken hours of completely useless work, but it was tradition. Each Sunday we exlaimed about the brilliant splendour of the carriages, the suppleness of the leather, and the brightness of the bits—a tribute to the coachman and the grooms. The grooms were everywhere, ornamental rather than useful. They sat on the box beside the coachman and sprang to the ground before the carriage stopped, to open the door. They sat back to back with the driver in dogcarts. They galloped thirty yards behind me when on horseback, throwing my horse into a panic. They stood with folded arms before the heads of stationary horses." And there were also, of

* The staff—after the stables, with the English coachman and innumerable grooms, had been given up—consisted of fourteen: a housekeeper, a butler, two footmen and a parlour-maid, three in the kitchen, two housemaids, two chauffeurs, a laundress, and a night-watchman. The same staff was employed in New York, where, until the 30's, there was also an outdoor night-watchman, shared by several families on the block, who patrolled the area, checking doors and windows. He was on duty on even the bitterest winter nights, from 10 p.m. until the early morning.

Outdoors, the Westbrook gardens and grounds required for their upkeep eighteen men, as well as a superintendent and two men in the dairy.

course, a proportionate number of carriages, from the humble buckboard and buggy to the four-horse brake or coach and two-horse victoria and brougham. When they finally were crowded off the roads by automobiles, the splendid horses were shot and the carriages sold for a song. Our coachman, retired on a pension, was inconsolable, and could not understand that anyone should prefer a hideous automobile to the beauty of another age.

"What would you have done with the carriages?" Justine asked him. "I would have built a shed at the foot of the lawn and kept them all there, just to have something pretty to look at."

"I wonder," Justine added, "whether he was not right."

Westbrook, however, had not always been my grandparents' home. In their youth they had first known some lean years—which were not perhaps entirely necessary, but may have added a flavour to the possessions that came in later life, and which were certainly entirely in accordance with the American principle that 'young people should begin simply'. Although both of them, later on, belonged to the society described in Edith Wharton's *The Age of Innocence*, neither of them spent their childhood in New York. My grandfather, William Bayard Cutting (since his mother had died when he was a child, and his father, for some reason which was never revealed to us, lived in France), was brought up, with his brother Fulton, in a small town in New Jersey called Edgewater, just across the Hudson, by his maternal grandparents, Mr. and Mrs. Robert Bayard. His grandfather was distinctly well-off, having inherited the fortune made by his father in trade with Europe and with the East and West Indies, as well as having substantial railroad interests himself; but he was also frugal, and both William Bayard and Fulton were brought up in an atmosphere of industrious austerity, and—in the words of my aunt Justine—of "high if narrow standards", with the understanding that they would have to make their own way in the world. My future grandmother, too, Olivia Peyton Murray, had had an austere up-bringing. Born in Illinois in 1855—the second pretty daughter of a family of six—she possessed a Presbyterian father whose own education, in Jamaica, Long Island, had been 'enforced dexterously with a flat ruler', and who disapproved on principle of all gaieties, 'dreading for his daughters any association with children more wealthy than they'. Even after the family had returned to New York, he restricted their acquaintance to an extremely small circle, and it was quite exceptional that Olivia should have been permitted to attend the Commencement Exercises at Columbia College, where she had a first glimpse of her future husband, as he delivered, with great fire and aplomb, the year's valedictory address. 'From that moment he became her hero.' There was a brief exchange of words, followed by one happy evening, when, having come to call upon her elder sister (since Olivia was not yet old enough to have a caller), Bayard was entertained by the younger one instead—and then—seven years of waiting. Even when their marriage at last took place, they had so little money that they were at first obliged to live with Bayard's grandparents in Edgewater, and it was not until the following year that Bayard could at last afford to rent a very small house of his own in 24th Street, only twelve and a half feet wide, but absorbing nearly half their income. When one of their first visitors asked Bayard why he had brought his bride to so very small a house, he replied, "I cut my coat according to my cloth."

When, however, Bayard was twenty-five, his grandfather turned over his business interests to him—largely in railroads, which were then opening out in the Middle West and Far West—and after this prosperity came swiftly. The young man was certainly both judicious and fortunate in his operations, and at twenty-eight he was already the President of the St. Louis, Alton and Terre Haute Railroad, while later on he also became a director of the Southern Pacific and opened up some new railroads in Florida. The extent of his interests in this field is suggested by the fact that, whenever he and his family travelled on any of these railroads, a 'private car' was put at their disposal, which included a sitting-room with bunks, a 'master's bedroom', a drawing-room and kitchen, and an observation car in which you could enjoy both the soot and the view—and which (though some people preferred to take their own chef with them) was also equipped with a Negro waiter, a porter, and a cook. In such a car one could live in the greatest comfort in any siding in the Middle West, where the roads were still few, and the hotels both few and bad. In the words of Mrs. August Belmont, who also belonged, after her marriage, to the small number privileged to travel in this manner: "A private railroad car is not an acquired taste: one takes to it at once!"

My grandfather was always extremely scrupulous in his business dealings and indignant against the sharp practices of the 'Robber Barons' of his time, who bought out the little land-owner and cheated the small investor—so much so, that his children were never allowed, later on, to accept invitations to their houses. He was responsible for the development of a large tract of what was then worthless land in South Brooklyn, the digging of the Ambrose Channel, which opened up New York and Brooklyn Harbour to large shipping interests, the starting of the sugar-beet industry in the Middle West, and later on he became a vice-president of the New York Chamber of Commerce. But he also found time for many other interests. A lover of the country and of sport, he was a keen fisherman and a good judge of horses, and for many years drove his own four-in-hand and tandem. He was one of the founders of the New York Botanical Gardens and the Zoological Society, and he also belonged to a small group of men of taste—John Cadwallader, Egerton Winthrop, Walter Maynard, Stanford White, Pierpont Morgan—who were beginning to change the life of New York by their active interest both in art and letters, in architecture and old furniture. He became one of the founders of the Metropolitan Museum and of the New York Public Library, and a Trustee of Columbia University. By then he and his wife were living in the square, massive brownstone house ("the ugliest stone ever quarried," as Edith Wharton justly remarked) on the corner of 72nd Street and Madison Avenue which remained their New York home for the rest of their lives, and which contained also, like many others of its kind (for their taste, though not ostentatious, was also not distinctive), a Louis Quinze drawing-room, a dark panelled library, a dining-room hung with French tapestries, and a large central hall which could also be used for a dance (as occurred, for the last time, on the occasion of my 'début' in 1920). The rooms were well-proportioned, the furniture 'good,' the upkeep, as at Westbrook, perfection itself, but the total effect was curiously impersonal, and to me, at least, somewhat oppressive. But to my grandparents the house was undoubtedly a source of much pleasure and pride, and to gather fresh treasures for it was one of the chief objects

Images and Shadows

of their almost yearly journeys to Europe. Such trips, indeed, were by then becoming part of an habitual pattern of life for the small section of New York society to which they belonged. 'From my earliest infancy', wrote Edith Wharton, whose background was very similar, 'I had always seen about me people who were either just arriving from abroad or just embarking on a European tour'—but she added that these journeys were generally artistic or sentimental pilgrimages in the wake of Scott, Byron, Washington Irving or Hawthorne—or, of course, shopping expeditions to the dressmakers of Paris or the tailors and curiosity-shops of London. It was only very seldom that they also became an occasion for forming European friendships. 'The Americans who fought their way into good society in Europe were said to be those who were shut out from it at home.' One might of course have a few personal friends in England or France, or, like my grandparents, one might become connected with a European family by the marriage of one of one's children (though this was still comparatively rare) but for one's real social life one came home again.

This life, as I have heard it described, seems to have possessed at least one quality notably absent in the New York of today: leisure. Many of the men, of course—my grandfather among them—worked extremely hard in office hours, but there were also some (such as the Astors and Goelets) whose fortunes, made in previous generations by the purchase of real estate and automatically increasing with its rapid rise in value, chiefly required fostering by careful administration. Others were bankers, lawyers, architects (never politicians, except in the case of Theodore Roosevelt, whom some considered a traitor to his class), and certainly many of them enjoyed sufficient leisure for week-day lunch parties of both sexes to be possible, as well as long weekends in their country places in Newport, Lennox or Long Island.

For the women, the standard of housekeeping was extremely high. However polished the English butler and French maid, however efficient the housekeeper and the large staff, a careful hostess was expected to take a personal and expert interest in her linen-room, garden and kitchen, and most of them possessed a number of carefully-guarded recipes transmitted by their grandmothers or aunts, written out on yellowing pages in exquisite

24

copper-plate hands. The cellar, of course, was the province of the master of the house, but it, too, was a matter for specialised knowledge and grave ceremony—a taste and a tradition which my grandfather transmitted to at least two of his children. Engraved invitation cards to formal dinners were usually sent out at least three weeks in advance, and the menu would often include, as well as every variety of oyster, such delicacies as terrapin and canvas-backed duck, broiled Spanish mackerel, soft-shelled crabs and peach-fed Virginia hams cooked in champagne. Great care was taken not to give such a dinner on an 'Opera Night', when instead a small party of six or seven (the men always a little difficult to find) would sit down in the house of one of the box-holders to a somewhat earlier and shorter meal. My grandfather was one of these box-holders—men who had founded and financed the Metropolitan Opera Company of New York, and who paid its annual deficit. Each of them was entitled to a first-tier box in the 'dress circle'; but here trouble arose, for when the architect's plan was examined, it was discovered that there were not enough boxes for them all; and no-one was willing to move to the second tier, where one heard better, but was not seen so well. So the architect was asked to extend the horse-shoe circle, providing a few more boxes, but damaging the acoustics—a matter which only distressed a very few music-lovers, since most of the audience merely considered the singing 'an interruption to good talk'. For indeed the Opera House in New York (as in Italy in the eighteenth century) performed a more complex function than that of providing fine operas. In a society lacking a king and court, it became the focal point of social life, providing occasions for the display of the first essential of an aristocracy, exclusiveness, for hospitality to distinguished guests, and for such a show of evening gowns and jewels as would elsewhere have graced a court ball.

In all this, of course, there was a great emphasis on possessions —country-houses, horses, carriages, yachts, gardens, pictures, furniture—but certainly not (except among the more ostentatious new arrivals, who, precisely for that reason, found it difficult to penetrate the inner circle) on money in itself, and I think that most 'Old New Yorkers' instilled into their children, at least by implication, the precept taught to Edith Wharton by *her* mother (and which is, of course, in itself, one of the privileges of the rich): "Never talk about money, and think about it as little as possible." There was also a very strong sense of charitable duty; not only in terms of money, but of time and trouble. My grandfather purchased some large blocks of slum-tenements on the East River and replaced them with decent, cheap apartments, and from the earliest years of her marriage, my grandmother belonged to a weekly 'sewing-class', which was still flourishing when she and the other surviving members were over seventy, and still referring to each other as 'the Girls'. During the whole of their life, my grandparents—both devout Episcopalians—devoted a great deal of thought and care, as well as a large proportion of their income, not only to gifts to public charities but to individuals in need, and my grandfather was also a member of various hospital boards a Trustee of the Children's Aid Society and the President of the Improved Dwellings Association of New York.

My own recollections of him, since he died when I was ten years old, are very nebulous. I think he must have been a charming man—wise, humorous, and urbane, with an unusually happy touch with people, a cultivated mind, and a tender heart. But I can only remember a warm voice and a kind smile, a pointed beard which pricked—and on my own lips, the unattractive sentence, "Granapa will pay", which became a family saying. Certainly he had paid, by his hard work and his foresight, for the luxury in which we all lived, and which some of his children, later on, found oppressive, but which I suspect he himself chiefly valued as an adornment and setting for his young wife.

Very lovely my grandmother must have been, according to the portraits I have seen, and also animated by a vivid zest for life and by strong, possessive affections. When first I clearly remember her, in her late forties, she was handsome still, but sometimes a little formidable—a skilful and experienced hostess, an elegant woman of fashion, a loving but rather imperious mother, a leading figure on charitable committees and art exhibitions, very much the mistress of her household and of her life. I can see her sitting very erect, as was required of a well-bred woman, with her long-gloved arm resting on the red plush rim of her box at the Metropolitan Opera House, most elegantly gowned, gloved and bejewelled, in the company of friends of equally irreproachable

26

character, breeding, and appearance, entertaining some distinguished (and often more dowdy) foreign guest, and receiving a
little court of callers during the interval. Any wish or whim of
hers that my grandfather could satisfy, he always did: but I am
told, too, that, for all his gentleness, it was always his hands
that held the reins. Certainly, in the long years after his death,
she constantly referred to his opinions and felt the loss of his
guidance so much that, at one time, she had frequent recourse to
automatic writing by planchette and received nebulous messages
which it was difficult not to consider merely emanations of her
own need, rather than an answering voice. But she also retained,
until the day of her death at ninety-four, a bright glint in her eye
and an eager interest in any new guest or fresh event—whether
a visit from Dr. Schweitzer or the first bloom of a new rhododendron in the garden. And so, too, she continued to take a constant
pleasure both in the appurtenances of her house and in her own
appearance, and remained, with her beautifully-dressed, snow-
white hair, her well-cut suits of white frieze or purple tweed, her
summer dresses of trim prints and her black velvet evening gowns,
the most decorative and soignée of old ladies. It is not, I think,
sufficiently recognised—since it does not occur to them to put it
into words—how sensitive young children are, not only to the
appearance but the fastidiousness of the grown-up people with
whom they live. Certainly both to myself, and later on to my
children, one of 'Granama's' chief attractions was, not the warmth
of her embraces, which I think very few children enjoy, but the
fact that she always looked so pretty and smelled so good. She
became, too, the centre of the whole family life: it was at Westbrook or in 72nd Street that large family gatherings took place
on Thanksgiving Day or Christmas—dreaded by her own children,
but I think enjoyed by the uncles and aunts and cousins—and it
was to her little pale grey sitting-room upstairs, with its family
photographs and Whistler etchings, that brothers and sisters,
nephews and nieces, and in due course great-nephews and great-
nieces, too, came to tell the story of their lives, attracted not only
by the generosity that often solved their problems, but by the
unfailing eagerness of her interest, and the common sense of her
comments.

Yet, in the course of reading old letters and hearing family stories, it has been borne in on me that, beneath so much prosperity, such deep and genuine ties of family affection, the youth of my father's generation was marked by tensions quite as acute as those which may affect families today. It is of course a commonplace that the members of each generation in turn tend to reject the values of the preceding one and to derive little satisfaction from what has been handed down to them ready-made. But I still think that the Cutting children (my father Bayard, his brother Bronson, and his sisters Justine and Olivia) were particularly allergic to the taste of their silver spoons, unusually determined to carve out new paths for themselves. There is a photograph of all four of them (varying in ages between twenty-two and eleven) sitting on the steps of the Westbrook 'piazza', in which the moody rebelliousness which they themselves referred to as 'Westbrook gloom' is plainly carved on their features. They partly attributed it (except Olivia, who was always happy there, and later on took an active part in running the farm and planting the park) to the damp and relaxing climate of Long Island. But another more personal factor was also just beginning to affect their lives: the shadow of ill-health, which (except for my grandmother and Justine) fell upon each of them in turn. My father (of whom I will speak more fully in another chapter) contracted tuberculosis at the age of twenty-two and died eight years later; both Bronson and Olivia, in a lesser degree, were attacked by the same disease and spent several years of their youth in fighting it. My grandfather—heart-broken at Bayard's death and attacked by the two prevalent complaints of his generation and class, heart-disease and gout—died only two years after his eldest son. It is hardly surprising that, with this family history, apprehension and solicitude should have overshadowed the lives of the survivors, while a constant preoccupation with health and comfort ruled the ordering of each day. The afternoon rest, the morning walk, the great glasses of creamy milk from the prize Jersey herd, the reading-light falling at precisely the correct angle over one's left shoulder —these were the outer tokens of a concealed but oppressive apprehension. But I think that what the younger generation minded most was something more subtle: the gentle, constant awareness of an unrelenting care for their happiness and preoccupation with their plans. They felt (in my youth I felt it, too) entangled in fine, suffocating cobwebs of solicitude and affection. An old friend, Olivia's contemporary, to whom I recently showed these pages, has commented that while she thinks the general picture to be true, I have omitted the *fun* they had in youth: the house-parties, the lawn-tennis, the canoeing on the river, the blazing of paths in the woods and, above all, the unceasing laughter. That this was so at week-end parties I do not doubt, and when guests such as Elizabeth Lindsay (then Hoyt), Laura Chanler or Alice Longworth were in the house—but how difficult it is to catch the echoes of past laughter! And certainly, for all Olivia's love of Westbrook, she could not deny (when I questioned her) the existence of the atmosphere I have described, though she never found it as oppressive as it seemed to Bronson and Justine (and, after his boyhood, I believe, also to my father).

It was from this world that all my grandparents' children, except Olivia, escaped in turn, to carve out new, if widely different, paths for themselves. All four of them possessed inquiring, original minds, singularly intolerant (at least in youth) of any form of conventionality or stodginess, and almost morbidly afraid of seeming to possess anything (especially money) that made them different as they grew up from the new friends they made. Each of them very soon broke away from the family orbit, or at least discarded, in different ways, the manner of life of their parents. Not one of them took pleasure in luxury in itself, and they all found something faintly ridiculous, as well as distasteful, in the solemn rites connected with the possession of money, whether the visits of the family lawyer or of the manager of the family office, or the ceremonial visits to the bank to 'cut off coupons'. Moreover Bronson and Olivia, in particular, felt an intense sense both of responsibility and discomfort at possessing a large private fortune. I remember my grandmother telling me that when, at the age of twenty one, Bronson was told that he was about to receive his share of the family fortune, he at first bluntly refused to accept it and then—realising that this was impossible —shut himself up in his room for two days, in solitary gloom. Later on, however, according to his sister Justine, he became 'very indifferent to money' and, in New Mexico, spent almost all of it (except what was required for his political campaigns) on the poor people of the State, while his Will broke up his fortune into innumerable small legacies, mostly to people to whom the relatively small sums were of great value. Olivia too, when not living with her mother at Westbrook, arranged her life in New York for many years on a much more modest scale than her income would have allowed, and chose some of her friends, too, from an entirely different world than that of her youth. As for Justine, she wrote that, to her, money had been 'simply a convenience. What I loathed was the stuffy, unreal type of existence it often produced.' She was, however, a woman of great taste, and certainly she got much pleasure from the fine Chinese bronzes and vases and French tapestries which adorned her Washington house, as well as the excellent French wine and food that she offered to her guests—though the bulk of her fortune, together with her talent, energy and almost all her time were devoted to her method of teaching Gregorian Chant to children, which, as it developed and took root, became the main interest of her life.

Justine had been, from childhood, the arch-rebel, egging on her brother Bayard (the other two were much younger) to daring and defiance, laughing at all that seemed to her 'stuffy' in their upbringing, and demanding from her parents the only gift that they were not prepared to give her—freedom. Possessing great musical gifts, she passionately longed, at fifteen, to go to Europe to study music there, but this, in the New York of the 1890's, was even more inconceivable than it would have been in the corresponding Victorian world in England. 'Never let anyone know that you play the violin: it would wreck your career!' was the advice given by the celebrated lawyer and Ambassador to England, Joseph Choate, to the promising young lawyer George Ward (whom Justine married later on)—and as for allowing a girl to take it up as her profession! Even the most cultivated and enlightened parent would have drawn back, as may be gathered from the following story, which Justine told me herself. One day, when she was still a schoolgirl and was practising on the drawing-room piano, the door opened and her mother brought in Edith Wharton, to show her a tapestry. Justine naturally stopped playing and stood up, but no-one addressed a word to her. As Mrs. Wharton was leaving, however, she turned to her husband and remarked in a loud voice, "Well, Teddy, it may be just as well that we never had any children. Just think, one of them might have been musical!"

It is curious, incidentally, that it should have been Edith Wharton to make this remark, for she herself had suffered, as a successful writer, from a very similar social ostracism. 'My literary success', she wrote in *A Backward Glance*, 'puzzled and embarrassed my old friends far more than it impressed them, and in my family it created a kind of constraint which increased with the years. . . . The subject was avoided as though it were a kind of family disgrace which might be condoned, but could not be forgotten.' And music, indisputably, was still worse. "Having a child that was musical," my aunt remarked to me, not without some retrospective bitterness, "was like having an epileptic in the family or a hunchback. My parents were to be pitied for their misfortune. The attitude changed towards the turn of the century, perhaps owing to more contact with the European point of view, but that came too late for me."

In her later life, in the beautiful house on the outskirts of Washington which her brother Bronson had left her, Justine led a life wholly dedicated to her vocation, and almost entirely cut off from her family and from any conventional social life. She was married in 1901 to George Ward, and in 1904 she became converted to Catholicism. She did a good deal of writing on musical subjects, particularly after Pope Pius X's Encyclical on Sacred Music. It was then that her work caught the attention of a remarkable man, Dr. Thomas Shields, then head of the Education Department of the Catholic University in Washington, who encouraged her to prepare a most original and lively series of textbooks for teaching singing to children, but, when she came to Gregorian Chant, she realised that she needed further preparation herself, and started studying the subject under the great Benedictine musician Dom Mocquereau, first at Quarr Abbey on the Isle of Wight and later on at Solesmes, spending half of the year in the little town of Sablé-sur-Sarthe, a few miles from the Abbey, and the other half teaching in Catholic schools in New York and Washington. Eventually her method spread to almost every Catholic country in Europe, as well as to South America and Canada. Once, for two days, I stayed with her in Sablé, in a serene little white house in a silent provincial street, to which life was brought only by the constant sound of the swift waters of the Sarthe just outside the window, and one morning she took me to the great Abbey to hear the Plain Chant of the Mass—a glimpse of a world of serene and austere perfection, of subtle and complex harmonies, such as I had never conceived. It was then that I realised how far she had travelled from the Westbrook lawns and the brownstone house in 72nd Street, and guessed at the strength of the impulse that was leading her to attempt, after a long period of arduous self-training, to transmit something of this tradition to the Catholic children for whom her method was intended, and who still, in over a hundred convent-schools in Belgium, France, and the United States, are being taught to sing by it. To her family she only came back, even after her return to America after the Second World War, for brief, fugitive visits: her life had taken on too different a pattern. In old age, as in youth, she retained the quick wit and strong will, as well as her passion for hard work, and much of the elegance and gaiety of of her youth, and—together with a devoted friend, Agnes Lebreton—led for many years in her secluded house in Washington a life which was a remarkable mixture of austerity and luxury: two elegantly-dressed old ladies following an unswerving routine of early rising, work and prayer in a setting of Ming vases, 'Tang horses, Persian carpets, French cooking and French wines —cut off from the world, but not in the least unaware of it; free, self-sufficient, humorous and serene. Even now—though Agnes died three years ago and daily life has become lonely—Justine, at the age of ninety-two, has been teaching Gregorian Chant herself for a whole winter, in a teacher's absence, to a class of children in Washington.

The life of her younger brother Bronson followed a very different course. In childhood a thin, serious, spectacled little boy, passionately addicted to the study of the classics and spending most of his holidays abroad in the British Museum or the Louvre, he promised to become a distinguished scholar, but distressed his elder brother in his boyhood at Groton, by his refusal to show an interest in any form of sport, or any attempt to be a 'good mixer'. It would have been difficult to imagine then that that studious, silent, and introspective little boy would ever become a public figure in American politics, but a sudden haemorrhage during his last year at Harvard, brought about, as well as an interruption of his studies, a complete transformation of his personality. In the company of Justine—who seems to have felt that a removal from family life, quite as much as the dry air and sunshine of Arizona or New Mexico, were essential for his recovery —he set off for the West. "As we got off at a little station on the way to Santa Fé," she has told me, "we noticed some Spanish peasants cooking on outside stoves, with the characteristic smell of burning pine and tortillas, and saw beyond them a little Spanish village, with a few Indians. Bronson, silent as usual, gave me a look which said, 'This is our place.' "

It was, indeed, the beginning of an entirely new life for him, as remote, in its very different way, from his point of departure, as Justine's at Sablé had been from hers. After a first year of outdoor life and rest, to recover his health, he had planned to join a group of archaeologists, but as soon as he began to see something of the life of Santa Fé, he developed an intense interest in local politics, identifying himself with the cause of the 'under-dog': the Spanish population of the State and the Indians who still survived in their reservations and villages. He built a house on the outskirts of the town, bought up a local paper, the *Santa Fé New Mexican*, chose for his friends a group of Spanish Americans and a wild Irish journalist, Brian Boru Dunne, used all his energy and influence to protect the interests of the Indians and to clean up the corruption of local politics, and eventually, at the age of forty, returned East as Republican Senator for New Mexico— a large, inscrutable, powerful politician, an ardent supporter of FDR's New Deal, an opponent of prohibition, an expert on foreign affairs—as silent as the young man who had gone West some eighteen years before, but very much more formidable.

When I stayed with him in Santa Fé, I still found all the classics Greek, and Latin, English, French and Italian—in his bookshelves, and sometimes, without a comment, he would hand me a new poem by Yeats, or, when no-one was about, would sit at the piano playing Bach. But in the company of his New Mexican friends, no trace of these interests was allowed to appear, partly no doubt from a natural distaste for what he would have considered a form of showing-off, but especially owing to the feeling which Justine has described as 'indignation at any form of inequality between human beings, including inequality of education or opportunity'. Today it would be called a repudiation of privilege.

'I remember', Justine once wrote to me, 'an occasion when I was sitting talking with ten or twelve of Bronson's men friends in Santa Fé. They were discussing a subject with which Bronson was thoroughly familiar, and he knew the answer to what was puzzling them, but he never opened his lips. Afterwards, I asked him:

"Why didn't you tell them, since you knew?"

"Why should I? They had a right to their own opinions." '

And she commented: "I have never heard Bronson use his superior knowledge to put anybody on the right track. It seemed to me that he felt that his superior education was an unfair advantage; the fact that he could speak several languages, another unfair advantage; the fact that he could live in a comfortable house when others could not do so, another unfair advantage."

The degree to which this sense of injustice weighed upon him is shown in another story. One day, after he had returned to Westbrook from New Mexico for a visit to his mother, they were walking together down one of the well-tended paths of the arboretum and passed one of the workmen who had been employed on the place for some forty years. My grandmother said a pleasant word to him, but Bronson pointedly looked the other way.

"Don't you remember Louis, Bronson? Why didn't you speak to him?"

"I was ashamed to."

"Ashamed of what?"

"Ashamed to think that a man's whole life should have been spent in tidying paths for us to walk on."

Bronson was the only member of his generation in our family to achieve success, in terms of public service—but at the cost of an outer transformation and an inner solitude at which one could only guess. He shared with Justine, as well as a love of music, a keen delight in the ridiculous, the grotesque, which would cause his large immobile face to expand into a slow irresistible smile; but it was only in the company of a very few people that he allowed this to occur. During his visits to us in Italy (for he came to Europe every year, and was better acquainted with European

34

politics and ways of thought than any American I have ever known) he would drop some of his armour; and with my son Gianni, with whom he clearly felt a real affinity, he would hold long conversations on the Westbrook piazza—both the small boy and the large man entirely absorbed, happy and at ease. But after Gianni's death he wrote to me that, though sympathising with my grief, he could himself only rejoice that the child had not lived to grow up, since he could not bear to contemplate the suffering that would have lain before him—a remark which I felt to be a sufficient comment on the writer's own 'successful' life.

In 1935 he said to Justine that he was convinced that there was no place in America left for a man of his type.

"Then why do you plan to campaign for another year in the Senate?"

"Because I can't let go, on account of the men who count on my support. I can't let them down."

Less than a year later, before he had been able to accomplish most of the public work he had planned, he died in an air crash on a flight back to Washington.

By then—since my grandfather, too, had died in 1912—only my grandmother and Olivia were left at home. Olivia, after a girlhood saddened by her father's and brother's death and by several years of ill-health, had made a marriage that had not been happy, and after its ending, had come back to Westbrook. It was there (except for a few winter months in New York) that she lived until her mother's death, running the dairy-farm and managing the estate, planning her mother's walks and rests (not without some occasional protests from her extremely active patient). She alone, owing to her deep attachment to Westbrook and her protective love for her mother, remained within the family orbit —but not without cost. She was a woman of great potential ability, of a singularly clear mind and judgement; she possessed a fine and discerning taste, she was immensely and sensitively generous; she performed valuable service in the First World War selecting personnel for the American Red Cross Overseas; she possessed, besides, a very deep (if carefully concealed) need for tenderness and affection. In her later years she seemed to me in the position of a person who has a dollar to give but of whom only change for a quarter is required. So she filled each hour of the day with self-appointed tasks, working on the boards of a few excellent charities, playing an active and constructive part in the activities of the Foreign Policy Association (which was then trying to educate American public opinion to a better knowledge of European affairs), giving support and help to a great many more people than anyone knew, walking about the house with little lists, sleeping badly, worrying about the welfare and daily routine of everyone she loved. Reticent, critical, unself-confident and generous, she had not found full scope for her qualities of either mind or heart; but in the last few years of her life—thanks to the companionship of a wise, cheerful and understanding friend, Nathalie Hopper, and to her own deep inner religious life —she achieved a certain serenity in accepting even this.

It was to her, and to my grandmother that, in 1923, I first brought my Italian fiancé, before our engagement was officially announced—somewhat disconcerting him, on the day of his arrival, by presenting to him the sight of a well-brought-up American family eating corn-on-the-cob—and it was there that we spent, with our engagement approved, one of the happiest months of my life, canoeing on the river and sailing in the Bay. It was to Westbrook that, after the Second World War, we both returned, bringing with us our two little girls of six and three. As we entered the hall and the grandfather clock began to chime, and my children ran to the French window with cries of delight at their first glimpse of the croquet-lawn and the river at its foot, all the war years were suddenly swept away. Here at least, I felt, nothing has changed! The shrubs were still as trim, the great trees as majestic, the milk as creamy, the house's appointments as impeccable, as before the war. Moreover my grandmother, though already approaching her ninetieth year, still kept, as she did to the year of her death, the keen enjoyment of the present moment which was one of her greatest charms: the guest to lunch, the drive in the electric car through the woods, the game of Scrabble after dinner, the small family festivity. I can see now the joint celebration on a later visit, of her birthday and that of my younger daughter, with the candles lighting up precisely the same expression of alert, unclouded delight on the faces of both the great-grandmother and the child.

In my children's recollection, indeed, Westbrook has remained an earthly paradise, and the months they spent there, the happiest part of their childhood. There was so much to do and see: the thickly-wooded islands to explore (feeling as safe and remote as Huck Finn or Robinson Crusoe himself), the river for canoeing, the barns on the home-farm which housed the fine herd of Jersey cows, the long-legged nuzzling calves, the trees of the arboretum, some of them with low, spreading branches which formed a green tent into which one could creep and lie, savouring the aromatic secrecy and darkness. As I watched my children enjoying these delights, I renewed the happiest recollections of my own child-hood, and saw them fascinated, as I had been, not only by this carefully planned and planted world, but by what still remained of the original wild life of the island: the snapping turtles which laid their eggs on the sandy riverbanks, and of which the bite, we were warned, could take off a man's leg, the squirrels and chipmunks and opossums and the vast variety of birds, and most of all, the family of wild swans on the river, at first so shy that they would take flight at any human approach, but gradually becoming so tame that they would glide up close to the river-path as we approached and dip their slender necks into the water for bread-crumbs. On one exciting day they even emerged onto the lawn, their ungainly gait on dry land a singular contrast to their majestic progress on the water. Sometimes, too, we would all go driving with my grandmother in the high, out-dated, open electric car, in which, until her eyesight failed, she drove herself over the roughest tracks in the woods. Always, though 'Granapa' was not with us, she would point out the trees and shrubs that he had planted and the paths he had planned, so that we still felt him to be our invisible, protecting host. Perhaps, indeed, the greatest gift of Westbrook was one which was never explicitly put into words: an awareness which could not fail to reach us, that what we saw was the creation of a completely happy marriage.

There was also another side to those last years—one which the children did not know and were too young to imagine. It consisted in the deep emotional undertow which, except in the hours in which they were with her, continually swept their great-grandmother back towards the past. The sorting and re-reading of literally thousands of old letters, each bundle carefully in-scribed and dated in her own hand, the ordering of old diaries and photographs—these, with her own Bible readings, filled the hours upstairs in her own room, until her eyesight failed her. Old joys, old sorrows, even old grievances and resentments filled her thoughts, and gradually, too (with no intention but one of love and piety), the very images of the dead became somewhat blurred and conventionalised, faded as it were in the light of their own haloes, until one could no longer clearly perceive the original human face.

Moreover it was impossible not to feel—especially coming from war-time Europe, where so many great houses had met with destruction and so many others, though still standing, could not hope to return to the life of the past—that we were existing in a world without a future, one which only my grandmother's presence rendered justifiable at all. In this, of course, Westbrook was only sharing the fate of many other large American houses, both in the country and the town, which had not suffered material destruction, as in Europe, but merely belonged to another way of life, in a country in which no tradition obliged one generation to continue what the preceding one had built. As early as 1905 Henry James, returning to his native land to observe 'The American Scene', had foretold the inevitable future decay of all the great houses that were then still rising on the Eastern seaboard, and of the life that was being led in them. 'Private ease,' he remarked, in Europe, was justified by the fact 'that old societies are arranged exactly to supply functions, forms, the whole element of custom and perpetuity.' But in America, he pointed out, precisely the opposite was true. 'For once that we ask ourselves in Europe what is going to become of a given piece of property, whether palace, castle, picture, *parure*, or other attribute of wealth, we indulge in the question twenty times in the United States—so scant an engagement does the visible order strike us as taking to provide for it.' And he proceeded, in one of his imaginary addresses, to upbraid the great houses of 'Uppermost Fifth Avenue': 'What are you going to make your future *of*, for all your airs, we want to know? What elements of a future are at all assured to you? . . . What you are reduced to for "importance" is the present, pure and simple, squeezing itself between an absent future and an absent past.'

These remarks might already have been addressed to Westbrook, as to many other houses of its kind, when first I stayed there as a girl—and twenty-five years later, they seemed still more pertinent. But I was mistaken: Westbrook still had before it a more stable and useful future than I could have foreseen. Long before then Olivia had fully realised that, much as she loved every stone and tree, it would be neither possible nor desirable to continue such a mode of life alone, after her mother's death, and it was she who, with her usual liberality and good sense, formed the plan which was perhaps the only way of saving the place. The farm, by then, had already been sold, but all the rest—house, grounds, and woods—was made over by my grandmother to the State of New York, with the proviso that Olivia might remain there during her lifetime, with an endowment of one million dollars, to be used as a botanical garden and park, open to the public, while the house was to be turned into a central office and tea-room. Picnics and amusement-parks were forbidden and cars were to be left near the entrance, so that visitors could enjoy, undisturbed, 'an oasis of beauty and of quiet for those who delight in outdoor beauty'.

This indeed is what has taken place. For two years after her mother's death Olivia, with a board of trustees, prepared the necessary changes, and then, with the arrangements completed, moved out for good. What she must have felt at leaving one can only surmise, but I think that later on she found a real satisfaction in the success of the scheme, and in watching Westbrook, in its new aspect, coming to life again. In the first year that it was opened to the public (1954) it was at once evident, by the number and type of visitors, that it met a real need; and ten years later the number of annual visitors had risen to 134,000.

So at last—after the death of almost everyone who originally lived there—a new pattern has taken shape. The beauty which my grandparents created for themselves and their friends now gives pleasure to thousands in a way which their children, too, would have fully approved, and which again brings the past to life. Children still hide under the sweeping branches of the willows, family parties explore the woods, young couples stand beside the azaleas at the water's brink. But I must confess that I myself have not had the courage to return there; and what has happened to the wild swans, I do not know.

39

2

Desart Court

For nothing is better or more precious than when
two of one heart and mind keep house together,
husband and wife ... But they know it best
themselves.

ODYSSEY, VI, 183*

THE ATMOSPHERE of the other house in which my childhood's holidays were set, the home of my mother's Anglo-Irish parents, Desart Court, was in many ways very different from that of Westbrook. Far more beautiful in appearrance—since it was an Italianate house built towards the end of the eighteenth century of the grey local limestone known as 'Kilkenny marble', with an austere central block of classical design linked by two semi-circular passages to the wings for children and guests—it stood in gently rolling parkland, looking across the gay, untidy patchwork quilt of what had originally been designed as a formal Italian garden, towards the misty purple outline of the mountain Slievenaman. But its neglected, overgrown shrubbery of laurel, laburnum and lilac, hawthorn and rhododendron, and its brick-walled garden where the grass was thick under the apple-trees and blackbirds were almost as numerous among the currant-bushes as rabbits in the flowerbeds, would have horrified any of the Westbrook gardeners, and reflected a way of life that was at once less luxurious and more easy going. Yet both houses had one thing in common: a child felt safe there. And Desart, too, was the creation of an unusually happy marriage.

Of my Irish family's history I only know that our ancestor Joseph Cuffe—the great-grandson of a Henry Cuffe who was executed on Tower Hill for taking part in Essex's rebellion—served under Cromwell in Ireland and was presented by him with the lands of Desart, 'Cuffe's Desert', in the sense of reward. His

* Translated by W. H. D. Rouse.

40

grandson, John, the first Baron Desart, married Dorothea Gorges, whose mother, my great-great-great-great-great-grandmother, Nicola Sophia, the daughter of Hugh Hamilton, Lord Glenawly, was the protagonist of a well-known Irish ghost story, one which fascinated us as children and to which we gave the name 'The Black Velvet Ribbon'.

Nicola, who was born in 1666, was left an orphan at an early age and was brought up, together with a young cousin, Lord Tyrone, in an idyllic country childhood, in the manner of *Paul et Virginie*. They were, however, both inculcated with the 'baneful principles of Deism', and when, having reached the age of fourteen, they were separated, they both came into the hands of guardians determined 'to extirpate the erroneous principles instilled into their youthful minds' and to teach them the truths of the Christian faith. Before parting, they exchanged a solemn vow that whichever of them died first would reappear to the other, to reveal which view of the universe was the true one and when, after Nicola's marriage to Sir Tristram Beresford, they met again, they repeated their pact. Shortly afterwards, when Nicola and her husband were staying with some neighbours, the Magills of Gill Hall, she came down one morning to breakfast looking pale and distracted, wearing around her left wrist a wide black velvet ribbon—but to all her husband's inquiries she merely replied that, though she had never refused any other request of his, this was a matter that she could not explain. She would never, she added, be seen again without the black velvet ribbon.

At that moment a footman entered, delivering a letter sealed in black. "It is as I expected," Lady Beresford exclaimed, "Tyrone is dead."

Still, however, she refused to reply to her husband's inquiries, and a few years later, having received from her a son and heir, he died, without apparently ever learning that on the night in question his wife had received a visitor from another world. This was, of course, Lord Tyrone, whom she suddenly awoke to find 'sitting on the bedside'.

"For Heaven's sake, Tyrone," she cried (this part of the story is told in her own words), "for what purpose have you come here at this time of night?"

"Have you forgotten our pact?" he replied. "You must know

41

that I departed this life on Tuesday last at four o'clock and have been deputed by the Supreme Being to appear to you, to assure you that revealed religion is the only true one."

He then went on to tell her that the child she was then expecting would be a boy, and would in due course marry his own daughter. Soon after the baby boy's birth, he added, her husband would die and after a time she would be married again to a man who would make her very unhappy; she would have four more sons and daughters and would die when she reached her forty-seventh year.

She then asked for some outward token, which would serve next day as a proof that he really had visited her and had not merely been a figure in a dream. First he lifted up the heavy red velvet bed-curtains through a hook high above the bed (but this, she objected, might have been done by herself in a nightmare), then he laid two fingers upon the chest of drawers, charring the wood (but this, she said, might have been an accident). Next he wrote a few words in her pocket-book—but these too, she said, she might doubt the next day. Finally he told her to stretch out her hand, and she obeyed.

'He touched my wrist—his hand was as cold as marble—in a minute the sinews shrank and every nerve withered.'

He then warned her never to let anyone see her wrist—and was gone.

Time passed and, one after another, Lord Tyrone's prophecies came true. Lady Beresford's son was born, her husband died and, though, in the hope of avoiding the fulfilment of the latter part of the prophecy, she moved to a small country village where the only man of her own class was an elderly clergyman, he unfortunately possessed a schoolboy son, Richard Gorges, who, in due course, grew up, made love to her, persuaded her to marry him, gave her two sons and two daughters and made her as miserable as Lord Tyrone had foreseen.

She then awaited with some apprehension the coming of her forty-seventh birthday, but it passed uneventfully and when the forty-eighth drew near she decided to give a small party to celebrate the event, in the belief that her cousin's predictions had at last worn themselves out. She invited a few friends to spend the day with her, her guests including the Archbishop of Dublin and an old clergyman who had baptised her in infancy. In the course of the day she told them that this party was to celebrate her forty-eighth birthday. But the old clergyman interrupted her; he had recently, he said, examined the registers of the parish where she was born and could assure her ladyship that she was only just reaching the age of forty-seven!

"You have pronounced my death warrant," Lady Beresford replied and, inviting the Archbishop of Dublin, who afterwards testified that this had occurred, and her son Sir Marcus Beresford (then a boy of twelve), to go with her into her bedroom, she told them the whole story. She also told her son that he would un-doubtedly one day marry Lord Tyrone's daughter, Katherine de la Poer, and exhorted him 'to conduct himself so as to deserve that high honour'. She then lay down upon the bed to compose herself and when, a few hours later, her son and daughter returned to the room, they saw that she had already left this world. Then they at last unbound the black velvet ribbon from her wrist, and found it as she had described it, with 'the sinews shrunk, every nerve withered'.

Her son, as had been foretold, married Katherine de la Poer and became the first Marquess of Waterford, and one of her daughters by her second husband, Richard Gorges, married John, the first Lord Desart. The connection of the 'Lady of the Black Velvet Ribbon' with Desart Court was thus indisputably not very close, but her story haunted my imagination and added a touch of romance to the stately grey house and the distant blue hills. Was the veil between the two worlds quite easy to lift? Besides, there was one room at Desart—a guest's room overlooking the drive, to which I was promoted when I was considered old enough to leave the nursery wing—in which there was a lingering atmo-sphere of deep apprehension, of overwhelming sadness, which I at once felt on the first night I slept there. My grandfather's elder brother, I was told later on, was a hard and reckless rider to hounds, and day after day in the hunting season, as dusk began to fall, his young and anxious wife would stand with a candle in the window of this room, looking across the stretch of rolling park-land and waiting for him to come home. She *knew*, she said—though of course he only laughed at her—that one day he would have a fatal accident, and though in point of fact this did not occur, she left in that room, still lingering there some fifty years later, her long-drawn-out, unbearable grief and fear.

Several years later—this story was told by my mother—my great-uncle Otway Cuffe, who (unlike my grandfather) was much interested in psychic matters and who had spent some bad nights himself in 'the north room', drove over to Desart late one evening, in my grandfather's absence, with Mrs. Standish O'Grady, who had some psychic gifts herself, and they were both surprised to see a light shining in the north bedroom window, and a faint figure standing there. "The maids should be downstairs now," he said, "and there is no-one else in the house!" As he spoke, the figure disappeared, and the light with it, and when they went upstairs they found the door locked from the outside.

When my grandfather was told this story, he was much annoyed. "Really," he said, "I don't know whether the idea of poor Ellen standing at that window or of Mrs. O'Grady seeing her there makes me more uncomfortable. No wonder our guests can't sleep in such a crowd!" The room was re-papered, and naturally none of us children was told the story. But when, after my first night there, I shyly said to my grandmother that it seemed "a very sad room", she at once briskly moved me back to the nursery wing, where each day succeeded the other in a safe and carefree routine, well rooted in the world of every-day.

*   *   *   *   *

I have before me a photograph, taken in 1904, which shows my grandparents as they were then, and as I still clearly remember them: waiting for our arrival at the foot of the double stairway of grey stone leading up from the gravel sweep of the drive to the front door—Gran wearing a feather boa and a hat perched high on her head, and Gabba* a well-worn knickerbocker suit of greenish-grey Irish tweed, smoking his after-breakfast pipe, with his spaniel sitting on the balustrade beside him. It was thus that we would find them when—tired and grimy after the long night-crossing of the Irish Channel, the train journey to Kilkenny and the leisurely fifteen-mile drive in an Irish car through the gentle

---

* I do not remember the origin of this nickname for my grandfather, but neither my cousins nor myself ever used any other.

landscape of green fields and low stone walls—we at last caught
sight of the familiar house, and Gran and Gabba standing before
it. Whenever in childhood I thought of them, it was there that I
saw them, recalling, too, the faint aroma of his pipe and of her
lavender water. But in fact they had been married for many years
before they came to live at Desart.

The younger son of an impoverished Irish peer, it had been
made clear to Hamilton Cuffe from childhood (as to my American
grandfather in *his* youth) that he would have to make his own
way in the world, and at the age of twelve, after a brief period as
a naval cadet on the training-ship *Britannia*, he was already seeing
service in December 1861 in a wooden frigate, the *Orlando*, bound
for Halifax. The account of his three years in the Navy—set down
only to please his grandchildren, since he himself did not really
consider it worth telling—gives a remarkable picture of the hard-
ships and responsibilities which little boys were then expected to
bear. The frigate was leaking so badly that it was a miracle that
she ever reached her destination; the food consisted only of salt
beef, pork, an occasional shark at sea and ship's biscuits, the latter
so full of weevils that the boys used to cook them before eating
'so that these somewhat disagreeable insects might at least be dead
before we consumed them', and the hours allotted to sleep were
so few that the boys, still hardly more than children, lived in constant terror of falling asleep on watch. From Halifax they proceeded
to the Bermudas, where Ham Cuffe was promoted, being then just
thirteen, to the rank of midshipman and was placed in command
of one of the ship's boats. These boats often spent a part of the
day on shore duty and it was the midshipman's task to see that all
hands, drunk or sober, got back to the ship safely, 'in spite of the
temptation to the men to slip away on shore, for the purpose of
enlisting in the blockade-runners of the American Civil War'.
(These were smugglers who supplied the Confederate troops with
arms and food and rum, and from whom a competent sailor
could command very high pay.) To maintain order over a crew of
fifteen large men, often drunk and insubordinate, was more than
a slight ordeal for a boy of thirteen, and was only rendered possible by the backing of a stern and merciless authority on board.
My grandfather recollected, indeed, with real horror, an occasion
on which one of the midshipmen had been struck on shore by a

Images and Shadows

drunken sailor. "The man was brought before the Captain and flogged, all hands being piped to witness the torture. I do not think," he added with characteristic reticence, "that any purpose would be served by describing it in detail, but it was really a very terrible thing to see."

After two years, however, partly owing to poor health and partly to the fact that he was not really drawn to a sailor's life, he returned ashore and went to Cambridge to take his degree. The rest of his reminiscences are chiefly of interest, I think, to later generations for their glimpses of the society to which he belonged —one in which money (at any rate for a young bachelor) was of very little account but in which privilege rested wholly on birth and breeding. At Cambridge (where his college was Trinity) there were then four classes of undergraduates—the Noblemen (peers, or the eldest sons of peers, who wore a very full silken gown), the Fellow Commoners (distinguished in Hat Fellow Commoners, younger sons of peers, who might wear a high hat) and Ordinary Fellow Commoners (who wore a mortar-board of velvet) and finally the ordinary undergraduates or 'pensioners'. Noblemen and Fellow Commoners not only dined at the High Table with the dons and had special seats in chapel, but were permitted to take their degrees after only seven terms at the University instead of the usual nine—perhaps from a vague idea that they would be needed sooner for public service.

Though not rich enough to afford hunters of his own, my grandfather had no lack of friends to mount him, and his weekends appear to have been spent in the smallest and barest rooms of some of the greatest English country-houses, in which luxury and glamour contrasted with extreme discomfort. At Belvoir, for instance, a private band played every night after dinner, beginning with a quadrille in which every member of the party, even the most elderly, was expected to take part, before the young people were allowed to indulge in a polka or a valse. Here Ham Cuffe's bedroom was in a very small turret at the top of the house, with windows all round letting in the icy air, and so small that he could only shave or brush his hair by kneeling on the floor. Moreover, on one occasion, when the Duke of Rutland's large party included royalty and some distinguished guests, the humbler members of the party, according to my grandfather's account,

46

were ordered by the Duke 'to shoot somewhere each day where we should not disturb the royal party. Since there were ten degrees of frost and we were sent to places where there was nothing whatever to shoot, we would rather have stayed at home, but the Duke was not a man to be crossed.'

At Chatsworth there were no bells at all, the assumption being 'that any male guest would bring his own servant with him, who would wait outside his bedroom', so that this young guest, who had never had a servant, was obliged to engage one just for a week. At Harewood, too, where he often stayed—until its doors were closed to him by his host's disapproval of him as a fiancé for his second daughter—there was a similar mixture of grandeur and austerity, the comfortable rooms and meals downstairs offering a remarkable contrast to the bare necessities in the bachelors' wing, and, to an even more marked degree, in the nursery quarters upstairs, where the children of the family lived, like mediæval Jews, in a grim and poverty-stricken ghetto, secluded, ugly and bitterly cold.

When, after taking his degree, Hamilton Cuffe returned to London, to eat his dinners and make his way at the bar, his social life continued in much the same manner, its diversions being 'archery and cricket in the summer, shooting and hunting in the winter'. 'I was introduced to society,' he wrote, 'by the simple process of my mother's leaving cards for me on her friends and relations. . . . An impecunious young man had his definite place in society, but might not presume upon it. All that he required was a suit of dress clothes and its appurtenances, and enough money to take a cab on a particularly wet night. . . . To have suggested taking a young woman out for the evening, however near her relationship, would have been considered an outrage, and to invite one's hostess, an impertinence.'

All this was very pleasant and carefree, until long before it was 'suitable' to do so—he fell in love. One of the houses in which he then sometimes stayed was the great, formal pseudo-Palladian house in Yorkshire belonging to Henry, Earl of Harewood, and presided over by his second wife—a handsome young Yorkshire-woman who had married him at the age of only nineteen and who had already added five more children (yet two others were to come later) to the six he had received from his first wife. These children played, however, a remarkably small part in the visible life of the great household; indeed there was a legend that, on meeting two of his younger children in a pram in Hyde Park, wheeled by a pretty nursery-maid, Lord Harewood had stopped to ask whose children those babies were: "Yours, m'Lord." Lady Harewood's duties as a hostess and her passion for the hunting-field left her little time to pay much attention to her large brood, who ran wild over the grounds, priding themselves on being 'bears by crest and bears by nature', and who turned for such mothering as they required to the second of their elder sisters, Margaret, since the first, Constance, an exquisite Dresden-china beauty, was already 'out' and planning to take flight from Harewood as soon as possible. It was 'Peg', warm-hearted and high-spirited, who shared some of their escapades and bound up their cuts and sprains, and it was on her—still in the schoolroom, as plump and bright-eyed as a young thrush and socially non-existent—that, on a cold winter's day in 1870, Ham Cuffe's choice fell. The whole tribe of children had, for once, joined the grown-up party to skate upon the lake, and Peg, as usual, had fastened on the skates of all 'the little ones' and was trying to warm her hands to buckle on her own, when her distant cousin, the quiet, pleasant young man who, in virtue of his cousinhood, had once or twice been allowed to climb up to the cold schoolroom to teach her to play chess, knelt down on the ice and put them on for her. No-one had ever done such a thing for her before. On the tide of her blushing gratitude and his protective tenderness, they fell in love—for life. In the year after their golden wedding, which was also that of Gran's death, my grandfather wrote to me: 'After fifty-six years of love and fifty-one of marriage, our love in *all* its forms was identical with that of our youth, when, after long years of waiting, we left for our honeymoon.'

It is hardly surprising, however, that at first the romance was not smiled upon. Ham Cuffe, however pleasant and industrious, was only a younger son, with no money and no prospects—not at all the husband whom Lord Harewood (when he thought about his children at all, which was seldom) had in mind for one of his daughters—and Margaret herself was only just seventeen. There was one love-letter, slipped into the pages of a copy of Byron's poems, and one other meeting, at a ball at Bridgewater House

48

to which, owing to a timely illness of her elder sister's, Margaret was sent at the last moment in Constance's dress (the programme, with her name written on it seven times, was kept by my grandfather until his death). Then, Lord Harewood issued an edict: they must not meet again. For the first two years, even letters were officially forbidden, but a few were in fact exchanged through Margaret's sister and a kind cousin—and Margaret's own family can hardly have been unaware of her feelings (however little importance they attached to them) since, after that first season, she refused to go out in London again.

All his life my grandfather kept the letters of their long time of waiting—letters which were sometimes a child's and sometimes a grown woman's, sometimes merely accounts of her dull country life, or descriptions of her father's indifference ('You know he does not like me and I think he never will'), her step-mother's coldness and her brother's demands, and sometimes, too, accounts of the constant pressure put upon her to give him up, until she began to wonder if indeed it was fair to him to ask him to go on waiting. 'Even if we are married', she wrote, 'you will always have the hardest share of the burden to carry. Poverty is so much harder for a man than a woman, they feel all the little discomforts so much more than we do' (here one seems to see the shade of Papa in the background) 'and I can't bear to think of you enduring all this for me.' But as to her own feelings there is never a shadow of doubt, even though each letter is also marked by a touching humility which is perhaps one of the signs of 'true love', and which certainly reveals a young girl very uncertain of herself, and very unlike the brisk, affectionate, decisive woman who was the 'Gran' we knew, and who would, perhaps, never have become so but for the love and support of her 'Ham'. But she was then still only eighteen and—after all the years of being snubbed by her father and step-mother and of unthanked fagging for her brothers—she found it quite impossible to believe that anyone, 'least of all a young man as brilliant and kind as Hamilton Cuffe', should really want and value her. 'It seems so very strange to me', she wrote, 'that anyone can love me in the way you do. It is such a new sensation that I am worth caring for or fit for anything but just to be useful.' Yet year after year, she went on writing—unselfish, courageous, tender, loving—and, in the last years, very very weary of waiting. These were letters he could never bear to destroy. I have them still.

Then, at last, the situation slightly changed; there was an improvement in Ham Cuffe's position and prospects, for his father had died and only one brother stood between him and the peerage, while he himself was said to be doing very well at the Bar. The young couple were allowed to meet again, though only once, in a cousin's house; there was an interview between Ham and Lord Harewood, and on the following day Margaret wrote in surprise that her father 'though he would say nothing to me, seemed quite impressed by the fact that you care for me and are working hard'. Letters between them were now countenanced, but no further meetings. 'I watched you from the window going away that day until I could see you no longer, but it felt like a bad dream, as if I were quite numb and powerless to move or do anything but watch you.' Yet she admitted that it was 'less bad' than their former parting at Bridgewater House, and that some hope now lay ahead. For another year the situation dragged on, with the young couple as firm in their determination as ever, but obliged to content themselves with letters and an occasional 'accidental' meeting at the theatre or in the Park. But gradually, by the sheer passage of time, the family's opposition was worn down and, when Margaret's grandmother, Lady Clanricarde (perhaps with this purpose in mind) left a small legacy to her favourite granddaughter, Lord Harewood was again approached. This time a telegram—its faded ink lies before me now—went off from Lady Harewood to Ham's chambers in the Temple: 'Henry says yes.' A few weeks later, in July 1876, they were married at St Margaret's Westminster, and settled down, as was suitable to their small income, in a very little house in Pelham Crescent.

The picture of their early married life used to fascinate me in my childhood, when already it seemed to belong to a world almost as remote as it would to my children now. The house was, as I have said, very small, but my grandmother's trousseau did not match it: it consisted of twelve dozen of everything—chemises and nightgowns and stockings and flannel petticoats—made of such good material that forty years later, in my childhood, she was wearing them still. She brought with her, too, a dressing-case fitted with gold and tortoise-shell and her share of the family

jewels, suitable only for a great hostess, and the silver plate and
cutlery was so abundant that the only helpful piece of advice that
her great-aunt, the Duchess of Buccleuch, could find to give her—
"since I hear, my dear, that you will not be very well off"—was to
have all of it gilt to save cleaning! All these objects were, of course,
swiftly sent to the bank, but the wedding-gown, of stiff white
satin, was reshaped and dyed (first pale pink, she told us, then red,
then purple) and worn as her best evening gown for nearly as long
as the underclothes beneath it.

Throughout their married life, money was of very little account,
but privilege was taken for granted. The comfort of Westbrook
or the fine furniture of 72nd Street were things that the Desarts
would never have dreamed of possessing or even desiring, but,
for all their personal modesty and quiet unassuming manners, it
never occurred to them to doubt that certain *égards* were due to
them. My grandfather's dress-suit might be a little shabby and
Gran's gown was dyed, but they took it for granted that, for a
party at Buckingham Palace, they should have the 'entrée' (permission to enter by a side-door, thus avoiding the long queue of
carriages before the main entrance), that if there was a party at
Devonshire House they would be among the guests, and that, in
the modest *pension* in Switzerland or on the Italian Lakes, where
they took their holidays abroad, the head-waiter should automatically assign to them the best table. "Great friend of mine,
Mario," my grandfather would say benignly, as he sat down,
"always looks after me."

Such parties and holidays, however, were few in number in the
early years of their marriage: first came many years of frugal living
and hard work. The promise of my grandfather's early career in
the law was relinquished when, in 1878, Disraeli offered him the
post of Assistant Solicitor to the Treasury, a post providing a
fixed income and consequent security for his wife and two little
girls, my aunt Joan (later on, Lady Joan Verney) and my mother,
Sybil. It was then that the whole family moved to the tall little
house, as tall and narrow as a sentry-box, in Rutland Gardens (a
small side-street off Knightsbridge), which became their London
house: a basement kitchen, two rooms on each floor, and, uniting
them, the steep stairs up which the maids carried, not only every
morsel of food, but the heavy Victorian tea-trays and dishes, and

the tall cans of hot water for the children's baths. There was indeed one bathroom, with a coffin-like bath encased in dark mahogany, beside my grandmother's bedroom; but the children or guests used tin hip-baths—and indeed to many Victorians their bath was a highly personal possession, almost like their clothes. One of my great-uncles, for one, refused all his life to use any hotel bathroom, saying that it was a nasty, dirty habit to wash in a public tub.

That his house was ugly troubled my grandfather not at all. "I look *out of* it, not at it," he would say, and indeed the view was pleasant enough, since the windows gave out upon a great plane-tree, and the secluded street, being no thoroughfare, had almost a country stillness, only broken by an occasional cab or barrel-organ or the cry of "Lavender, sweet lavender!" As for interior decoration, Gran kept the drawing-room fresh with the brightest and crackliest of chintzes, and hung the walls with water-colours of Desart and family portraits; but her husband placed no objects of his own in his study, in the course of some fifty years, but a complete set of the Navy Record Society and a very ugly pipe-rack.

The truth was that, but for Desart, he attached very little importance to the house he lived in, except as a frame in which he could see his wife and children and do his work. Every morning, wet or shine, Gran walked with her husband as far as Hyde Park Corner (she was still doing so forty years later, when I stayed with them as a child, sometimes looking in at Harrods, on the way home, as a treat). Every evening at six, his latch-key was heard in the door, and he had the hour in the drawing-room with his wife and daughters (and later on with his grandchildren), which was for him the happiest time of the day. His family and his work were his whole life. After the death of his elder brother and his accession to the peerage, in 1898, he resigned from the Treasury, but worked no less hard in the House of Lords, taking part in any debate about Ireland and belonging to many Parliamentary Commissions; he was appointed a member of the Privy Council, served on the International Court of Arbitration at The Hague, became an Irish magistrate and the Lord Lieutenant of his county, was appointed Treasurer of the Inner Temple; and finally, at the age of seventy, was a leading figure in the small group of Irish Loyalists who, at the Convention in Dublin and Belfast in 1918, made a last despairing effort towards the settlement of the Irish question. 'With short intervals', he wrote to me in his old age, 'I have served the Crown all my working life, that is, for something over fifty years.'

"Your dear father", said Bernard Berenson to my mother, after having shown him his celebrated collection of Italian pictures without eliciting more than an intelligent interest, "always makes me think of the Roman prefect, in one of Anatole France's stories. . . . Yes, don't you remember? The prefect, hearing that Saint Simon had been standing on a pillar motionless for a year, was shocked to think how little he had done in that time for the State!"

It is singularly difficult to give a true picture of my grandfather, even though I have a great deal of information to draw upon, both in his own memoirs and the book in which my mother completed them, in many packets of letters, and above all, in the close tie of affection and sympathy between us, since I was three years old. For any portrait of him, to be authentic, should be etched with a very light pen—as fine, as unemphatic, as the one used by Chinese artists to depict their sages. He, too, was, by temperament and by conviction, a dweller in the Middle Kingdom.

Though a man of strong moral convictions, his mind was always open to the 'other fellow's' point of view. I remember my mother telling me that, when the news of the Jameson Raid had just reached England and all her young friends were ardently championing the 'gallant raiders', she wrote to her father, who was then abroad, a youthful letter reflecting this enthusiasm and received, by telegram, a damping reply: 'Facts not yet ascertained: reserve opinion.'

I think, too, that this natural impartiality was reinforced by an aristocratic conviction that too great vehemence, or too extreme an expression of opinion, were slightly ill-bred. I remember exclaiming as a child, in full assurance of being approved of: "I *hate* so and so; he says Ireland should break away from England at once!"—and being suppressed, as he glanced at me over his spectacles, by the quiet reply: "But, my dear, one doesn't *hate* people on account of their political opinions!" Since then I have been acquainted with two generations of Nazis, Fascists, Communists and their aftermath, in a very different climate, and know that such a comment was the product of a more stable, more secure and more self-confident generation. It was the only attitude possible for a man like him, and it was not shaken even when, only a few years later, his own Irish house was burned to the ground in 'the Troubles'.

A similar moderation—together with a quiet refusal to be swept off his own ground by other people's enthusiasms, or by what seemed to him merely a matter of prestige, whether social or aesthetic—coloured his taste. My mother has described how on one occasion, after having spent a long morning with her in the picture-gallery of Siena, looking at a long series of *fondi d'oro*, he showed signs of having had enough.

"But you *like* Italian pictures," she said, "you always took us as children to the Italian room in the National Gallery!"

"I took you perhaps twice a year," he answered firmly. "I like a *little* Italian art—not too much, and not every day. What I should like now is a country walk."

A countryman he always was, both by inheritance and taste, and it was to his father's house in Ireland, which had been his home in boyhood, that his affections were most closely bound. It was not until middle age, however, that the death of his elder brother, in 1898, caused him to inherit both the earldom and the estate and, though Desart then at once became the true centre of his life, he was only able to live there for as much of the year as his work in London would allow. Then, at last, he could throw off the burdens of a harassed civil servant and become the easy-going country gentleman that his father and grandfather had been before him; a good landlord, who improved the grass for his cattle and cared for his woods, who kept his cottage and farms in good repair and often closed an eye on the quarterly rent-day—and also a host who liked to keep open house, as in the days when, as he himself wrote, 'No-one cared if you came in a donkey-cart or a coach-and-four to a garden-party, and any officer who possessed a horse was welcome in any house to dine and sleep before a meet.'

So, as in the old days, they all came to the 'Big House', and Gran (while struggling hard, by small economies, to make both ends meet) came to accept her husband's dictum that 'nobody cares what you give them to eat in Ireland'. Safely hidden in the boughs of a leafy copper-beech, my cousins and I would peer down

54

at the guests, as we heard carriage-wheels bowling down the drive, and decide whether or not we wished to join the party. Sometimes it would be a young English officer posted at Kilkenny, inquiring about hunting prospects for next season, sometimes the courtly Trollopian Bishop of Ossory—aptly named Dr. Crozier—for lunch; or the Kilkenny solicitor or doctor and their wives for tea, or the neighbours with their house-parties to see the garden with its long rows of tall sweet-peas and clumps of delphiniums, or some young people for tennis and croquet on the rough lawns, and children to swing with us under the trees, to creep under the gooseberry and strawberry-nets in the kitchen garden and eat and eat, to present carrots and sugar to Sally the donkey in the paddock and to coax her to let us climb on to her dusty, boney back. Once a year, too, there was the school party, with long trestle-tables laid under the trees and some seventy tangle-haired, bright-eyed children with their schoolmaster, Mr. Collins, rather too deferential. There were races and competitions and small prizes so attractive that we all secretly longed for them, too. And in the centre of all these occasions moved my grandparents—she as gay, as innocently pleased by these small gaieties as when she had been a young girl; he with the air of being equally at ease, equally relaxed in every sort of company, that is perhaps a peculiarly Irish gift.

Looking back upon those days, it is difficult to realise that beneath this gay and friendly surface—for every farmer and cottage-woman, too, appeared devoted to their landlord and called him 'the spitting image' of his own father—so much hatred (of religion, class, and race) was stirring, that the years of the Great Famine were less than half a century away, and 'the Troubles' just ahead. How much these preoccupations, in those first years, troubled my grandfather I do not know, but certainly by the time that I was growing up they filled a large part of his thoughts and even from the first they may have accounted for what seemed to my mother in *her* youth a somewhat intolerant impatience with the cult of Irish folk-lore, superstition, and poetry which was then just coming into fashion and which so greatly appealed to her. She could not understand that her father should prefer the Ireland of 'An Irish R.M.' to that of Yeats and Synge, of A. E. and Lady Gregory, and tried hard to convert him. But he only smiled. "I know you think me a Philistine," he told her, "of course there is charm in all these fancies, but sooner or later they lead to cruelty and trouble. There is danger in every denial of reason." He felt a faintly amused irritation, too, at the activities of his younger brother, Otway Cuffe—my mother's much-loved 'Uncle Dot'—a great traveller and a confirmed theosophist who in his later years settled down on the banks of the Suir, and extended his enthusiasm for the wisdom of the East to Irish lore and the nationalism of 'Young Ireland'. When Otway told my grandfather that, according to Yeats, the divulgation of Irish folk-tales among educated people and the association of literature with popular music, speech and dancing might "so deepen the political passion of the nation that all—artists and poets, craftsmen and day-labourers—would accept a common design", he dryly replied that this was precisely what he feared. But Otway followed his own course—wearing a highly picturesque costume which he (but no-one else) declared to be the Irish national dress, setting up workshops for wood-carvers and bookbinders in the manner of William Morris, collecting folk-stories about the 'Little People' and changelings, and encouraging the study of Erse. Of this last my grandfather disapproved not only on practical grounds but because he believed that all differences of language tend to divide, and that what Ireland needed was unity.

As for my grandmother, she did not concern herself much with these matters, but interpreted what came before her eyes with realistic and kindly common sense. One day (the story is told by my mother in her reminiscences) she had driven with an English cousin and her brother-in-law Otway down the straggling, poverty-stricken street of a neighbouring village. "They need poetry, poetry and music," said Uncle Dot as they drove away. "Perhaps," said Gran a little doubtfully. "What they seemed to me to need *most*, though, was buttons and teeth."

*   *   *   *   *

It is with the recollection of Desart that my own story becomes intertwined with my grandfather's, since it was, for my cousins and myself, our home in the holidays—and our earthly Paradise.

Can these holidays really have been as long and as untroubled as they seem in my recollection? Was the house so stately and the shrubbery so thick and dark, the park so green, the woods so deep in bluebells? I could walk about the house, if it still existed, blindfold today.

The square entrance hall, in which stood the post-box of which my grandfather held the key, was flanked on one side by the dining-room with its great oval table over which my grandparents presided and at which at least twenty people of all ages generally sat down to lunch, my grandfather carving the roast beef or leg of mutton at one end and my grandmother the fowls at the other. On the sideboard stood the bowls for the dogs' dinners and for the chickens—both prepared by my grandmother herself, not without an occasional anxious glance at her guests' plates for fear that they would not leave enough; while another sideboard was given up to the delicious hot-house fruit, which no child might touch until every guest had helped himself. On the other side of the hall was my grandfather's study, with its well-bound 'gentleman's library' and family portraits; behind, looking over the garden, was the drawing-room, with its gay chintzes, smelling of sweet-peas, wet dogs and fresh roses, and the pianola on which some child was always playing, while a fine double staircase led to the bedrooms upstairs.

The kitchen was in the basement, together with the house-keeper's room, the servants' hall, the still-room and the pantry, all linked by a wide, damp, stone-flagged underground passage, which led into the cobbled stable-yard. Here stood the loose-boxes for Gabba's hunters, the carriage-horses and our ponies, the saddle-room, with its delicious smell of leather and fine array of old harnesses and saddles, and the dairy, in which we learned how to make rich, golden butter. It all suggests great lavishness, yet I know that, in order to keep it up at all, my grandparents often denied themselves many small personal comforts, and to local eyes their reign seemed economical, if not stingy, compared with that of their predecessors, for the tramps who came into the stable-yard used to complain, "In the old Countess's time there'd be legs of mutton for the picking on the dust-heap every day!"

Freedom, that was the dominant note of our life at Desart, the spice of our delight—freedom within a rule of order. Punctuality, in my grandfather's eyes, was not relative but absolute: you were late for lunch, unless you were standing in the hall *before* the gong had finished ringing. (I must add, however, that since we were in Ireland—where, as in Italy, rules are mercifully flexible—the old butler went on ringing the gong until a glance over his shoulder told him that the last breathless grandchild had arrived.) Good manners, too, were not so much required as taken for granted: they were an instinctive response, in all his grandchildren, to his own urbanity, and my mother used to say that the same was already true in her childhood. 'The sound of his latch-key in the door', she wrote, in her reminiscences, 'was the signal for the straightening of sashes and the steadying of behaviour; to be boisterous or mannerless in his company was somehow inconceivable.'

It was not that he was sharp with us; indeed I can remember him waiting for a long time on his horse in a cold wind, patient and amused, beside one of the park gates, while I, on a restless pony, struggled clumsily to open it and hold it back with my riding-crop for the others to pass; but it never occurred to him to let me off this small act of good manners; nor did he admit shyness as an excuse for any lack of friendliness towards the bedridden, complaining old women he took me to visit in the dank, musty cottages.

A few well-defined duties, too, were demanded of both my cousins and myself: to help Gran with picking sweet-peas and raspberries and, after lunch, with the dogs' dinner and feeding the chickens; to collect the eggs beneath broody hens (this I disliked very much, when they squawked and pecked); to pick up windfalls in the orchard—often with a great soggy slice of ginger cake from the cook, as a reward for a full basket—and to learn the Collect for the day by heart before breakfast on Sunday mornings. When all this was accomplished, the rest of the week was ours.

To an only child like myself, the daily companionship of my Verney cousins—the good-looking eldest boy, Gerald (for whom, since he was my mirror of perfection, I would even carry home dead rabbits by the ears), my immediate contemporary and close companion Ulick, and the two younger ones, Desmond and Joy—was intoxicating in itself, and indeed my mother used to complain that at Desart my good manners suffered as much as my pretty clothes, though she did not know that, as soon as I was out of sight, the long white muslin dresses in which she took such pride

58

were tucked into my bloomers, and the floppy hat hung on a bush. But it was the freedom that was the real delight; to explore the woody tangle of laburnum and laurel in the shrubbery, where we had a 'secret' hut, thatched with branches and carpeted with hay; to climb the apple-trees and pear-trees and munch their sunny fruit; to bicycle, when I was a little older, on the road outside the lodge gates, though terrified, whenever my cousins outdistanced me and disappeared from sight, that the bogey we had all been warned against, a tramp, might suddenly emerge from behind a hedge.

"Wait for me! Oh, wait for me!"

A certain anxiety, too, attended my first ventures on a pony. It was delightful to set off across the park in the early, early morning, always hoping, as one entered the beechwoods, for the glimpse of a vixen with her cubs slinking across one of the green rides. I never really had, however, the makings of a good horsewoman; my pony was often too fresh, I was always too nervous, and there was a certain relief in the pronouncement—after a bad toss on a stony road had resulted in some days in bed with concussion— that I had better ride no more that summer.

Only unmitigated pleasure, however, attended the yearly excursion to the wooded hill of Ballykeefe, where the thickest blackberry bushes grew, and where, every year, we had a picnic to celebrate jointly my grandfather's birthday and my own. Picnics in those days were no matter of thermoses and neat plastic boxes. Gran drove the donkey-cart in which all the provisions were packed and a great kettle besides, while we followed on bicycles or on foot, and when the picking was over and we had all come back with purple hands and mouths and full pails, she was waiting for us in a clearing in the bracken near the hill-top from which, on clear days, we could look down over several emerald counties to the Tipperary hills. Then we would build a fire and boil the kettle and roast potatoes in the hot ashes. Never has food tasted quite the same again.

There was only one day of the week in which a rule was imposed upon us, Sunday—and that, too, had its own charm. Many children, I think, are interested and attracted by recurrent forms and ceremonies and external forms of observance fulfil a real need for them, if not necessarily a spiritual one. Certainly, though I hated the starch of my white Sunday frock and the prickliness of my clean woollen combinations, there was a distinct pleasure in coming downstairs in the morning in our best clothes, ready for church—a sixpenny bit for the collection pressed as firmly against our hot palms as the day's Collect was embedded in our minds, and with the sense that this was the day to be clean and good.

All the house-party would be assembled in the hall, the men in dark London suits, the ladies in summer gowns, feather boas, and trimmed hats rustling and leaving behind them a faint aroma of lavender and Parma violet. In the drive the carriages were waiting: the large brake for the household, the light wagonette with two horses which my grandfather drove himself, with a fortunate child beside him on the box; and for my grandmother and the older ladies, a more staid landau in fine weather, or a stuffy brougham when it was wet—since it made Gran nervous, she said, to go "whizzing along in the wagonette". I realise now that the party from Desart must have formed the larger part of the congregation, since we were a very small Protestant community in a Catholic world, and I remember the carpenter's son coming home from school in tears with a black eye, received for being 'a bloody Protestant'. In church Gabba read the Lessons and I felt a conscious pride at his reading them so well, and also a snobbish satisfaction in the deference shown to him by the rest of the congregation and even by the clergyman himself, when we stood about afterwards in the churchyard, greeting our neighbours.

On Communion Sundays, however, we children—not having yet been confirmed—were sent out early, to start slowly homewards on foot. I remember the keen sense of release at coming out of the dark little church into the sunlit lane, the blackberries in the hedges and the foxgloves on the banks, the mares and foals in the fields, the sense that this sunny morning (sometimes I suppose it must have rained, but I cannot remember it) would go on and on. Then the wagonette would come rolling up behind us and we would climb in and trot home to roast beef and Yorkshire pudding. After tea, when decorous drawing-room games had been played or a Sunday story read aloud, we would gather round my grandmother at the piano and, with more enthusiasm than melody sing the familiar hymns chosen by each child in turn: 'Abide with me', 'Jerusalem the golden', 'There is a happy land', while outside the shadows lengthened on the lawn and the scent of tobacco-flower and cherry-pie floated in through the window, and one last riotous game of tag among the flower-beds ended the day, before we went to bed.

So each summer passed—serene, immutable, unending. Were they really so many or so long? I know that they were not, since, after 1914, I spent the greater part of the First World War in Italy with my mother and did not return to Ireland until 1918, when the shadow of 'the Troubles' had already fallen. It hardly matters how many they were. Green sleeping parkland, deep woods, peaches on a sunlit wall, laughter and freedom—they have been enough to fill a lifetime.

*   *   *   *   *

The story of the end of Desart is sadder than that of Westbrook. Like many other Anglo-Irishmen whose family had been settled there for over three centuries, my grandfather's feelings were both profoundly Irish and intensely English, and the attempt to conciliate these two allegiances formed the tragedy of the latter part of his life. Himself a man to whom compromise came easily, he found it impossible to realise how alien it was to the Irish temperament, and he fastened his energies and his hopes on the cause of the Southern Loyalists. But the clouds were gathering. In 1909 the Home Rule Bill in the House of Lords had caused preparations for rebellion in Ulster and the muster of the Loyalists in the South. The trouble was that while the North had a strong leader in Sir Edward Carson, the landed gentry of the South had had a tendency for more than a century (in the words of Lord Midleton) 'to concentrate on country life and to regard themselves as a British garrison', an isolated minority, almost completely out of touch with Irish political life. The controversy went on and on and, after the struggle between Ulster and Asquith's government had come to a head in 1913, feeling ran high on both sides. Bullets flew freely in the Dublin streets, country houses were burned, Loyalists were denounced from the pulpit, and even to be seen speaking to one of the hated British militia, the 'Black-and-Tans' (who, for their part, were also responsible for many outrages) was enough for a Catholic to incur a threat of excommunication.

In the mistaken belief that the real crux of the Irish question, even more than a craving for independence, was a hunger for the land, my grandfather had promptly sold his own, under the Land Act, keeping only the demesne and, up to the time of the Convention in Dublin in 1918 for the settlement of the Irish question, he still believed that some compromise might be found and Irish unity preserved. He was asked by Lord Midleton (the leader of the Southern Loyalists) to be one of the ninety-six representatives at the Convention, and attended it very conscious, as he wrote to me, of 'how very thin the ice is'. 'It was probably', Lord Midleton wrote, in a tribute to the part that his friend and colleague had played, 'the most important event of his public life . . . in Ireland.' He went on to observe: 'The spirit of compromise is virtually non-existent, and a premium is placed on disruptive influence which is denied to constructive statesmanship. Ulster glorifies herself by a lonely furrow. . . . After a surfeit of oratory, Desart felt that, as no other party would show its hand, we Southern Loyalists, few as we were, should make definite proposals for a separate legislature and taxation.'

To these proposals Redmond replied by expressing his willingness to serve under Carson in a National Ministry, but the premature death of the Irish leader and the backsliding of some of his colleagues caused the proposed settlement—which had won almost unanimous acceptance—to fail. 'If Desart's colleagues were still alive', Lord Midleton commented, 'they would bear testimony to the extent to which his single-mindedness and freedom from pique or prejudice contributed to the attempt. History takes little note of policy which has failed, and gives no credit in any department of life to those who have prevented evils by timely concessions.'

From that day my grandfather himself felt that any hope of reconciliation between England and Ireland was over. 'It breaks my heart to think of it,' he wrote to me in 1921. 'The complete apathy in England adds to one's despair. Football, cricket in Australia and things of that kind fill the bill for the mass of our reading public, and Ireland and Germany are only headlines to them. A half-educated population in its results is worse than an ignorant one.'

Nor did he find much more understanding in higher quarters.

On his return to England—the story has been told me by one of his nephews, who had it from himself—he was sent for by the King, and went to the Palace in the belief that he would be asked to give an account of the situation in Ireland as he had left it.

"I suppose you must have had a great deal of interest to tell His Majesty," his nephew commented.

"He never gave me a chance," was the reply. "'Ah, Lord Desart,' was his cordial greeting, 'I'm delighted to hear that you still wear nightshirts, just as I do! Can't bear those new-fangled pyjamas!'"

The rest of the conversation ran upon nightwear, entirely oblivious of the Irish question. I have always thought this a peculiarly English story.

Having done what he could, Desart was not a man to dwell upon his failure, and it was not until, in February 1922, raiders from Tipperary burned down his beloved house in a single night, that he recognised that his life, too, in Ireland had come to an end. He was in London at the time and hurried over at once to Desart by the night boat which had so often brought us all over for the holidays. On the lawn before the house there was a small heap of objects saved from the flames by a courageous and devoted house-maid, Loma. Everything else was a burned-out shell. 'Everything of value,' Gabba wrote to my American grandmother, 'family history, papers, portraits, was there and has perished'—as irrevocably destroyed as his own hopes for his country. He never went back to Ireland again.

'The wound is deep,' he wrote to me then, 'and there is no cure for it. The only thing is to go on and do one's work and be as useful as one can in other spheres, but I sometimes feel I can hardly bear it—and at my age, how can one plan out a new life?' Eventually he and Gran moved into a rather ugly, unpretentious little country house in Sussex, Hawkhurst Court, from which he could easily get up to London for his Parliamentary duties and where she could do a little gardening. I do not remember, during their years there, either of them even suggesting that they found the new life and house more restricted than that which they had once known. Only once, ten years later, when my grandmother had died and he was quite alone, one of Gabba's letters to me re-echoed the old sorrow: 'I can't bear to think of Desart—it is sadness itself. All gone, all scattered—and we were so happy there.'

*   *   *   *

In the year after Desart was burned, I became engaged to be married, and the centre of my interests naturally turned to my new Italian life. Yet it was, I think, at that time—perhaps because I was growing up myself—that I fully became aware of how large a part my affection for Gabba and his for me had played through all my childhood and youth. It had been, and remained for both of us, one of the happiest relations of our lives. The bond between grandparent and grandchild can be in many ways a freer and easier one than that between parent and child. There is less responsibility, less daily friction, and above all, an absence of emotional undercurrents: both are free to make themselves agreeable—and to be themselves. The gulf in time (in our case, of fifty-four years) may form not a barrier, but only an enrichment: each of us brought to the other (although of course his gift was the greater) glimpses of an unfamiliar and sometimes disconcerting world. From my first visit to Desart at the age of three, when he wrote for me my first poem—a little sentimental and humorous in the Victorian manner—until his last visits to us in Italy after Gran's death, an unfailing, carefully veiled tenderness warmed and lit our friendship. In 1908, when I was six years old and my parents were spending the winter in Egypt, I stayed with him and Gran in Rutland Gardens, sharing the serene, restful routine of their daily life, which had changed so little in the thirty years of their marriage: going for little walks in the Park (and envying the fortunate children with ponies in Rotten Row), visiting an old governess of my mother's in Trevor Square, shopping with Gran at Harrods 'for a treat' and, on Sundays, sometimes walking to the Round Pond with Gabba or (this was an occasion for great pride) going to church with him in my grandmother's seat at the Temple, hearing the Christmas carols in the Round Church, and being introduced to some of his colleagues as 'my little granddaughter'. Always, as when his own daughters were young, his return at tea-time was the culminating moment of the day. I would carefully prepare spills for his pipe, and he would teach me to play picquet or backgammon and read aloud and still today some chapters of *David Copperfield* and *The Rose and the Ring* and *Ivanhoe* are enriched for me by the echoes of his voice.

Between the end of 1914 and 1918, when I was in Italy with my mother, he wrote me long weekly letters—some of which I shall quote later on—which were a deliberate attempt both to keep me in touch with the English point of view and to keep our friendship alive, but in which he also fully replied to all my childish outpourings about my troop of boy scouts, my studies, and my friends.

As the war dragged on, he wrote, 'From a purely personal standpoint, I think I feel most the long severance from Mummy and from you. She perhaps will be much the same when we meet again, but you are at a time when every day, month and year changes your outlook and standards. . . . You will be a different Iris when we meet, and I shall have to begin knowing you again. You may no longer think of me as an amiable elderly relation, but an obsolete old buffer out of touch with your interests and sympathies. But believe me, I shall never be that.' In a later letter, even though at that time he was already caught up in the anxiety and strain of the Irish Convention, he returned, more seriously, to the same subject. 'I shall have lost the child I loved so well, but perhaps find the young woman I shall love even better. Our outlooks may be different, but love is the most real thing in life, and there are certain elemental things which to old and young are equally applicable. You have too much sense of humour to allow yourself, with the different ideals of another generation, to be contemptuous of what older people think and do. It is the intolerance of the young and the want of sympathy of the old that produces much unnecessary unhappiness in family life, and I trust we may avoid it.'

Certainly, in so far as our friendship was concerned, we did. When I returned to America after the war, it was to him that I wrote about my distress when I realised how deep a rift had grown up between my mother and my American grandmother (caused by the former's determination to take me back to Europe during the crucial years of my upbringing) and about the problems of my divided loyalties.

'I hardly know, dear child,' he replied, 'what to write about all you say. . . . In truth the situation and its difficulties can only be faced as you are doing it and I could add little or nothing to the counsel you have taken with yourself. I do not mean to pay compliments, but I think you have got from some hereditary source balance and practical common sense which will help you through difficulties, and the sympathy which will enable you to understand the views of others.' (If indeed there was any truth in this, 'the hereditary source' is very apparent.) 'I am very sorry for Mrs. Cutting, but you have divided duties, each of which you must recognise in its due proportion.'

As soon as Antonio and I became engaged, and indeed before the engagement was announced, Antonio went to London to call upon him and was asked to dine with him at the Travellers'. They liked each other from the first and came to feel a mutual affection and respect, but their conversation at this first meeting was characteristically elliptical. Antonio had expected, perhaps not unnaturally, that at some point of the evening his host would make some enquiry about his position and prospects or at least would refer to our future. But the evening passed pleasantly in talk about public affairs, farming and the recent war, with not a breath of any personal matter. Later on Gabba wrote to tell me how very much he had been attracted by his guest, but it was not until he took leave of him at the door that he made the slightest reference to the person who was the only link between them.

'You'll find her very extravagant in stockings!' he said with a smile and there the conversation closed.

Gabba followed, however, with great interest all the phases of our engagement and especially the purchase of our Tuscan farm, La Foce. ('It is intensely interesting to me. Is it a big house? is there a fine view? and what will you grow? Olives and grapes and I suppose maize. Is it country for riding and is there any shooting?') And though he could not attend my wedding he sent me, a few days before, his blessing and his 'high hopes'. 'For you I hope it is all happiness both now and forwards—and it will surely not be other than a pleasant thing to you to know that all your life you have brought nothing but happiness to your loving grandfather.'

On our first visit to England, we both stayed at Rutland Gardens, Gran having made touching efforts, as I now realise, to meet modern and 'Continental' usage by placing a bidet in my bedroom, but our first family breakfast was marred by an unfortunate choice of subject. Antonio, still unaware that this was not Gabba's best moment of the day, mildly observed to the table in general that the crossing on the previous afternoon had been very disagreeable, and expressed a hope that before too long the need for such journeys would be obviated by the building of the Channel Tunnel. Gabba, who was helping himself to some ham at the sideboard, turned around sharply.

"I hope I may never live to see the day!" he exploded.

Silence fell, and Gran nervously offered Antonio a scone.

Such brief outbursts of irascibility in Gabba's later years— though plainly only a superficial matter of nerves—were disconcerting to us, being so unlike his fundamental equanimity. I think they were largely caused by a constant, nagging anxiety about his wife's health, for she suffered from acute rheumatism and became subject to sudden, progressively severe, heart attacks. His preoccupation unfortunately took the form of scolding her for doing too much, followed by deep depression, so that we all knew that Gran's first gasping words, as we ran to her with the smelling-salts or the capsule that checked the attack, would be "Don't tell your grandfather!" I remember, too, wondering how it was possible that Gabba, so plainly a kind man, who loved his wife so dearly, should yet apparently grudge her (however grey with cold she might be, however tightly she pulled her cashmere shawl about her) the extra piece of coal on the fire which would have made the last hour of the evening pleasant for her. I did not yet know how many ways there are of denying what it is too frightening to admit.

During all my visits to England after my marriage I would dine once a week in Rutland Gardens, and once a week Gabba would dine instead with me, generally at a quiet table in my hotel, the Berkeley. For these occasions, knowing that it pleased him, I would prepare as carefully as for a formal party, wearing a dress of which he approved, and choosing the food and wine that he liked best, for he considered a knowledge of good wine to be a necessary part of a lady's education. Sometimes we would then go on together to a Shakespeare play at the Old Vic, but more often we would merely sit on talking, each of us trying to choose such subjects as would interest or amuse the other. Does all this sound a little absurd and unspontaneous to members of the present generation? I expect it does, yet I can assure them that we both looked forward to these evenings with equal pleasure; and I believe it was precisely the faint touch of formality in our relationship that prevented it, over so many years, from ever becoming stale or dull.

There were, however, strictly defined limits to the range of subjects which my grandfather considered suitable for my ears, or indeed, I presume, for those of any woman of his own class. I remember once—when I was already a married woman, and had been reading some book about Oscar Wilde—asking him, since it was he who was the King's Proctor at the time of the poet's trial, what his real opinion was of the whole episode. "He was a very wicked man, my dear," was his reply.

*   *   *   *   *

Two years after our marriage, in 1926, Gran and Gabba celebrated their golden wedding, and that summer they were able to attend a big party at Bridgewater House, the scene of the ball at which they had first danced together fifty-five years before. But it was already plain to us all that Gran's health was failing, and by the end of the following year even Gabba could no longer conceal his anxiety, though he still wrote of being able to 'stave off attacks'. He admitted, however, that she was no longer able to come downstairs to give him his breakfast (a thing she had not failed to do for fifty years), and that she could no longer get about the garden 'except on level ground'. This letter alarmed me, and I telegraphed asking if I might come to stay the following week, but before I could get there the end had come. The family was scattered, and Gerald with his wife Joycie (both of whom he dearly loved) were alone with Gabba during the terrible last two days, during most of which Gran was too exhausted to speak. He spent part of the time in writing me a long, factual account, hour by hour, of what was happening, still not without hope and retaining his usual restraint—but at the end he added, 'I am not to talk to her. But if she passes without a word between us—*oh my dear.*'

When, two days later, I joined him at Hawkhurst, he was almost too worn out for grief—a very thin, frail old man. Yet he thanked us all, with his usual gentle courtesy, for coming, and made a great effort, very soon—so that his family should not feel him to be a burden—to resume normal life again. The constant support and companionship of his daughter Joan was a great comfort to him, as was that of all his grandchildren, particularly his youngest grandson, Desmond, who went to live with him in Rutland Gardens.

When, later on, he came back for brief visits to Italy, it was at La Foce that he was most at ease. In Florence, among my mother's 'artistic' friends, he often looked lost and alone; he could offer no small talk about Venetian lacquer and the baroque, and they did not care about the reform of the House of Lords. But walking about our farm with Antonio, taking an interest in the successful crossing of our Large White pigs, imported from Yorkshire, with the lean black Tuscan swine, or comparing systems of tenant-farming, talking to me as I gardened or did the flowers, or playing with his small Italian great-grandson, he was upon more familiar ground.

His letters to me during those years are too moving and too intimate to quote. It was almost as if, in some indefinable manner, he had transferred to me a portion of the love that for fifty years had bound him to Gran, or rather it was like a continuation of the same love. When, in 1933, our only son Gianni died, he identified himself with our loss, almost as if his own were being repeated— yet he expected of me (as he had of himself) to take up life at La Foce again without any fuss. 'I think', he wrote, 'that you and Antonio have chosen wisely in going back to La Foce. No-one could advise in such a moment, but I think work and duty the nearest approach to an anodyne. . . . You have done great work for your people at La Foce, and, apart from its inherent value, I am convinced that its continuance will be something of a solace to you.'

It was on his next visit to me in Italy that he gave me the gold Victorian locket—engraved with the word Mizpah, 'God watch between us two'—which he had given to his fiancée, sixty years before when they were separated from each other, and with it some rough verses that were, I knew, his farewell to me:

> In my old age on you I lean
> As in my youth I turned to her.
> Here or elsewhere in world unseen
> In some shape may both loves endure.

In a letter, a few days later, he added: 'In the circumstances in which Margaret received it from me, it was steeped in love, and was her companion in the many years of separation. Now, my darling, it goes to you with the same symbolism. . . . Margaret and you are the outstanding loves of my life.'

These words were written only a few months before his own death, in 1934, seven years after his wife's. During those long, lonely years his natural reticence and his feeling that he should not impose his sorrow upon younger people kept him from speaking very often about her, though I think there was hardly a moment of the day in which he did not miss her. For even then, his sense of proportion, his perfect reasonableness, did not fail him: he did not ask for exemption from the common lot. Being totally without self-pity, he dwelled upon the fullness of the past, not the leanness of the final years. Shortly after her death he wrote to me, 'I believe that love in marriage is better than anything in life. Ambition and success are not in the running with it. My real life has always been my home—wife, children and grandchildren, and she saw and rejoiced in her great-grandchildren. It is a happy record.'

I think he would have liked me to end with these words.

3

My Father

WHEN I THINK of my father, it is difficult for me to distinguish what I really remember from what I have read or have been told, just as my visual memory of him has been overlaid by portraits. It seems to me, however, that I remember him very much as he was in a snapshot taken in California with me, when I was about three years old: very slight, very young, in spite of the pointed Vandyke beard which he grew after an accident to his lip and which gave him both distinction and a curiously Latin look (though perhaps French, rather than Italian), looking down with both tenderness and amusement at the very cross little girl sitting beside him. He was, according to everyone who knew him, a person very difficult to forget. Even now, half a century later, I sometimes meet a friend of his, who says, 'I remember the first day I met Bayard.' But my own recollections, since he died before I was eight years old, are only fragmentary, and it has been from letters and photographs, from school and college reports and family stories that I have had to piece together some aspects of him, almost as if I were writing about someone unknown to me, and to try to reconcile them with the glimpses that I myself remember.

The serene and successful years came first. By all accounts, he was a singularly attractive child and boy, modest and affectionate as well as gay and brilliant, and at school, as gifted for games as for work, as popular with his contemporaries as with the masters. At home, though later on he was to react impatiently against the combined pressure of too much comfort and too much solicitude, he had a most affectionate relationship with his father and a very close alliance with his sister Justine, who stirred him up sometimes to rebellion and adventure. At Groton and Harvard his record was one of unbroken success. At Groton, where he was under the famous head-master, Dr. Peabody, he was, according to the school magazine, 'by far the most remarkable scholar we ever had'; he was also the editor of the school paper, vice-president of the debating society, member of the baseball Nine and bass-violin in the orchestra. At Harvard he specialised in history, economics and philosophy, and, after three years, took his B.A. degree *summa cum laude*, but he showed an equally keen pleasure in the social side of college life. He was elected to the Phi Beta Kappa, the Delphic Club and the Porcellian; he played golf and football, he rode, shot, made music.

Perhaps this unflagging energy, this need to achieve success in *every* field, already held a trace of the restless quest for perfection, for filling every cup to the brim, which is often to be found in those in whom the seeds of tuberculosis are already latent. Certainly, however, there were no symptoms of this as yet. The philosopher George Santayana, whose pupil he was at Harvard, wrote after his death to his father:

> His intellectual life was, without question, the most intense, many-sided and sane that I have ever known in any young man, and his talk, when he was in college, brought out whatever corresponding vivacity there was in me in those days, before the routine of teaching had had time to dull it as much as it has now . . . I always felt I got more from him than I had to give, not only in enthusiasm—which goes without saying—but also in a sort of multitudinousness and quickness of ideas.

In the summer of his Junior year, Bayard was offered the position of private secretary to the American Ambassador in London, the Hon. Joseph Choate and, deciding to give up his Senior year at Harvard to accept it, he sailed for England. His letters to his friends and family, however, show that he was not really suited to diplomatic life. 'It's the drag of utterly insignificant work that galls . . .' he wrote to Ben Diblee, one of his oldest friends at Harvard, 'not the fact of working. You won't anyway have the feeling I have that you are wasting endless hours in buying clothes or attending teas or dropping cards . . . this infernal social act.'

He derived, however, considerable amusement from the spectacle of the Opening of Parliament in 1901, which he felt to be 'both the finest and most impressive ceremony, and also the most bizarre and ludicrous that I have ever seen'. I cannot resist quoting a few passages from his account, in a long letter to his mother, for the combination they show of eager interest and of the amused, critical detachment of a spectator who was not an Englishman.

When we got in, the peeresses and peers were beginning to arrive, the ladies all in black or with ermine capes [mourning for Queen Victoria], and the men in full robes . . . I was astonished to see how cheap and almost tawdry the robes looked. It was like a chorus in an opera, and after they had filed in and taken their places, you expected them to break into a Glee . . . [The Dukes] were hardly a fine-looking lot, for the Duke of Northumberland is the typical Englishman of a French farce, red whiskers and all, the Duke of Marlborough is the meanest looking little fellow in the world, and as to the old and red-faced ones, their cheeks appeared to be on the point of bursting with a pop . . . Lord Rosebery looked old and fat, yet still wore the bad-boy expression . . . On the right front bench were the bishops, dressed as Spiritual Barons, in great ermine capes—rather fine. "You're the kind that used to do all the fighting five centuries ago," said Mr. Choate to the Archbishop . . . The peeresses, all in deepest black, were in low-necked gowns, and were allowed to wear diamonds and pearls, so that when, at the last moment, all of them flung off their capes and furs for the arrival of the King, there was a tremendous effect . . . I should say that the Duchess of Devonshire's tiara was appropriately the most massive and the ugliest. Altogether the effect was tremendous.

Then followed a description of the Royal procession:

The Duke of Devonshire carrying the crown on a velvet cushion and looking as if he'd drop it any minute, Lord Salisbury as Old Father Christmas goldsticks and silversticks and other fantastics . . . and finally the King and Queen, who were both quite gorgeous.

Then, summoned by the Black Rod, arrived the members of the House of Commons.

We could see the Speaker, in wig and gown, walking towards us, and behind him a running, shouting, pushing, fighting riot of members. It was the most comical thing you ever saw. The Speaker grave and slow, saluting three times to the House, and the crowd of the members making this infernal row behind, while policemen shouted "Steady!", or tried to close the doors. The Commons kept up the best traditions of their order for turbulence and disregard of royal authority . . . Finally, (after the King's oath against transubstantiation) the King stood up and put on his hat. He spoke loud and clearly with much dignity, but with quite a German accent . . . It was most perfectly medieval. They were bold barons and haughty prelates and fair dames and pliant courtiers, not the men and women one sees every day . . . The details were everything; the perfection of each detail was what made the whole so superb. Not a person there that was not plainly labelled so-and-so, by dress and position.

Gradually, Bayard's circle of acquaintances and his range of occupations in London had become wider. He attended frequent meetings of the House of Commons, he spent twenty-four hours with George Santayana in Oxford ('I never saw any place that came anywhere near it'), he joined a golf club, he met Sidney Colvin and Mark Twain. ('Every word he said in his drawling twang held you more and more thrilled, like a great actor in a fine play.') Gradually he began to see less of his official colleagues and more of some new English friends. In the spring of 1900 his daily rides in Hyde Park, in attendance on his Ambassador, had been enlivened by frequent meetings with an Irish peer, Lord Desart, and his pretty daughter, Sybil, and it was natural enough that, while Mr. Choate and my grandfather exchanged stories of legal and political interest, the two young people should ride ahead, engaged in no less animated, but far more theoretical, conversation.

I have before me a photograph of my mother as she was then: rather plump, very fair, with soft unmoulded features that in no way revealed the strength of her determination and the quickness of her mind. In her, for the first time, my father met a girl with whom he could talk and argue as freely as with a man, and who possessed a mental alertness that was to him a constant stimulus and delight. The Boer War, the Irish Question, the Indian Question, these alternated with discussions of the philosophers and poets. He lent her Santayana and William James and Royce; she brought *The Stones of Venice* and Shelley. And was Platonic love indeed possible? And what should a young man do with his life? So they talked and talked, ambling gently along Rotten Row—breathless, eager, extremely young. It was, at this stage, almost entirely an attraction of the mind, as sexless and yet intense as only the ardour of the very young and very intelligent can sometimes be.

During that summer, young Mr. Cutting was one of the guests invited to Desart, and was writing to Ben Diblee that his hosts were 'some of the nicest people I have met in England'. There were long rides down the wide avenues of the summer woods, long talks between the tall hedges of the kitchen-garden, and finally, one whole day together in the sunlit heather, climbing the mountain of Slievenaman.

I have found myself wondering whether Bayard really wanted to get married quite so soon, or whether either of them yet quite knew their own mind, and one of his letters to my mother confirms this impression. 'After Slievenaman', he wrote, 'I knew we were very close. I ought to have gone home, or at any rate been careful and strong. I couldn't resist.' But he added, 'Thank God I couldn't.'

During all this time, as their letters show, he was still calling her 'Lady Sybil' and they still behaved so formally in public that they believed their secret to be theirs only, though perhaps her parents were not quite so unobservant as Sybil liked to think, for one day, picking up a book that she had dropped—Locke's *Essay on the Human Understanding*, with 'W.B.C. Jr.' on the flyleaf—her father returned it to her with a smile and a muttered Latin tag.

"What does that mean?" she asked.

" 'In how many disguises the god' . . ." said her father. "That's roughly it."

All the same, like most parents, he still thought of his daughter as a child, and it was a shock to him, no less than to Bayard's own parents, when, only a few weeks later, he received a letter from the young American, formally requesting permission to ask for his daughter's hand. Very soon afterwards Bayard, by his parents' wish, returned to New York and discussions on both sides of the Atlantic repeated an eternal dialogue, each set of parents trying to impose what seemed to them best for their own child, and the young people resenting any interference, yet perhaps more swayed by their parents' influence than either of them would have liked to admit. Certainly Bayard's parents, who had cherished a dream of a charming American daughter-in-law, felt that it was too soon for him to commit himself, and perhaps he, too, now that he was home again, would have been willing to accept their suggestion that he should postpone any decision for a year, spending the interval in the West. But Sybil's insistent letters came by every ship, stirring both his tenderness and his chivalry, while on their side, her parents, remembering how much they had suffered during their own long time of waiting, refused, if a further delay were required, to allow the engagement at all. So, early in the spring Bayard returned to London and, on April 30, 1901, after a good deal of family discussion about the date, the marriage took place, at All Saints' Church, Ennismore Gardens.

A letter of my father's at that time gives an inkling of how very little freedom was allowed to a well-brought-up young girl to see her fiancé, even in the last months before their wedding. 'They won't let me act as her escort in the evenings', Bayard wrote, 'or go and stay in the country with her at her relations' houses, or even go to see her when they are out. I dine at Rutland Gardens about three times a week, but they don't like her to go out the other days. So it really comes to tea and every other dinner, and never very long at a time.'

My mother has described the day on which, after their honeymoon, she and my father sailed for America. My grandfather went with them to Southampton to see them off. 'Together,' she wrote, 'we showed him our little cabin, deep in the bowels of the great sumptuous ship. "Very nice, very convenient," commented my father, "but a little like sleeping in a housemaid's cupboard in Buckingham Palace." ' She laughed, of course; but after they had come up on deck again for all visitors to go ashore and saw her father standing on the quay looking up at her, she suddenly realised, for the first time, that she was indeed embarking on a new and very different life.

It was a year before the young couple returned to England

again. Almost at once, the first shadow fell. During the winter in New York, my father had driven himself too hard, working at Columbia for an examination, and very soon after his return to London, three months before my birth, he had his first haemorrhage.

'They tell me that I have got a weak spot on one of my lungs,' he wrote to Ben Diblee, 'but they can't find the spot'; and he added, with the optimism so characteristic of his complaint, 'It is a mere weakness and no disease and they expect I shall be able to lead a normal life after a month or two.' He had only eight more years to live.

Meanwhile, however, he was sent to convalesce in a sanatorium in the Cotswolds; and it was in a cottage nearby, in the small village of Birdlip, that—on August 15, 1902—I was born. My christening, however, did not take place until nearly three months later, at Desart, and rather against my father's will, since he was then going through a phase of intolerant agnosticism and considered it, as he wrote to the same friend 'an awful shame to make pledges for her in her infancy'. 'Indeed,' he added, 'I don't think I should allow it in the case of a boy.' As to my name, 'Sybil wishes to call her Iris, and therefore will, I expect,' but the officiating clergyman maintained that this name was to be found in no Christian calendar, so that my grandmother's name, Margaret, was added. The associations in my mother's mind were entirely classical—the messenger of the Gods and the rainbow—but, unfortunately, since the rest of my life has been spent in Italy, my name is more frequently associated with one of Mascagni's minor operas, or a cheap soap made with orris-root.

The remaining years of my father's life, and in consequence the first eight years of my own, were mostly spent in travel from one country to another, in the vain pursuit of health.

The first two years of their marriage, after a difficult winter in hotels at Portofino and Sestri Levante, were spent in California, an experience to which they had both looked forward with great expectations, but which at first they found somewhat disappointing. The little town of Nordhoff in the Ojai valley seemed to them uninteresting and remote, their cottage was dirty, unsanitary and ill-furnished, and the sense of isolation much greater than they had expected. Gradually, however, the beauty of the surrounding scenery and of the climate, the wonderful rides up mountain tracks, the making of a few close friends and, for my father, the editing of the local paper, *The Ojai*, reconciled them to their life there, though it did not bring my father the recovery he had hoped for. Then the relentless quest began again: first a sanatorium in the Adirondacks, where he was given a 'tuberculin' treatment which was then new, but appears to have done him more harm than good; then two winters in a chalet at St. Moritz, some months in a sanatorium at Davos, springs and autumns on the Italian lakes, and two winters in Egypt.

Re-reading the letters of that period—impatient, rebellious, courageous, reckless, unbearably poignant—I have often thought (though tuberculosis was then considered a disease from which only the rich could recover) that these years would have been less tormented if *every* possibility that money could provide had not been open to him. California or St. Moritz? A sanatorium in the Adirondacks or in Switzerland? His distracted parents would advocate one course, his young wife, still hoping to keep some element of adventure and beauty in their lives together, would press for another. His parents undoubtedly sometimes felt that, in her wish for a more normal and varied life, as well as owing to her preoccupation with her own health, she did not fully realise how ill her young husband was. Friends and relations contributed their advice. Endless letters and cables—all full of good-intentions, all showing a deep undercurrent of anxiety and desire for control on the part of the older generation, and of an exasperated desire for independence on that of the younger—crossed and re-crossed the ocean. A further complication, too, was added by my father's determination only to go where he could do some work. 'I don't know why I want so much to work,' he wrote to Ben Diblee, 'but I'm quite sure I shall never be satisfied until I do.'

It would, I think, be entirely mistaken to measure this craving, which certainly shortened his life, in terms of achievement: no-one realised more clearly than he how little there was to show, and I feel sure that ambition, too, is not a sufficient explanation. A strong sense of public duty was certainly one factor, as well as an intense interest in American public life, which, in spite of the example of Theodore Roosevelt, was still considered a very odd field for a gentleman to enter; to this was added the constant sense of 'Time's wingèd chariot'. 'I was reading a book yesterday', he wrote to his brother Bronson on the latter's fourteenth birthday, 'which makes a birthday to me a very sad time.' (He was then twenty-two.) 'It was the life of John Stuart Mill, who by the age of thirteen was not only acquainted with every masterpiece of Greek and Latin literature, had studied Euclid and the differential calculus, but had attained such a mastery of political economy that from his summary of conversations with his father the latter was able to write a book on the subject that made an epoch.' He went on to enumerate Mill's other achievements before the age of twenty-three, commenting, 'This seems to me to throw Napoleon and every other youthful genius far into the shade,' sadly adding, 'I always hoped to accomplish something, and I feel that your chances are twice as good as mine once were . . . Of course I may get all right and be good for something, but what a time wasted!'

Six years later he was condoling with Bronson on the latter's first hæmorrhage and the interruption of his work that it inevitably entailed. 'Nothing', he wrote, 'can make it anything but desperately hard to bear. For years you are going to be handicapped; you are going to see other fellows go ahead of you all along the line, and must learn not to mind. You'll have to think about fiddling matters of health which seem at first a destruction of manhood.' But he also believed (and rightly) that his brother would recover and be able to undertake the public work which he already knew to be, at least partially, closed to himself.

'If I were your age,' he wrote to Bronson, 'there is only one thing I could think of doing today—going into politics . . . I am too ashamed of the figure we cut as a nation—possessing as I think we do the best individuals, the best raw material, to be found anywhere—to take even a moderate interest in other aspects of American life, compared to the political.'

Meanwhile, wherever he happened to be, he flung himself with intense activity into whatever interest was at the moment available: learning Italian and making Italian friends, in particular Guido Cagnola, and developing a great addiction to the opera in Milan, studying architecture and painting in Tuscany, and, when laid up in Switzerland, collecting with passionate absorption every fragment of evidence with regard to the Dreyfus case.* One of his most striking characteristics, according to Justine, was 'his flaming fury at any wrong done to someone else, regardless of the person or how remote that person might be from his own life. Any injustice or wrong aroused this indignation', and an immediate desire to do something about it. In the case of Dreyfus, this of course was not possible, but this characteristic was certainly one of the deepest reasons why he could not resign himself to being cut off from public life. He never gave up the hope of being 'good for something' at last and, meanwhile, through all his years of illness he always found something to which he could turn his hand, even if the actual job was not in itself very interesting or important. In California he edited the local paper, *The Ojai*; in Italy he accepted the post of American Vice-Consul in Milan, and relieved his rather pedestrian duties by writing a paper on international law for an examination for the diplomatic service, which is still preserved in the State Department as a model of its kind, and an official report on *pellagra*, then prevalent in some parts of Northern Italy. Above all he never allowed himself to give way to any form of invalidism: whenever any kind of work seemed possible again, life and hope returned with it.

After his death Edith Wharton, with whom, in spite of the difference in their ages, he had a close and lively friendship, wrote some perceptive comments on this aspect of his character:

> It might almost be said that the only way in which he betrayed his lack of strength was in his constant untiring struggle to live as if he were unaware of it: to be forever up and doing with the careless unconsciousness of health. The effort to crowd so much endeavour, so many impressions, so much work and so much enjoyment into his measured days confessed, perhaps, to a haunting sense of their brevity; yet there was nothing feverish or rebellious in his haste . . . The impression one had to the end was that, though he knew he was gravely ill, and had early to make his terms with that knowledge, yet he knew so many other things more interesting, more impressive and more immediate, that his individual plight was

* He left all his books and papers about the case to Harvard, where his father also founded a History scholarship in his memory.

quite naturally dismissed to the remoter planes of consciousness . . .

Perhaps the distinctive thing about him, in this respect, was
that his tastes were so inwoven with his personality. I have
never known an intelligence in which the play of ideas was so
free, yet their reaction so tinged by the elusive thing called
'character'. Coolness of thought and ardour of moral emotion
dwelt together. He cared passionately for politics, economics,
all manner of social and sociological questions, and cared for
them practically, reformingly, militantly. Yet he contrived—
young as he was—to keep a part of himself aloof from the
battle and above the smoke, and to look down on the very
conflict he was engaged in.

Two gifts of his rich nature helped him to this impartiality:
his love of letters and his feeling for beauty. Nothing so clari-
fies the moral sense as a drop of aesthetic sensibility . . . The
result was a receptiveness of mind and a tolerance of heart . . .

When, on December 28, 1908, the tragic news came of the
Messina earthquake, Bayard at once set off for Sicily, to re-
establish an American Consulate in Messina, and to act as a
special representative of the American Red Cross. His official
report, while giving a tragic picture of the general devastation,
is unlike other such documents in one characteristic respect: the
scene before him was described with deep and active compassion,
but also with the intellectual detachment of a historian. Beneath
the debris, the flames and the curling smoke he saw, in the lie of
the land, of the harbour and the hills behind it, 'the real Messina,
what an ancient phraseology would call its formal and final
causes. With those fertile hills, with that spacious harbour situ-
ated on a principal trade route, Messina will always be a city.
Houses and inhabitants there will always be to embody the
Messina idea, to fulfil the Messina purpose.'

Meanwhile many thousand dead lay beneath Messina's ruins—
and perhaps as many more were buried there alive. One of the
things that first struck my father—apart from the sheer horror of
the human suffering before his eyes—was 'a strong impression of
the Oriental affinity of the Sicilians. Their mood was one of sub-
mission, unsurprised and unassertive, to the hard hand of fate.

They did not rebel or complain, and on the other hand they would not strive. It was folly to think of building a comfortable house, when there was no-one left to occupy it, or to earn money which could bring no sweetness. So most of them sat idly in the streets, or under the roof of the market, and took what food was put before them. The few who worked, like our boatmen, did not care what pay they received. A piece of bread they were glad to get; but when it was a question of money, one lira or five were all much the same.'*

Much of my father's report is naturally very similar to the experiences of everyone who has done relief work of this kind and it would be irrelevant to quote it here. What does stand out, however, is how very swiftly the relief ships—British, Russian, and American—reached their destination, and how admirable their collaboration was with the local authorities in the distribution of the stores they brought. In particular, my father was immensely impressed by the Russian sailors, who were, he wrote, 'a revelation to those who did not know the quiet common sense, the tactful sympathy and the unassuming heroism of the *moujik*. The Russians were the only people who always had everything on the spot.'

The American ship, carrying twenty-four nurses and three doctors and fitted out to receive two hundred hospital patients and one thousand refugees, brought clothing for two thousand persons, medical stores for five hospitals and large quantities of food and tools. But already by the time it arrived, the greatest need was no longer at Messina but at Catania, where twenty-five thousand refugees from Messina had arrived, and it was there that much of this relief was devolved. One thing that also strikes

* I remember hearing similar comments from people who did relief work, several years later, in the earthquake of the Abruzzi. But certainly this was not so, in my experience, after the devastating flood in Florence in 1966. Here, during the first week before the extent of the disaster was realised elsewhere, the early stages of relief and reconstruction were undertaken entirely by the Florentines themselves, with a courage, an absence of self-pity, a kindness and a sense of humour beyond all praise—digging in the stinking mud and rubble, distributing food and water and drugs, blankets and clothing, salvaging works of art and precious manuscripts, saving old people and patients in hospitals who had been marooned. Communists working beside parish priests, Red Cross nurses beside young students. Later on, of course, generous help came from all over Italy and Europe, but for the first week Florence stood and worked alone; and it was the tenacity, endurance and resourcefulness of her workmen and craftsmen that set their city upon her feet again.

one about the report is the unobtrusive and tactful manner in
which all this help, which included the shipment of three thousand houses and the foundation of an agricultural school, was
bestowed. 'The aim of the Americans', my father wrote, 'has
never been to act independently of the Italians, but simply to
put at the service of the Italians their eyes and brain as well as
their money.'

Of his own part in the work, the report says nothing, but I
think that those weeks, which undoubtedly damaged his health,
but during which he was able to lead again a man's life of active
work, were probably the happiest he had known for many years.
When he returned to Milan to report, it was with the intention of
returning to Sicily as soon as possible to continue the work, but
a letter to his father mentions, very much in passing, 'a little
attack of pleurisy, very slight'—hardly surprising, since in Messina
he had not taken his clothes off by day or night; he had also been
up to his neck in sea-water during a storm, helping to tug in a
rowing-boat carrying stores, which had nearly capsized. There
was no question of his returning to Sicily, and indeed hardly had
he returned to Milan than an order reached him to report to
Washington, with a view to taking up an appointment as secretary to the American Legation in Tangier. By the end of March he
was writing from Washington, eagerly looking forward to his new
post. 'The correspondence with Tangier is *fascinating*. It is only a
question of how thorough one is, how much work one has to
do.' But before he could take up his appointment, he had another
hæmorrhage, undoubtedly the result of his exertions in Sicily, and
it was not until the summer that he could rejoin his family in Italy.

It is at this point that my own clear recollections of my father
begin. Looking at his letters, I realise that, long before then, he
had both spent much time with me and had written about me, in
a tone in which humour is allied to the prophetic hopes common
to all young parents. Before I was three months old, he was
writing that I seemed 'to have been born with company manners', and three months later, he was asking for his old books of
French nursery songs because he was sure that I would be musical.
'She loves to be sung to, but weeps bitterly at any sad tune.'

'I have a notion', he says in another letter of the same period,
'that she may be like Justine [his sister]. Her roars of rage are so

loud and so *funny*, and she is able to change with such speed from despair to smiles.'

By the time I was three he was writing, from a sanatorium in the Adirondacks, enchanting long letters to me. One of them, which contained a long story about a chipmunk, ended with four kisses of different shapes: 'Fat kiss for Fatty; Kite-shaped kiss for the Mischief; Giant heart-shaped kiss—'m!; and Small bullet kiss for the bullet-headed girl.'

In the following winter, at St. Moritz, my education in skating and dancing began. 'She is *not yet* an expert skater,' says one letter rather testily, 'seems unable to bend her knees' (I was four years old) but soon after progress is reported: 'She cannot get her edges yet, but skates ahead with fine form and swing.' In that same winter, too, before a children's party at the Kulm, 'We have been dancing with her till she can do the valse and two-step very nicely'; and I am also reported as talking and reading fluently in English, Italian, and German. My father, later on, wrote to a friend, 'She has become a speaker of German, and is rapidly ceasing to be a speaker of English. "Stand here, horse, to the post, I want to hang you on!" '

My own personal memories of being with my father only begin with the summer of my seventh birthday, which occurred at Camaldoli, in the heart of the great pine-forests that stretch along the ridge of the Appenines; and these memories are inextricably mingled with the smell of freshly-sawn wood and of wild strawberries. Every day, my father would walk up with me to the clearing where the great timber logs were sawn, and when we came back I would hunt for strawberries in the sunny meadow beneath the hotel, bringing a few to him on a large green chestnut-leaf. My mother dressed me in long white muslin frocks, old-fashioned even then, and large, floppy muslin hats, held on by a wide blue ribbon under the chin; the brim flopped into my eyes, as I bent to pick the fruit.

On our walks my father would pause, sitting upon a log, and then we would act scenes which were, as I now realise, my first history and geography lessons.

"You are the Little Duke and I am your faithful Squire, and we have just set out from Normandy for the Holy Land. Which way shall we go?"

The next memory, I think, belongs to the same autumn. Every morning, after breakfast, I would visit my father in his bedroom at Varenna and say a verse of poetry to him—from the *Lays of Ancient Rome*, or *Hiawatha* or Henry V's speech before Agincourt. This I loved—the sounds of the words themselves and also, of course, the pleasure of being approved of. But on one particular occasion I failed.

'Fair stood the wind for France—As we our sails advance.'

That was easy enough; but the end of the verse was too difficult:

'And be our oriflamme today—the Helmet of Navarre.'

Never had I heard of an oriflamme before, nor apparently did my father explain it to me—I am a little vague still—and when I got to that line, I broke down.

"Never mind, Fatty," my father said cheerfully, "you'll say it right tomorrow."

But the next day I broke down again, and again, quite patiently but firmly, my father said that I must repeat it right tomorrow. At the third failure I ran sobbing from the room—but not so far as not to hear, through the half-open door, my mother say:

"Aren't you a little hard on her, Bayard? She is so very little!"

"Not too little," he firmly replied, "to distinguish between knowing something and half knowing it."

It was a distinction which—unlike the word oriflamme—I at once understood, and have never since forgotten.

Any impression, however, that my whole time with my father was spent in lessons, or that I was in awe of him, would be quite wrong. The quickness of thought and movement, the infectious gaiety which charmed his friends, was no less irresistible to a small child. I can never remember his 'talking down' to me, but I *can* remember an occasional feeling of slight bewilderment, a wish that I could understand better what it would be so fascinating to know.

During that Italian summer my father's plans had taken a new turn. If he could not accept a regular appointment, surely he could take up, at his own pace, the study of British colonial administration, and fit himself to give a course on the subject at

Harvard? His old university welcomed the plan and so, on his return, did his wife. 'I have set my *face* towards Harvard', he wrote to Mrs. Griscom, 'and the feet will follow. Meanwhile we intend to spend parts of a number of years in investigating the British Empire, travelling to as many colonies as possible . . .'

In all these plans his wife, as resilient, as irrepressibly active as he, fully shared. 'It fills us with excitement', he wrote. 'Sybil will come in and say to me: "Oh, I've been reading a fascinating chapter by Milner, he's the most extraordinary man" . . . And the days pass peacefully in discussion of the Debt or of irrigation, out in the pine-woods of Camaldoli.'

So, in December 1909, sailing up the Nile on a private *dahabeah* (this luxury being a gift from my American grandfather) my parents—travelling with their own doctor, Freddie Bishop, their close friend Gordon Gardiner, myself and my governess—returned to Egypt for the last time.

'We start with a crew of ten,' wrote my father, 'and one of these is a singer—his only function being to sing while the crew work or row. He is treated with great consideration, for if he is at all discontented, none of the crew will work, and as a result he is insufferable. Like all singers here, he is a great opium-eater, and as yellow as a Chinaman.'

The first weeks in Egypt were full of activity and hope. In Cairo my father was able to collect some political information, incidentally discovering that in order to get to Government House it was still necessary to ask for *Beit-el-Lord*, The House of the Lord (a name going back to the days of Lord Cromer, the Lord *par excellence*), and at Minia, too, he was able to interview the Moudir and a young Englishman representing the Finance Department. 'It will be our own fault', he wrote, 'if we don't make something of this.'

As for the journey itself,

'A sailing *dahabeah*', he wrote, 'knocks a steamer into a cocked hat. A tug is necessary, one only makes $2\frac{1}{2}$ to $3\frac{1}{2}$ miles *with* it, against this current, but the motion is delicious—you don't perceive that you are moving . . . The charm of the Nile is as great as the first time, and the interest greater. It is all perfection. This winter, under these conditions, is an *absolute* test of what climate and rest can do.'

My Father

By mid-December we were anchored beside a wide, lonely valley a few miles before Assiut, with high cliffs on either side. Here a camp was pitched, consisting of two tents in which my father and mother slept, a day-house of matting thatched with palm-leaves, and a shelter for their live-stock: three donkeys, some turkeys, a cow, and 'the sheik of the cow'. The rest of us slept on board. Along the shore stretched a band of some fifty yards of cultivated land of the emerald green of Egypt, and beyond was the desert—still, majestic, lonely. At night a couple of Kaffirs with guns guarded the camp from jackals, wolves, and thieves.

I remember this camp very well. In the early mornings, before the sun was high, I would go out riding in the desert on my white donkey, which wore a wide necklace of turquoise blue beads to keep off the evil eye. Then I would 'do lessons' with my Swiss governess, Mademoiselle Nigg, in a shady corner of the deck, and gradually, as the sun rose higher and my head drooped over my book, the figures of Sophie and Maître Corbeau faded into a landscape of tawny rocks and shimmering sand, while the voice of Mademoiselle was drowned by the low monotonous chant of the Nubian ship-boys, rowing out to us with the provisions and the mail. The boat would bump against the ship's side—a grinning white-turbaned figure would bring me a bunch of bananas—and then, as the mid-day breeze sprang up, the river would be studded with little white or orange sails. Close beside our ship a woman was bending down, to fill her water-jar, and a little further off, a group of fuzzy-headed Bishareen children were dancing like small black devils round a blind beggar.

'*Mais voyons, Iris, tu ne fais pas attention! Qu'est-ce qu'il disait, Maître Renard?*'

No, I was not paying attention. For, by the camp on the shore, I had just seen my mother returning on her camel from her morning ride, her long green veil floating back from her sun-helmet, and there was my father coming to his tent-door to meet her. Soon, after my siesta, I would join him, too, for every day I was allowed to spend an hour in his tent, while he read aloud to me or told me stories. From his letters that I have read since, half a century later, I now realise how strong a current of grief and anxiety must have underlain those hours, how much he wondered what was going to happen to the child whom he read to and played with and gently laughed at—but never kissed.

Later on I discovered that, in the Will he drew up then, he tried to ensure for me what he considered the best of all gifts, a measure of independence, by a small legacy to come into my hands at eighteen and a larger one at thirty 'so that she may be able to decide her own life, whether married or not'. In a long letter to my mother, written shortly before his death, he said that his chief wish for me was that I should be brought up 'free from all this national feeling which makes people so unhappy. Bring her up somewhere where she does not belong, then she can't have it. I'd rather France or Italy than England, so that she can really be cosmopolitan, deep down . . . She must be English now, just as she'd have been more American if I'd lived and not you. That is natural and right. But I'd like her to be a little "foreign", too, so that, when she grows up, she really will be free to love and marry anyone she likes, of any country, without its being difficult.' This letter was shown to me by my mother many years later, after I had grown up in Italy and was engaged to an Italian. But of what my father *said* to me in those last days, as I sat on the carpet of his tent beside his day-bed, I have only the haziest recollection. He was learning some of Shakespeare's sonnets by heart and he recited some of them to me, in accordance with his belief that it is not necessary, nor even desirable, for a child to understand *all* that is said to it: the sights should always be placed just a little too high. He taught me poker-patience, too, and wrote with amused pride to his father about my skill. 'I think she will have a card mind.' But what I remember best is his voice itself, and his quick smile, and the intense feeling of companionship and well-being, as I leaned against his knee while the last story or poem drew to an end, while through the open flap of the tent, the sky changed to gold and green and the rocky hill grew darker. Then a lean, dog-like shape was suddenly outlined against the sky, the first jackal's shrill yelp broke the stillness, and it was time to say good-night.

At Christmas my father was a little better, and Iskander Haik— our dignified, gentle, omniscient Syrian dragoman—prepared a Christmas party on board. I can still recall the wonder of being up so late on the deck festooned with bright paper garlands, the songs of the boatmen, the scents of the Eastern night and the bright lights of the Christmas-tree beneath the stars. I myself was dressed in a Turkish fancy-dress with long trousers of white gauze and an embroidered gold jacket, which my mother had brought me from Constantinople, and in the cabin the grown-ups, too, had improvised some kind of fancy-dress. Even my father had a white turban and my mother a shimmering dress, and the ship-boys their best scarlet sashes over their long white gowns. There were crackers and toasts and presents and songs—until the flickering lights of the Christmas-tree and the stars in the sky and their reflections in the river were all blurred in my sleepy eyes, and I was carried below to fall asleep to the sound of more singing and of the Nile lapping against our keel.

That was the last untroubled evening. It had already become evident that the violent alternations of cold and heat, which at first had seemed so bracing, and the strong, cold sand-laden desert winds, were as dangerous for my father as they have proved for many other invalids. Four days after Christmas he had another hæmorrhage, and in a faint pencilled scrawl, to reassure his father, he wrote: 'I hope my little hæmorrhages no longer give you the same horror as at first. To me they are merely a nuisance.'

Dr. Bishop, however, was not so sanguine, and as soon as possible we sailed on to Assuan, within reach of medical help and hotels. There we pitched another camp in a little bay on the west branch of the river, beyond Elephantine Island, out of sight of the town, but looking on one side towards a wide golden valley leading to the open desert. 'It is really almost a pleasure,' he wrote to his father from his cabin, 'to lie in bed in such a beautifu, place.'

His friend, Gordon Gardiner, wrote later on to his parents: 'I think that the little cabin, the shining river, the palms and the desert, the sense of isolation which fell with the night and with the calls of the jackals and wolves—I think that all these things appealed to him, and that he liked to feel the touch of adventure which always supports a true traveller.'

By then my governess and I had been moved to a hotel on the mainland, and my English grandparents, realising how dangerously ill my father was, had come there to join us. On his worst days I could not, of course, see my father, but as soon as he was a little better the rowing-boat came to take me across the Nile to the *dahabeah*, and I spent an hour by his bed, or, when he was too weak for even that, stood for a minute or two at his cabin door.

'Yesterday I saw him for just one second,' I wrote to my American grandfather. 'He seemed a little better, he smiled and said that I was an excellent child.'

I do not think that his appearance or manner can have changed much, for I remember no sense of strangeness or apprehension (though from this I may have been protected by the egocentricity of childhood) but I do recollect the intense excitement on each occasion of the long row across the Nile and around the island, waiting to see him.

The next memory is of an afternoon two or three days before my father's death. My grandfather, too, had suddenly fallen ill, with one of the sudden high fevers that so often attack European travellers to Egypt, and I remember Gran taking me into his room, where he lay in bed with his eyes closed, and saying briskly:

"Gabba is ill, darling. I am going to your mother, and you must stay with him. Sit quite still on that chair, give him a glass of barley-water if he wants it, ring the bell if he tells you to, and don't talk."

For two hours I sat there—filled, I fear, not with anxiety but self-importance. When my grandmother came back, her eyes were red. But it was only two or three days later, returning from another visit, that she took me on her knee and gently told me that my father was dead.

Even then, I did not really understand. I cried a little, because Gran so plainly expected it, and my governess cried too, and tied a black sash on my white frock; and the stout Italian housemaid whispered "*Povera piccola!*" As I walked demurely down the long hotel passages to my supper I was thinking almost exclusively about my black sash.

"I am an orphan," I said to myself, "like Sophie."

It was many years, remembering that self-picturing, before I could refrain from blushing. Indeed, I was right to blush and should do so still, for one form of self-picturing or another has been one of my greatest weaknesses all my life. All that I have

learned since then is that it is a sign of insecurity and of vanity—
but not necessarily of a cold heart.

My mother rightly considered that I was too young to go to
the funeral, though later on, before leaving, I was taken to see
my father's grave in the stark, lonely little cemetery outside the
town, separated only by a low white wall from the desert and the
rocks, where he lay beside a few English officers and soldiers who
had died in the Sudan, most of them as young as he and nearly
as far away from their native land. On the day after his death, I
was taken to my mother, in the tent that had stood beside my
father's; his had already been taken down. She tried to take me
in her arms but I drew away from her tears and ran back to the
boat. I looked into my father's cabin and into all the other cabins;
they were all empty. Without a word, I ran to the ship's side and
signalled that I wanted to be lifted into the rowing-boat; swiftly,
in silence, the Nubians rowed me ashore. The hot desert wind, the
Khamsin, had sprung up and as I climbed up the short hill back to
the hotel, it blew the burning sand into my eyes. I became
acquainted then with loneliness and grief.

How can one measure what might have been? Often in my
childhood I cried for my father; often, later on, I thought, 'If he
had been there, I would not have made this or that mistake.'
Reading his letters and talking to his friends, I can see some of
the characteristics that I may owe to him; a natural affinity with
the Latin world (one that was always closed, in spite of her love
of Italian landscape and art, to my mother), an interest in many
different kinds of ideas and people; a satisfaction in tackling
intellectual problems (though not with equal brilliance) and also,
the sharp, sudden impatience which his illness made so much
more excusable in him than in me. But what the later years of our
friendship might have brought, I shall never know.

His greatest gift to me was assuredly that he became the personification of a myth. A large part of childhood is spent in a
legendary world, peopled by myths and heroes: it is through
them that beauty and valour are first apprehended. But it is
generally a shadowy, secret domain, wholly cut off from life.
When, however, a child can translate his myth into terms of
reality and can recollect his hero in flesh and blood, the vision is
unified: virtue and valour walk upon this earth.

4

My Mother

IN MY EARLY CHILDHOOD, my father and my English grandfather were the presiding deities; my mother being, in my
recollection, either a reclining figure upon a sofa or a moving
one, waving goodbye from a car. It was not until after the age of
ten that I began to discover what she was like—or at least what
the facet was like which was turned to a child's eye. After two
years of widowhood she was still (as I now realise) only thirty, a
young woman just awakening, in the freedom and independence
of her new life in Italy, to the full flowering of her own personality. All my memories of her, during those early years in
Florence, are coloured by her intense vitality, her infectious
eagerness. Though she had little regular beauty of feature, the
brightness of her hair, of the colour of burnished brass rather
than gold, and never faded either by illness or old age, the clear
china-blue of her round childlike eyes, the swiftness of her
speech and movements, the gay colours she chose for her clothes,
gave the effect of a humming-bird or a kingfisher, always in flight.
Her clothes, too, then seemed to me extremely beautiful: I can
still remember a scarlet duvetyn cloak, a little black velvet tri-
corne with a Cavalier's sweeping feather, and, in the evening, a
succession of the Fortuny tea-gowns which had then just come
into fashion: long straight gowns of finely pleated heavy silk,
girdled like those of figures in a Greek frieze, or coats of velvet
and brocade, in the designs and colours of Venetian or Florentine
Renaissance pictures—sapphire and crimson, deep green and
gold. Dressed myself in the suitable 'pinafore-frocks' (dark blue
or purple serge in winter, pale green or blue linen in summer)
which had replaced the white muslins of my earlier childhood, I
felt her clothes to be as dazzling and unattainable as the swiftness
of her mind.

As I grew a little older, however, I began to gather courage.
Although not really a child-lover and content to delegate the routine
of my daily life to her maid or to a succession of governesses,

my mother had a remarkable gift for awakening a child's imagination: everything she told or showed one was exciting, because it clearly delighted her, too. It was in her company that I discovered the two greatest pleasures of my childhood, which have endured for my whole life—the pleasures of travel and of books. I would come down after tea in the '*sala degli uccelli*'—the Chinese drawing-room papered with exotic birds and flowers— and there, lying in her Fortuny tea-gown on the sofa of greyish-blue brocade, she would read aloud to me in her quick breathless voice. "Shall it be *St. Agnes' Eve* today, or *Kubla Khan?*" Like Charles Lamb, she believed in awakening 'that beautiful interest in wild tales which makes a child a man, while all the time he suspects himself to be no bigger than a child'—and indeed her own enjoyment was still as untarnished, as childlike, as mine.

A few years later, when she was compiling an anthology, *The Book of the Sea*, I not only helped her with the mechanical tasks of copying and typewriting but with the work of research and selection. I would come into her bedroom (for a lingering form of jaundice kept her in bed for the whole of that winter) with some new find, generally in French or Italian, for with her own knowledge of English poetry I could not compete. On one day it would be a Piedmontese ballad, *O marinar della marina*, on another, a Breton sailor's prayer, *Protégez-moi, mon Seigneur: mon navire est si petit et votre mer est si grande*, or perhaps (for by then my classical education had begun) a fragment of the Homeric hymn to Castor and Pollux, or an epitaph from the Greek Anthology: 'Not dust nor the light weight of a stone, but all the sea that thou beholdest is the tomb of Eurisippus . . .'—"Oh darling, that *is* a find!"

As proud as a spaniel who has retrieved his bird, I would settle down happily upon the hearth-rug, while my mother read aloud to me what she, too, had found in the course of the day, secure for an hour in the most delightful, and rarest, form of family affection—a real kinship of the mind. I would not then have exchanged her companionship for that of any child of my own age. Indeed I felt a bitter disappointment whenever a visitor's arrival would break into the precious hour, and would sit in a corner of the room with my own book, apparently demure and absorbed, inwardly seething with resentment.

The initiation into the art of travel was not without its discomforts. I was then an acutely self-conscious schoolgirl, anxious above all to be inconspicuous in public, and this, in my mother's company, was seldom possible. We would generally start, if going by train, with a triumphal procession down the station platform, my mother not infrequently in an invalid chair and accompanied by a bevy of affectionate friends and servants, all encumbered (in addition to the suitcases borne by the porters) with hold-alls and tea-baskets, cameras and guide-books, rugs, parasols, and reading matter for a week. On entering the sleeping-car, my mother's bed had to be made up with her own pillows and rugs and fine Jaeger sheets ("all sheets in trains are damp") and the little brown cupboard of our washstand was filled with smelling-salts and lavender-water, face-cream and sympathol, and an array of pills; the conductor had to be coaxed to fill her hot-water bottle, and the dining-car man to bring the menu.

"No, I could not possibly touch any of this, but perhaps a very *fine* breast of chicken, lightly grilled, and a bottle of *cold* Vichy water." And then, to me, "Darling, I'm sure I smelled a cigar. *Would* you mind explaining to the man—no, not in the next carriage, I think it must be three or four doors off—that I am very delicate . . ."

I did mind. I minded so much that I would stand outside the offender's compartment praying for an accident before I had to go in.

"I am so sorry, but my Mother . . ." "*Scusi tanto, ma mia Madre* . . ." "*Verzeihen Sie* . . ." "*Veuillez m'excuser* . . ."

Sometimes my interlocutor was nice about it, and sometimes not. If he went on smoking, I would hurry back to our compartment, shut the door, hand my mother a book, and retreat in silent prayer that she would not notice, but in vain. A few minutes later:

"Darling,—I don't think you *can* have explained yourself properly. Would you call the conductor?"

I wished that I were dead.

Travel by car, too, had its embarrassing moments. The sight of a cypress avenue leading to a fine villa, or the mere mention of its existence in a guide-book was, to my mother, irresistible.

"Tell him to turn in, darling, we've just time before tea."

"But we don't *know* them, Mummy!"

"Never mind, people are always glad to show their house, if it's a nice one."

And a moment later the astonished owners, sitting at ease in their loggia or on the lawn—Papa sometimes with his coat off, Mamma at her knitting—would see an English lady in the height of fashion, but swathed in a dust-coat, rapidly descending from a large Lancia, followed by a plump, self-conscious schoolgirl carrying Baedeker, the Guide Bleu or Mrs. Wharton's *Italian Villas*.

"I know you won't mind us glancing around for just a moment —such a delightful façade! And my daughter tells me that the frescoes in the hall are by Veronese, or at least his school. Yes, look, Iris" (for by then we were in the hall) "that balustrade is very characteristic, with the Negro boy looking over it—but surely that wall has been touched up a good deal? It is really delightful of you"—this to our dazed host, who had meanwhile caught up with us—"to let us see your charming room—and I see you have a little formal garden on the other side—rather like Maser, only of course on a smaller scale. Now do tell me"— confidentially—"what *other* villas of interest are there in this neighbourhood?"

Sometimes this technique was entirely successful. Our host, swept off his feet, would begin a lively discussion of the local works of art and we would all end up, with his wife and daughters, in a semi-circle on the lawn. But sometimes we encountered only blank stares and stiff manners.

"*Not* very agreeable people," my mother would say, as I miserably climbed in beside her and we drove on. "And the garden disappointing, too. The Italian taste for palms is really very misplaced."

To the morbid self-consciousness of adolescence this was misery. Yet I should be giving a very false impression of my journeys with my mother if I implied that they consisted of nothing but discomfort. The same driving energy which sometimes embarrassed me, also caused us to discover and visit many places of singular beauty: hermitages on mountain-tops (up which, all illness cast aside, she leapt with the grace and speed of a chamois), remote oases in the desert, exquisite half-vanished mosaics in crumbling chapels, or the arch of a ruined Roman

bridge at the end of a lonely valley. All these sights were enhanced and illuminated not only by the depth and variety of the
information she offered, but by a capacity for enjoyment which
was irresistibly contagious. For in all this there was no pose at all.
The persistence, as ruthless as a child's, which brought us to these
places, sprang from a child's single-mindedness, but also from a
love of beauty and an imaginative and informed historical sense
which neither illness nor, later on, advancing years, could ever
quench.

In following her swift steps and her darting, clear, inquiring
mind I have often been reminded of Madame de Charrière's
remark, "After all, it is necessary, is it not, to know where
Archimedes placed his lever!" To my mother, too, it was always
necessary to see, to know, to understand. She belonged to the
great tradition of eighteenth-century travellers—enterprising,
courageous, arrogant, totally immune to criticism or ridicule,
carrying their own world with them.

Perhaps the most suitable vehicle for her would have been
Byron's travelling-coach, drawn by six horses and furnished with
a complete library, but she would certainly have been at home,
too, on Lady Hester Stanhope's white camel. And I have no
doubt whatever that, if we had been in Istanbul at the end of the
eighteenth century, it would have been my fate to endure, together with Lady Mary Wortley Montagu's daughter, the first
vaccination against smallpox in Western Europe.

It was perhaps in a Venetian gondola, belonging to the palaces
lent to her by friends on various different occasions, that she
found the mode of progression most suited to her in our own
time, lying back on the black cushions, with a parasol over her
head and a guide-book open in her hand.

"Tell him not to miss San Zenobio," she would say to me,
"there's a small Bellini Madonna over the third altar on the
right, and an unfinished Tiepolo sketch in the sacristy."

The information was always accurate; the picture, church or
palazzo always worth seeing. Then, as the evening approached,
she would tell the gondoliers to row us out across the lagoon,
sometimes as far as the island where Byron used to visit the
Armenian monks or to the cypresses of S. Francesco del Deserto.
There, tied up against a pylon, we would eat our evening meal,

with the water lapping against the boat and the last breath of wind dying away with the sunset; then we would slowly row back under the stars, sometimes meeting or overtaking the great fruit-barges rowing out from the mainland with their cargo of ripe figs and peaches, cucumbers and water melons, for the morning market.

It was at such times that I knew—the anxieties and embarrassments of the day forgotten—that I was lucky to be with her. Indeed even the mildest afternoon picnic or a day's excursion into the Mugello or the Casentino could acquire, in her company, a flavour of adventure.

"Look, darling," she would say, poking me in the back as I sat beside the chauffeur, "I see a nice little road winding up that crag —and yes—I think there's a chapel at the top. Tell Valentino to turn up there."

Resignedly, Valentino would stop the car and ask a passing *contadino* if it was indeed a road, or only a cart-track.

"He says that no car has ever been up there before, *Signora Contessa*."

"Well, never mind, I expect we'll get up there somehow."

Very often we did, to a wonderful view, and if instead we got stuck, Valentino would carry the tea-basket to a chestnut wood or beside a stream, where we would sit contentedly drinking tea, munching biscuits and reading aloud until a yoke of oxen, detached from their plough, had pulled the car back upon the road again.

The discomfort of these incidents has long since faded; the love of new sights, and the awareness that a little persistence may lead to hidden treasures, has remained.

As I became a little older, our journeys took us further afield— to Sicily and Greece, to Algeria and Tunisia, where we even spent a night in Tebessa, to see the Roman ruins, in the most primitive of rest-houses. When sufficiently interested by new and strange sights, all my mother's love of comfort and invalidism fell away from her. Riding all day on a camel across the desert, driven by Greek drivers at whirlwind speed down the steep winding roads of the Peloponnesus, briskly pacing around the walls of Constantinople, she never missed a sight nor turned a hair.

It was on one of these journeys, motoring in North Africa, that I saw two scenes which, after half a century, are still imprinted on my memory, though I cannot remember the name of the place where the first one occurred. I only recollect leaving the clean, characterless French rest-house on the outskirts of a Tunisian oasis, in which my mother was lying down during the heat of the day, and, turning down between some tall palm-trees to a group of mud-huts, suddenly coming upon a coal-black scarecrow of an old man, dressed only in a lion-skin on his shoulders. He was performing, for a fascinated circle of Arab spectators, a 'lion dance'—a mimicry of a lion stalking and killing his prey—and the dance reached a paroxysm of excitement at the final moment of the kill. To the circle of watching Arabs the half-naked, possessed dancer was plainly as alien and barbarous a savage as he was to myself, nor have I any idea of how he came to be there. At the end, he fell to the ground slobbering and writhing in something very like an epileptic fit. His audience, returning to their huts, left him writhing there in the dust, while I went back to the cool white hall of the rest-house, where a French colonial officer in a trim uniform and his wife in black high-heeled shoes were still sitting, as I had left them, on cane-backed chairs, peacefully sipping their coffee.

The second scene took place outside the walls of the sacred Algerian city of Kairouan, a few days before the beginning of Ramadan. The desert tribesmen were already gathering for the great annual festival and, squatting round a fire, soon after sunset, some of them were listening to a story-teller. I could not of course understand what he was saying, but this was hardly necessary. Every phase of the story, every dramatic moment, was reflected in the bearded faces of the listeners—taut with apprehension as some crisis approached, quivering with sensual delight over a love-scene or with cruelty and blood-lust at the climax of a fight, rising to their feet to shake their fists and interrupt the narrator with hoarse comments and cries, shaking with Gargantuan laughter over some Rabelaisian episode. This, I thought—as more and more listeners came from their tents or camels to join the circle, the firelight accentuating the lights and shadows on every face, the story-teller's voice quickened by his audience's response—this is how Homer must have told the story of Polyphemus or of the stealing of Helen; this is how men must have listened to the tales of the quarrels of the gods before the camp-fires of Troy, and, in a later day, to the story of Tristan and Iseult and of Childe Roland's horn. Every written word is only a thin substitute for this, and perhaps it is man's desire to return to it that has brought about the success of the radio and of television: the need to have beauty and terror and laughter brought to us, not by books, but by a human voice.

The strangest of these journeys, however, and the one most clearly imprinted on my memory, did not take place in any exotic setting. It was a voyage across the Atlantic when I was twelve years old, in the first week of August, 1914.

For about a week beforehand, in London, the grown-ups had been talking in corners ("No, not just now dear, no, Doody can't finish the packing.") We were going to the United States, to stay with my grandmother by the sea in Maine, at North East Harbour, and though of course there always used to be a fuss before a long journey, it was not quite this sort of fuss. Usually it was about clothes and luggage and comfortable enough seats ("Are you *sure* that we are facing the engine and that it is an *outside* cabin?") and about not catching cold two days before leaving ("You started chicken-pox just before we left for Greece, and whooping-cough when I had planned to go to Sicily.") But now the grown-up conversations, or rather the scraps of them overheard, were full of new words and phrases: 'Sarajevo', 'the tinder-box of Europe', 'the Archduke'. (I knew about archangels, but what was an archduke?) It soon became plain to me that some unusual event had gone into the way of our plans; that my grown-up cousin Irene Lawley, who had never been to America before, was determined to go; that my grandfather, although he never interfered, did not approve; and that my mother, although she hardly ever let anything get in her way, was perturbed and perplexed. ("But, Irene, if it *should* happen, and we can't get back?")

But what was 'it'? It is not surprising that I did not know, since the grown-ups, for all their talk, did not really know either, even though Mummy had of course all sorts of important friends 'connected' with this or that department in the Foreign Office and the War Office and the Admiralty and the House—'Tommy' and

'Eddy' and 'Henry' and 'Jack'—for England was still ruled, as indeed it continued to be for some time longer, by a family party. (I remember reading, many years later, a book basing its attack on the Conservative Party on a family tree showing how many members of the House and the Cabinet were closely related to each other, and wondering why the author had bothered to set down what one had always known.) And the 'Tommies' and 'Eddies' looked in, on their way back from their offices in their black coats and striped trousers, rather tired; and some of them said, very emphatically, "My dear, don't start. It may come at any moment." Others said with equal firmness, "My dear, of course you can go. There's nothing in it."

Since both Mummy and Irene liked the second piece of advice better, we went.

We sailed on August 2nd, bound for Quebec, and the first two days were spent in a pleasant travellers' limbo—while, in our wake, the lamps of Europe were going out. Then, on August 4th, all passengers were summoned to the main saloon and the Captain read aloud the news he had just received by radio: Germany had invaded Belgium; France and England had come to her defence; Europe was at war.

The thing that was peculiar about this announcement—though of course I did not realise this at the time—was its starkness. No rhetoric, no propaganda, not even any details: just the grim bare fact that peace was over, war had begun. For four days, we sailed across a grey sea, between two continents, with this knowledge, and I think there was no-one on board for whom it did not take on a heroic stature. Then, with the first tug that steamed down the St. Lawrence to meet us, and the scramble on deck for the first papers, rhetoric came on board: 'Brave little Belgium', 'a Scrap of Paper'. But then those phrases, worn later on to a paper thinness, still carried with them a genuine impact, a true emotion.

After landing, an anti-climax: for one young passenger at least, the strife in Europe faded again into the distance, compared with her acute awareness of hardly less acrimonious, though always polite, dissension at home. My mother's one thought was, how quickly we could get back to Europe; my grandmother's, how to keep me in America. The pull of their two strong wills, with myself as their object, taught me what my later experience confirmed, that a major war also often arouses many small family conflicts, no less deadly. In this particular one, my mother was victorious. We sailed back to London from New York a fortnight after our arrival, on the last ship carrying civilians for many months.

During the second half of the voyage a strict black-out was observed; there was boat-drill, and a considerable sense of tension. In so far as I remember, no-one mentioned the word submarine in my presence, and everyone was very hearty at deck-tennis and shuffle-board. My mother and Irene were the only women on board and I the only child; all the other passengers were men, of widely varying professions and classes, but almost all very young, hurrying home from remote regions of America and Canada, to volunteer. No news reached us during the voyage. On the last evening—the portholes shuttered and sealed, the decks dark—the Captain gathered all passengers together for dinner. For the first time in my life I tasted champagne; for the first time I felt what it was to be in the company of a large number of people, all dominated by a similar but unexpressed emotion. At the meal's end, the Captain, a quiet, laconic Scotsman, made a short, matter-of-fact speech. We were expected to dock, he said, next morning at eight. He requested passengers to have their baggage ready by six. He thanked them for their discipline and cheerfulness during the voyage and gave thanks to Almighty God for our safe arrival. He hoped that some of us might some day meet again. And then: "God Save the King." The recollection of the intensity of emotion beneath those reticent words, and the silence of the listeners, has remained with me all my life; it broke out, at last, in the national anthem. Within a few weeks, every man present that night was in the front line; very few of them, at the end of the year, were still alive.

After that, the War was always there. Not *in* my life, because I had no father or brother at the front, but always just behind the door, like the fog of which the damp and the smell were always creeping in through the ill-shut windows. We spent that autumn in London, in a small, dark flat in Sloane Street, because, my mother said, "One really must do something." (The something ended by being the equipping of a Red Cross Unit for Albania.)

Rain, rain; one hung out of the window in spite of it ("You've got another smut on your nose, Iris") and *Tipperary* came in; troops were marching down the street, so young that they seemed young even to me; and quiet, white-faced women lined the streets, watching them. There was greasy wool all over the house, khaki and dark grey, and I wound it and knitted (like everyone else, though very badly) Balaclava helmets and seamen's mufflers, and the smell and grease of the wool got under one's finger-nails.

Once, on my way to Miss Woolf's class, I saw a blowsy middle-aged woman present a pale young man with a white feather, and knew, even then, that it was a very ugly thing to do.

In my mother's flat, people came in and out; but not the Tommies and Eddies any more, for some of them were at the Front and some in the Cabinet, and some were dead. Everyone was resolutely cheerful, but no-one talked much at breakfast after reading the casualty lists; later on in the day, someone would come in, looking very tired, saying, "I've just been with Jack's mother," or, "Sheila is wonderful—she went straight back to the canteen." And one day Irene brought us a slim, dark little volume, saying, "They've come—Rupert's poems."

Everyone who came in was working in a hospital or a canteen or an office, or else at Victoria Station meeting and allocating Belgian refugees, and then in the evening went home to the 'Belgiums' they had taken in, and later on told funny stories about them. (I formed an impression—which subsequent years have confirmed—that 'refugees' are not an amiable race, and that their hosts soon become unamiable, too.) The refugee in the house of Irene's mother, my Aunt Constance—how they met each other I cannot say—was, very suitably, a Russian princess. She complained, too, though in another style; she had—although, I was told, so poor—the largest pearls I had ever seen.

It went on raining, and my mother went on catching cold, and eventually, soon after Christmas, she decided to take me back to Italy. I was miserable, both at being checked in my patriotic fervour and at being torn away from Miss Woolf's enthralling classes. But we went. The Channel boat—on which I felt, even then, that my mother's scarlet cloak was out of place—was crowded with troops and nurses and French civilians returning home, and we were all very sick and wet and cold; and at Boulogne, there were turbaned Indian troops on the quay, looking even sicker, wetter and yellower than we. And that was the end of my first glimpse—through a thick pane of glass—of war.

It was after our return to Villa Medici, where we spent the war years in a state of mental and emotional segregation which I still find very surprising, that my attitude to my mother began to change: I was becoming aware that she had interests and needs of her own, which I could not share or fulfil. Certainly by the time that I was thirteen or fourteen, I had begun to realise that, in the varied procession of friends who came to the house, what she was seeking was a stable and protective affection. Beneath her egotism, her brilliance, and her taste for sophisticated talk, she had preserved a very simple and English romanticism. When, in 1917, she told me that she was going to marry Geoffrey Scott, the brilliant young architect and writer who had been working as Mr. Berenson's secretary, the turmoil of my feelings was instinctive rather than rational.

It was not that I minded, in itself, her marrying again. My image of my father was something so separate from daily life, so entirely my own possession, that I felt no resentment on his behalf. On my own account I was, I think, not so much jealous, as uncomfortably disturbed by watching my mother suddenly become both so much younger again, and also so vulnerable. But I tried to stifle these feelings and to believe that only happiness lay before her. My instinct, however, told me that her choice had not been wise; and of this confirmation came very soon. I have no intention of dwelling upon the complex causes which made this marriage unhappy, nor of setting down accusations against Geoffrey, whose friendship I kept even after he and my mother were divorced, and whom I continued to see in England and America until his early death in 1929. I think with much affection, after so many years, of his tall, ungainly figure, and of the mobile, ugly face lit by quick flushes of intelligence and laughter; the straight coarse black hair, eternally unbrushed and falling over his eyes, and the appealing, faintly bewildered look beneath his horn spectacles—the defence (sometimes misleading) of the shortsighted. He could be the most perceptive of friends, the most brilliant of talkers, and his disarming helplessness must, I think, have made more women fall in love with him than his brilliance. But he was not, by temperament, a husband—and, in any relationship, he was a disturbing human being, an iconoclast who had begun by destroying his own idols, a mocker filled with self-mockery. Moreover, the complete instability of his moods made him extremely difficult to live with; the uncertainty as to whether he would not awake, after an evening enlivened by his stories and his wit, to a morning blackness which, for three days, would envelop the whole house in a dank mist of silence and gloom. At such times, too, he became incapable of doing any work—an incapacity which my mother (whose own unflagging industry was only checked by illness) was constitutionally incapable of understanding. He had by then already made his name with *The Architecture of Humanism* and during the first months of his marriage he was contemplating *A History of Taste* which would certainly have been a fascinating and entertaining book. There was a great deal of conversation about it, and I still possess a large piece of foolscap which lay for many weeks upon the centre of his desk, bearing, in his fine scholar's hand, the following words, and these only:

A HISTORY OF TASTE
Volume I
Chapter I
'It is very difficult . . .'

So far as I know, the work progressed no further.

He was, however, writing at this time most of the poems—many of them, of great distinction and charm, published in two small volumes entitled *Poems* and *A Box of Paints*, and I remember the pride I took in being shown them as they took shape, and in even sometimes being consulted as to the choice of an adjective or turn of phrase. His chief work during those years was one in which he and my mother collaborated with great delight, his *Portrait of Zélide*. The idea for this book came to them on a wet November evening at Ouchy, where my mother was staying for one of her cures. All day the mist had blanketed the lake, the gulls had repeated their rapacious melancholy squawks, the guests of the Beau Rivage Hotel had been served their insipid diets in little individual green casseroles, and after luncheon Geoffrey, in search of the only distraction available, a new book, had taken the tram to Place St. Francois, returning from the Librairie Payot with a large volume under his arm, M. Philippe Godet's *Madame de Charrière et ses Amis*. This he read aloud to my mother after dinner; the next day they ransacked the Lausanne Library for every work upon Madame de Charrière available—including her own novels, which later on my mother translated into equally elegant, formal English prose.

Within three days, the *Portrait of Zélide* had begun to take shape, and thus, by a curious irony, a woman whose own emotional life had been singularly unhappy, brought, for a few months, harmony to another woman's marriage. In the absorption of bringing Zélide and Boswell, d'Hermenches and Benjamin Constant to life again, Geoffrey and his wife suspended the relentless analysis of their own feelings: they laughed and worked together. Perhaps, too, there was in all this a certain process of self-identification. Certainly Geoffrey possessed, as well as Benjamin's wit and his passion for 'reality of intercourse', a somewhat similar cleavage between mind and temperament, something of the destructive '*dédoublement Constantien*'; certainly Sybil shared, as well as Zélide's fine taste and love of learning, her unflagging zest. But the parallel must not be pressed too far; no other woman, perhaps, has ever been so relentlessly, unfailingly rational as Zélide.

Be that as it may, the result of these labours—Geoffrey's *Portrait of Zélide*, dedicated 'To Sybil'—was a remarkable and delightful book, a vivid portrayal of the life and vision of the eighteenth century, an acute and merciless portrait of a clever and unhappy woman. Here and there—as in most biographies worth reading—the biographer's intuition was called upon to supplement the facts: some of Zélide's own letters to Boswell, in particular, were lacking, and it was necessary to guess what they might have contained. In this case—with a good fortune which seldom falls to a biographer's lot—the pattern was eventually completed. I had the pleasure of being with Geoffrey several years later, when, as he was sorting and examining the fabulous treasures that had lain concealed in trunks in Malahide Castle, he came upon Zélide's letters and discovered that wherever he had only guessed, he had guessed right.

While this book was taking shape, I too had a small share in it —at least to the extent of eagerly listening to each chapter as it

was read aloud and to the discussions about its protagonists—
and I think it may be questioned whether so wholly rational an
attitude to life and love, so much stark and chronic disillusionment, was desirable fare for a schoolgirl, especially for one who
was, by nature, quite as naïvely romantic as her mother, and also
desperately afraid of showing her naïveté. Often I would go
upstairs, after an evening in which I had shown, I hoped, nothing
but an amused and intelligent interest, feeling much inclined to
burst into tears.

'Is this what love is really like?' I wondered—and then, with
the immediate egotism of the young, 'Is this really all *I* can
expect of life?'

I was far more conscious, too, than was good for me, of the
ebb and flow of emotion in the marriage before my eyes: I
learned too soon to be tactful, and, when necessary, blind. By the
time that my mother and Geoffrey had decided to part, I was
myself engaged and, when their divorce took place, I was already
married. In 1927, my mother married again—choosing this time
an old friend, Percy Lubbock, and I felt a conviction (which the
future entirely fulfilled) that she would find in him the protection
and care that she needed. What, however, we none of us foresaw
was an entirely different tragedy—the gradual increase of invalidism which (perhaps partly fostered by her husband's uncritical, unremitting care) began gradually to change her whole
personality, and eventually set up barriers which cut her off from
everything that she had once valued. How much of this was due
to physical, and how much to nervous, causes I should hesitate
to say, nor would most modern doctors set the problem in those
terms. "Sybil's always ill when she can't get what she wants,"
her mother used to say of her in her childhood, with the decisive-
ness of a tougher generation and a simpler nature. But the grain
of truth in the comment did not alter the fact that the illness was
always real. My mother was genuinely sick on our Egyptian
dahabeah—the only person, I imagine, ever to have been made so
by the waters of the Nile; she genuinely crashed to the floor in a
faint in the midst of a tedious party. She had an uncanny capacity,
too, for picking up any germ that was about in its most virulent
form: when I had a mild attack of measles she was laid up for
three months; when we attended the procession of the *Volto*

Santo in Lucca, she caught a form of infective jaundice which kept her in bed for the whole winter. My most vivid memory of her later years in Fiesole is of her figure lying in her sea-blue bedroom, hung with curtains of the same colour and adorned with Chinese prints—a room as fragrant with exotic flowers as the tropical hothouse at Kew, and of much the same temperature —but still, as she sent out directions to every member of the household, with her hand firmly grasping the helm.

The suddenness, too, of her attacks was as disconcerting as it was inconvenient. In retrospect, I seem to have spent a great deal of my girlhood at the telephone, changing the plans which some sudden minor illness had destroyed. "Mummy has *such* a bad headache today," I would say to an irascible elderly uncle or a distinguished foreign writer passing through Florence, "could you possibly come to tea tomorrow instead?"—"No,"—this was to Cook's, "I'm afraid we shall not be able to use our reservations for Taormina next week. My mother . . ." And so on.

Up to her early forties, these sudden eclipses were followed by equally sudden and complete resuscitations. One day she would be lying in bed in total darkness, the air pervaded with eau-de-cologne, and the next morning, entering on tiptoe, I would find her sitting on the edge of the bed, with her maid grimly handing her her stockings, a map open on her knees.

"Such a lovely morning, darling! Just the day for a picnic, and there's a new road in the Casentino . . . You were lunching with a friend? Oh, just call up and say that you can't come, oh, and darling,"—her voice rose as I was closing the door—"ring up Marchesa X too, and say that I won't be able to see her next week, as I shall be in Sicily." So the cavalcade would set off again.

It was only very gradually that her friends realised that the periods of illness had become longer, the recoveries less frequent and less complete. In Ceylon—where she went, with Percy, on her last journey to the East—she may have picked up some infection which accounted for her prolonged and debilitating intestinal attacks, causing fits of intense chilliness alternating with sweating attacks so violent that all her nightclothes and sometimes her bedclothes had to be changed two or three times a night. A night-nurse became a necessity, her diet became more and more restricted, and the number of days diminished in which—even wrapped up in a fur coat and with a footwarmer—she could go for a drive. But far sadder, to the observer, was the corresponding change in the responsiveness of her mind and heart. In the past her eager curiosity, her quick sympathy, had never failed to respond to any new stimulus; now, although not yet wholly muted, her responses were subordinated to the preoccupations of ill-health. The doctor's visit, the daily processes of digestion, the position of a pillow or a lamp—these came first. Gradually the objects which had been the means to comfort—rugs and hot-water bottles, soft carpets and cushions, fires and screens—became not her servants but her masters; they dominated her life. Gradually, relentlessly, the body took command over the spirit.

Then the Second World War began. From the moment when it became evident that Italy would soon be drawn in, it was also plain that my mother must not remain there. It might perhaps have been possible to obtain permission for her and Percy to live with my husband and me in our country-place, La Foce (instead of in one of the remote mountain villages of the Abruzzi or Calabria to which many interned Englishwomen were sent), but even if she stayed with us, how could we be sure of providing the luxurious food and tropical warmth that she needed? England too—the England of Churchill's 'blood, sweat and tears'—was plainly no place for her. With much string-pulling I succeeded in obtaining permission for her to leave, only three days before Italy's declaration of war, for Switzerland. Here, at Vevey and, in the summer, in a villa on the slopes of Mount Pélerin, she spent the last years of her life—and here, in the winter of 1941, I was able (thanks to my American passport) to pay her a visit.

I went to the Grand Hotel at Vevey from a country already at war, already bombed and short of food; from work in the P.O.W. office of the Italian Red Cross, from interviewing (after the Allied advance in Africa), day after day, women imploring for news of their husbands or sons—killed, wounded, or captured— from the soup-kitchens of Rome for hungry refugees, from the bombed cities of the Campagna. I found Switzerland as prosperous, smug and well-fed as it had ever been, with every table in the well-heated, well-appointed dining-room filled with elderly, well-dressed, rich refugees. Every day they took little walks by the lake in the mornings as far as the newspaper kiosk, to buy *The Times, Corriere della Sera* or *Figaro*; at lunch-time they would exchange the news, or gossip about any new arrival, and complain about the food; in the afternoons and evenings they played bridge. Sometimes one of them would go for the day to Geneva, to return from his Consulate with scraps of news which he would impart to a carefully chosen group of friends.

"Of course this must go no further, but the secret weapon . . ."

"Know it for a fact, a chap in the Consulate has a cousin who . . ."

Sometimes the Queen of Spain would come over from Lausanne for tea and bridge, providing conversation for the next two evenings.

"Poor Queen Ena! My sister used to live in Madrid, and she told me . . ."

They were the scavengers of War, more belligerent than any combatant.

And upstairs, in the midst of all this plenty, my mother was starving. This is not a figure of speech. Whether the intestinal infection she had caught in the East had really become much more severe, whether a body exhausted by years of alternations between sedatives and purges or stimulants had simply ceased to react or whether it was her nervous system that had broken down, is surely irrelevant. The simple fact was that the wish to eat, as well as the capacity to assimilate, had left her. Her fingers, always long, had now become so slender that her rings dropped off them; her arms and body were as thin as an Indian famine baby's. In the first year, on very fine days, she was sometimes wheeled in a chair down the long passage to the lift, and Percy and the chauffeur lifted her into the car for a short drive through the vineyards on the hill. But when the second winter came, she kept entirely to her room.

I saw her for the last time in November, 1942, having obtained a week's leave from the Red Cross—since it was plain that, when the advancing Allied armies moved on to the north of La Foce, we would be cut off entirely from Switzerland and I should not be able to get to her again until the war was over. I had brought with me some photographs of her grandchild, Benedetta (who had been born after her departure from Italy), but her interest in them was as perfunctory as in the news from England which her sister wrote to her. Everything had shrunk to the small space enclosed within the four walls of her sick-room.

The news of her increasing weakness continued to reach me, through Percy, for a few weeks longer—then all communication with Switzerland came to an end, and even messages of inquiry through the International Red Cross produced no reply. Finally, in January, I opened a letter in an unfamiliar uneducated hand, postmarked in Turin, '*La nostra amata Contessa è spirata il 26 dicembre, senza soffrire.*' That—a message smuggled by a partisan across the Alps—was all.

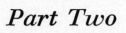

Part Two

5

Childhood at Fiesole

Sally go round the moon, Sally,
Sally go round the sun,
Sally go round the omnibus
On a Sunday afternoon.
Nursery rhyme

I AM NOT CERTAIN how it came about that my mother bought
the Villa Medici, on the southern slopes of the Fiesole hill
above Florence, but I do remember the spring day on
which, from the little villa at Rifredi which we had taken for a
few months, she took me for a drive up a long hill, first between
high walls over which yellow banksia roses tumbled and a tangle
of wisteria, then through olive-groves opening to an ever wider
view; and finally down a long drive over-shadowed by ilex trees
to a terrace with two tall trees—paulownias—which had scattered
on the lawn mauve flowers I had never seen before. At the end of
the terrace stood a square house with a deep loggia, looking due
west towards the sunset over the whole valley of the Arno. There
were three rooms papered with Chinese flowers and birds in
brilliant colours, with gay tiles upon the floor and upstairs I was
shown a little square room with green Florentine furniture,
painted with Cupids and garlands of flowers, which, my mother
said, would be my own.

"This is where we are going to live."

This, then, until my marriage fourteen years later, became my
home, and certainly no child could have had a more beautiful one.
The house had been built by the great Florentine architect
Michelozzo for Cosimo de' Medici on the foundations of another
villa belonging to the Bardi called *Belcanto*, and it has always
seemed strange to me that Cosimo's grandson Lorenzo should
not have kept its original name, for it was in this villa—as in his
other house at the foot of the hill at Careggi, the seat of the
Platonic Academy—that Tuscan Humanism reached its finest

flowering. It was at Careggi that Lorenzo gave a party every year on Plato's birthday, while Pico della Mirandola and Marsilio Ficino discussed the 'mysteries of the Ancients'. It was in the Villa Medici at Fiesole that Cristoforo Landino lived for a year, writing his Commentaries on Dante, and that Poliziano composed his long pastoral poem, the *Rusticus* (before he was sent off, as tutor to the Medici children, to the remote castle of Cafaggiolo in the Mugello, in the dreary company of Lorenzo's wife, Clarice); and it was at Fiesole that banquets were held by the Medici brothers on spring and summer nights, followed by the reading aloud of poetry, dancing, music and love-making—each with the zest and vigour which Lorenzo brought to all his pursuits—while often the whole company would ride off the next morning at dawn, to hunt in the Mugello. One of these evening parties, however, on the night of April 25, 1478, nearly had a tragic ending, for the bitter rivals of the Medici, the Pazzi, having been invited to a banquet at Fiesole by Lorenzo and his brother Giuliano in honour of Cardinal Riario, planned to take this opportunity of murdering their hosts at their own table. It was only a sudden fit of gout of Giuliano's that postponed the attack until the following day, when the murderers struck instead in the cathedral of Florence, Giuliano being killed by a dagger-thrust at the foot of the high altar, while Lorenzo barely escaped with his life.

Dutifully showing visitors round the Villa and telling them, like a diligent little parrot, about these events, I used to regret that the more dramatic scene of the conspiracy had not taken place in our own house; and sometimes, when my mother was out of hearing, I made up a story of my own about a daughter of the Medici murdered by her brothers for unfaithfulness to her betrothed, whose corpse had been buried beneath the stairs. Sometimes, I whispered, if my audience seemed sufficiently credulous, her ghost walked the house at night.

The main structure of the house, with its two deep loggias (one of which contained a bust of the last of the Medicean Grand Dukes, Gian Galeazzo), was still the same as it had been in Lorenzo's time, but in the eighteenth century the house had passed into the hands of Horace Walpole's sister-in-law, Lady Orford—a lady of dubious reputation but fine taste, to whom we owed the exquisite Chinese wallpapers which were designed especially for some of the drawing-rooms. She, too, held parties at Villa Medici, to which the English Minister in Florence, Sir James Hill, came, and Horace Walpole, and all the fashionable tourists of their day. The house was still in English hands when, in 1911, my mother bought it.

She restored the Villa's formal garden to its original design and furnished the house from the Florentine *antiquari*—at a cost which then seemed high but would now seem moderate—with the help of two gifted young architects, Geoffrey Scott and Cecil Pinsent, who were then working for the famous art critic Bernard Berenson, at his villa at Settignano, I Tatti, and sometimes with the Olympian advice of B.B. himself. What would be the novelty today, I used to wonder, as I came downstairs from the school-room for lunch. Sometimes it was a Capodimonte bird to adorn the red lacquer cornice of the library and once a bright-feathered one in a gilded cage, which, when you turned a key, spread its wings and whistled a little melancholy tune; sometimes an inlaid writing-table or a small bronze statue for the fountain; sometimes (from Geoffrey) the tale of the latest incident in the Loeser-Berenson feud, or (from Cecil) a map of an unexplored road in the Mugello, leading to a half-deserted villa. No picnic or expedition was complete without Cecil; no luncheon or dinner-party, without Geoffrey's stories.

For my mother, it must have been a fulfilling and stimulating time but, for my part, I must confess that the immediate effect of being exposed so soon and so intensively to so much art and culture was that I soon came to associate any talk about garden design, Venetian writing-tables, Florentine *cassoni* or lacquer cabinets, with a tedium which did not fade until, after acquiring a house and garden of my own, I suddenly found that I possessed information which I had consciously rejected, but which had somehow remained with me, like sea-wreck on the shore when the tide has gone out. Though whether this is, or is not, an argument in favour of introducing children early to subjects which still bore them I really do not know.

I have said that I was not consciously aware of the beauty around me; yet I now realise how much more I did take in than I knew, and how much I owe to the space and solitude of those early years. (An understanding of these needs was, I think, the most creative element in the theories of Signora Montessori, who never mistook for sheer naughtiness what she called 'a child's defence of its molested life'.) Whenever I was free of my governesses, I escaped into the garden, not to the formal terrace, with its box-edged beds and fountains where my mother took her guests, but to the dark ilex wood above it or the steep terraces of the *podere*, partly cultivated with plots of wheat or of fragrant beans, partly abandoned to high grass and to the untended bushes of the tangled, half-wild little pink Tuscan roses, perpetually-flowering, *le rose d'ogni mese*. This became my own domain. The great stone blocks of the Etruscan wall were as good for climbing, with their easy footholds, as were the low-branched olive-trees; the high grass between the rose-bushes was a perfect place in which to lie hidden with a book on a summer's day, peering down, unseen, at the dwarfed figures of the grown-ups staidly conversing on the terrace far below; and the deep Etruscan well in the midst of the ilex wood, its opening half-concealed by branches and leaves, was dark and dank enough on a winter evening to supply the faint eeriness, faint dread, without which the sunny hillside might have seemed a little tame. It was, I now know, a very small wood, but it was large enough to feel alone in. To dare oneself to venture into its shadows at twilight, to smell the dank rotting leaves and feel one's feet slipping in the wet earth beside the well, was, for a solitary child, adventure enough. It was not a dread of 'robbers' or even of any ghost from the past that overcame one then, but an older, more primitive fear—half pleasurable, wholly absorbing. It is one of the penalties of growing up that these apprehensions and intuitions gradually become blunted. The wall between us and the other world thickens: what was a constant, if unformulated, awareness, becomes just a memory. It is only very rarely, as the years go on, that a trap-door opens in the memory and a whiff of half-forgotten scents, a glimpse of the mysteries, reaches us once again.

The greater part of my childhood, however, was of course not spent in this private world, but on the everyday level of what one was told was real life: meals and lessons, getting up and going to bed, brushing your teeth and saying your prayers. Like other children of my generation, most of my time was spent upstairs, in the nursery or schoolroom. I came down, with my governess, to lunch in the dining-room, and again, when my mother was well enough, to the drawing-room after tea—for an hour of reading aloud, which I have already described. But the rest of my day was spent in a monotonous round of lessons and walks and early schoolroom suppers, and of meals as unvaried as my routine. My mother, having been treated for years for chronic colitis, following the cure of a Swiss specialist, Dr. Combe, decided to forestall any similar tendency in me by also making me follow his strict diet, so that every day, for over two years, the same wholesome, unappetising meal lay before me. I was not a particularly greedy child, but there were days in which the stodgy, unflavoured food simply would not go down, and I can remember the envy with which I would see other children at parties helping themselves to chocolate cake or ice-cream. Visitors to the house, too, made matters worse by commiserating with me, in particular the kind but silly wife of the famous French nerve-specialist, Dr. Vittos, who paid us a visit during that period.

"*Pauvre petite*," she would exclaim as she saw my meal, "*c'est affreux! C'est une torture!*"

I can still feel the facile tears of self-pity rising to my eyes, and hear the dry tones of her husband's reply:

"*Mais non, ma chère, c'est une discipline comme une autre.*"

I liked Dr. Vittos, and the plain common sense in his voice was at once convincing. I stopped, once and for all, complaining about my food.

As for company, some little girl chosen by my mother generally came to tea on Sundays, most often a well-behaved, gentle child called Marie-Lou Bourbon del Monte, half-Italian and half-American, whom for many years I considered my 'best friend', not because we had much in common, but because she had so sweet a nature that it was impossible not to become fond of her. Later on there was also a very fair, clever English girl, Elnyth Arbuthnot (who later on married, like me, an Italian, a delightful Florentine naval officer, Ferrante Capponi), and a gifted, musical little American girl, Paquita Hagemeyer. Together we formed the nucleus of what we pompously called a 'Cosmopolitan, Literary, Artistic and Dramatic Society', the CLADS, which met once a week and published a quarterly magazine. Then there was the weekly excitement of the Saturday dancing-class, the high-light of the week; and the rarer, still greater delight of the few parties to which I was allowed to go at Christmas and Easter. To these occasions I looked forward with an intensity denied to children who had company of their own age every day, though the pitch of my expectations made some disappointment inevitable.

I can still feel myself catching my breath with excitement as, in the crowded little dressing-room of the Florentine palazzo in which Miss Flint's dancing classes took place, we changed our shoes, smoothed out our accordion-pleated skirts, and then, as the tinny piano struck up, ran to our places. Skipping-ropes, clubs, the five positions, the formal measures of the minuet and gavotte, the valse and the polka, and then—Miss Flint's speciality —'expressive dancing'.

"Now, the dance to the Sun-God. Iris, you try it alone today."

Pride, alarm, ecstasy; rigid with these emotions I twirled, I knelt and raised my hands to heaven, I sank to the ground in worship. At the end came Miss Flint's verdict: "You'd do very nicely, dear, if you didn't try so hard."

At parties, however, I did not try at all, but was content to 'stand and stare'. They remain in my memory as a brilliant phantasmagoria: the day in Casa Rucellai on which, gently protected by the elder sister Nennina who became my life-long friend, I saw my first children's play; the annual Christmas party at the Actons', where the tree and the presents were larger and more expensive than anywhere else, but our young hosts' most valuable possessions—rare shells from the South Seas and small *objets d'art* —were locked away in glass cupboards before we arrived; and finally a wonderful fancy-dress dance in our own house, when I was about ten years old, which started at four o'clock for the children and went on until next morning for the grown-ups, and at which Marie-Lou and I, dressed as Renaissance pages, were allowed to stay up until the end, handing round a silver loving-cup.

These parties, glamorous as they were in recollection, took place too seldom for any real friendship to be formed with other children, even if I had known how to make friends. All I did was to look on—quite happily, and entirely unaware that to the other children, who saw me always watched by my governess,

restricted to my dull diet, forbidden to come at all if the weather
was bad, and often snatched away before the party's end, my lot
seemed a most unenviable one.

Much of their sympathy was misplaced. My childhood at this
stage was not unhappy: it was merely disconcerting, in its swift
alternations between excitement and tedium, between caviare and
bread-and-milk. At the age of twelve, for instance, in the last
weeks before the First World War, I was taken for the first time
to the theatre in London, to see *The Merchant of Venice* at the
Old Vic. The illusion was so complete that I resented my mother's
faint smile, when, at the words, 'how far a little candle throws its
beams', a brilliant shaft from the footlights lit up the whole stage.
A few days later, I was taken to Covent Garden, to see the Russian
Ballet. It was the last year in which Nijinsky was dancing in
London: I saw him in *Le Spectre de la Rose*, and, most unforget-
table of all, I saw Pavlova in the *Dying Swan*. It was then that,
for the first time, beauty and delight reached me through my eyes
and not through a book. Then we sailed for America and, a
few months later, returned to Italy, and I never entered a theatre
again (far less a cinema) until I was seventeen.

There was a hardly less vivid contrast at Villa Medici between
the social life downstairs, of which I had brief glimpses, and my
own schoolroom, in the undiluted company of my governesses
—a long and dreary dynasty. Fräulein Hodel, a round cheerful
girl, entirely absorbed in the young Italian *ragioniere* who (to my
great interest) played the guitar under her window at night, was
perhaps the silliest of these ladies; Mademoiselle Nigg was the
most sentimental, Mademoiselle Sanceaux the most neurotic,
Mademoiselle Gonnet (who frequently remarked that her neck was
considered to resemble the Duchess of Marlborough's) the vainest.
These weaknesses I observed with the cold, unwinking, inhuman
eye of childhood. The only governess from whom I learned something of value—a little German and some interest in history and
geography—was Fräulein Weibel, a good teacher and an able
woman and (I now realise) a very unhappy one, embittered—for
she had an illegitimate daughter, whom she called her niece—by
caring for another woman's child instead of her own, grudging
me the pretty clothes and the pleasures which she could not give
to her own Liselotte. At the time I merely dimly knew that she

disliked me for some reason which I could not understand, and considered me in every way inferior to the pig-tailed 'niece' whose photograph stood on her bedside table. "Liselotte would never do such a thing," was the daily refrain. I hated Liselotte.

Two things were harmful to me in the succession of these ladies. The first was that I spent my time in a constant conflict of loyalties (unknown to children today) between the standards of the drawing-room and those of the schoolroom. All of my governesses disliked my mother—partly, I think, from jealousy of her pretty looks and clothes and quick wit, of the agreeable men constantly in and out of the house, and of the general aroma of luxury, and partly because her charming manners to them imperfectly concealed an abysmal indifference. All this was conveyed to me, by sniff and innuendo, as soon as we went upstairs again.

My mother, on the other hand, never spoke to me directly about my governesses, except in terms of respect. "I hope, darling, you do just what Fräulein Weibel tells you"; "I do wish you could have as beautiful a French accent as Mademoiselle Gonnet"; but it would have been a very deaf child who did not overhear the aside, to one of her own friends, after Mademoiselle Nigg left the room, about the Swiss being a sentimental race—and a blind one, who did not observe that never, except to talk about my work, did she spend ten minutes in Fräulein Weibel's company.

I felt, in short, uncomfortable when governess and parent were in each other's presence. Moreover, my mentors were also bad for me in a more important way. I was, by nature, not only a law-abiding little girl, but one who *needed* to respect and admire her elders. When scolded my instinct was never to say to myself, as I have often heard my own children say, "Fräulein's so cross today", but rather to feel "How naughty I am!" This instinct, however, was undermined by undeniable facts. Fräulein Weibel was so irritable as to be unfair. Mademoiselle Gonnet flirted with the convalescent British officers who stayed with us after Gallipoli, shaking her chestnut curls and arching her swan-like neck, in a manner both embarrassing and common. I observed all this and despised these ladies—failing, however, to perceive the loneliness beneath Mademoiselle Gonnet's flirtations and the longing for her own daughter beneath Fräulein Weibel's crossness. Because I thought Mademoiselle Gonnet silly, I refused to learn, to my lifelong regret, what she could have taught me: correct and fluent French. I became, in short, a supercilious and self-satisfied little prig.

When I was fourteen, however, in the last year of Mademoiselle Gonnet's reign, I struck. I pointed out to my mother that all the things I wished to learn were being admirably taught by my classical tutor in Florence; that it was her maid who looked after my health and my clothes; and that, if she found it tedious to see my governess's face at luncheon, I found it still more so to spend all the rest of the day in her company. Might I not in future do without a governess at all? My mother agreed, and thenceforth I lived in my schoolroom in blissful solitude.

There were, however, two persons who brought a very different note into my daily life and whom I dearly loved: my first Italian teacher, Signora Signorini, and, from babyhood, my mother's maid Kate Leuty, whom I called Doody. Whatever governesses might come and go, Doody was always there. She had been my mother's maid even before her marriage and had afterwards followed her everywhere—the personification of a devotion and loyalty which never abrogated her right to 'know her own mind'; the embodiment of stability, kindness, and uncompromising British common sense. Unfailingly dressed in a neat black coat and skirt, her stocky figure stumped behind her mistress over the ranges of the Grand Canyon, through Grecian temples and Eastern bazaars, frequently carrying a small camp-stool or a hot-water bottle. She sat bolt upright on the low chair supplied for lesser travellers in the prow of Venetian gondolas, gazing expressionlessly across the lagoon; equally upright, and in the same black suit, crowned with a sun-helmet, she rode across the desert on a camel. When asked if she was tired, she would reply, "No, m'lady, we are here for pleasure."

Ships' stewards, Swiss concierges, Syrian dragomen, Arab houseboys, Italian housemaids, all instantaneously recognised her authority, and the prestige of the lady whom she served. At her bidding floors were scrubbed, tents were set up, kettles boiled, the necks of chickens were wrung. Again and again I have seen the miracle occur: the arrival at the end of a long day's motoring at a squalid inn in North Africa or Greece, the unloading of the innumerable suitcases, cloaks and hold-alls with which we travelled, and my mother wandering off with her companions to whichever ruin we had come to see.

"No, don't bother about the luggage. Leuty will see to things."

An hour later, when we returned, the metamorphosis had taken place: in my mother's room the bed was made up with her own sheets and cashmere shawls; the hot-water bottles were already in place and the tea-tray prepared; the engraved bottles and brushes were on the dressing-table; the medicine chest stood open; the guide-books and maps (and perhaps, a pocket copy of *The Golden Treasury* or *La Divina Comedia*) were on the bed-table, and the mosquito-net over the bed; an aroma of roast chicken rose from the kitchen and Condy's Fluid from the bathroom. Another corner of a foreign field was now forever England.

To my mother Leuty awarded the mixture of deference and bluntness of the privileged English 'upper servant', gratifying her caprices, while plainly showing that she recognised them as such; but in real illness or grief suddenly gentle as well as efficient. My grandfather fully appreciated her quality and, in one of his letters during the war, wrote to me: 'You must tell Leuty how grateful we are to her for her care of Mummy, and how we appreciate all she is doing. She is a real and faithful friend to us all and no family ever had a better one. Mind you tell her this for me.' To me she invariably referred, even long after I was grown-up, as 'the child' ("the child needs some more flannel petticoats"; "the child's looking white; too many parties"), under the impression, apparently, that by avoiding the use of any endearment in speech, she was concealing her complete, but never uncritical, devotion.

In all the changes of homes, of governesses, of plans, in all childish ailments and disappointments, Doody was my 'fixed mark'. It was she who tucked me into bed every night and later came back to remove the electric torch with which I was reading under the bedclothes. It was she who bought—unthanked— my warm woollen combinations and long black stockings, who taught me to speak the truth and to wash the back of my neck. She was, besides, a most agreeable companion, with a childlike capacity, beneath her placid manner, of enjoying the minor pleasures of travel. I remember, indeed, annoying my mother in Venice, at the age of twelve, by saying (it required some courage) that, rather than look at the Carpaccios with her, I would like to spend the afternoon in walking about the *merceria* with Doody, buying glass beads and animals, and having an ice at a café. No disapproval was actually expressed, but I started off under a cloud, well knowing that I had shown myself 'uncultured'.

It was with Doody that, on this and many other occasions, I spent some of the happiest hours of my childhood—secure and at ease, with no obligation to seem either better or cleverer than I really was. She discouraged, indeed, not in words, but by the mere lack of expression on her face, any form of showing off, and, later on, any airs and graces. She understood any real trouble, and wiped out, by her own disregard, any small humiliation. She ordered and put on my Confirmation dress; she inspected and appraised my governesses, my friends, and later on—with some anxiety and mistrust—my young men. Fortunately, she approved of my fiancé, Antonio (in spite of an initial national prejudice), and on my wedding-day it was she who, with an unexpected touch of poetry, wreathed my mirror with the garland of jasmine in which—so her own mother had told her—a bride should first see her face on her wedding morning. And (since my mother was ill) it was the sight of her stout, motionless figure, standing in the loggia, that was my last picture of home, as I drove away for my honeymoon.

When, six years later, a telegram reached me in Venice to tell me that, on a visit to England with my mother, she had been run over by a London bus, I caught the next train to England, but arrived too late. The thought of the hours in which she may have looked in vain for 'the child' are still unbearable to me. I realised then that, in all the years of my childhood and youth, I had never thought to say 'thank you'. This is an attempt—at last—to do so.

The debt that I owe to Signora Signorini is of an entirely different nature, but hardly less great. When she first came to me she was, as I now realise, a young woman, not yet thirty, and she must once have been beautiful, but her looks were already a little faded and her youth dimmed by hard work and resignation. Her life had consisted of fourteen years in a convent-school

—reading no book but those the nuns provided, never entering a theatre or a concert-hall—followed by a marriage which, after six happy years, had been obscured by her husband's dangerous recurring attacks of acute melancholia, which made it necessary for him to be shut away at intervals in a psychiatric hospital, and for her to support her children and herself, by teaching. For five years she came to me for two afternoons a week. I read *Pinocchio* with her, and then *Cuore*, and then *Le Mie Prigioni*; I learned by heart, in conventional slow succession, *Rondinella pellegrina* and *O vaghe montanine pastorelle*, and eventually *Il cinque maggio*. In her quiet, gentle voice she dictated to me the subjects for my essays —on themes intended to develop, rather than the intelligence, the heart: *Stasera Pierino è andato a letto contento di aver compiuto una buona azione—Una festa di famiglia—Chi dona ai poveri dona a Dio.**

Sometimes on a Saturday afternoon she brought her children with her—two little girls of much my own age in their best white frocks, carefully pressed and lengthened, both of them much neater and politer than I, both (as I dimly felt) more secure. I envied them, I did not quite know why. I thought it was because they went to school with other children and had their mother to themselves every evening. I think now that what they possessed was the stability of children living in a wholly homogeneous world, one in which there was a constant struggle with genteel poverty and anxiety, but none of the confusion of mind that had come to myself, a child living in a world too sophisticated for it, too varied, too rich. Through the Signorini children, I became acquainted with a world of small, frugal pleasures, long awaited: the *gita* by tram to Settignano, the new hair-ribbon as a prize for hard work at school, the rare treat of an ice at a café on a Sunday evening, listening to the band, the summer holiday in a small bare *villino* on the slopes of the Pistoiese hills. I was much surprised to learn that one of their greatest pleasures was coming to play with me at the Villa Medici: I could not think why.

As the years went by and we grew up to different lives, I ceased to see much of the Signorini girls. But my devotion to their mother and her unfailing affection continued until her death a

* 'Pierino went to bed tonight, happy, because he had done a good deed'—'A family celebration'—'A gift to the poor is a gift to God'.

few years ago. It was enough to climb up the steep stairs to the flat, in which she lived with one of her married daughters, and enter the cold, over-furnished sitting-room where she sat in an armchair in the corner—a little old lady now, in a seemly black dress—to feel myself back in the schoolroom again, in a smaller, safer world.

"So Donata [my younger daughter] did well in her exam of *terza media*? What a *consolazione* for you, my dear."

No touch of censoriousness marred her interest in what I had to tell her about my travels and my social life; to her it was all plainly 'as good as a play', and equally remote from anything she expected, or even desired, for herself or her daughters. *La discrezione*, that was her guiding virtue—*saper essere discreti*. Even when, in her later years, she was often bedridden with bronchitis and painful heart attacks, her demands upon life remained equally moderate. A religious woman, her piety had no touch of mysticism; a loving heart, she loved without demands. "*È troppo bello per me!*" she would say, stifling her cough, and trying to still her trembling hands, as I brought her a bunch of roses, a pretty dressing-jacket or a pair of fur-lined slippers; and I wish I could convey how genuine the cry was, how far removed from any false humility. She had been brought up and had lived in the true Tuscan tradition, unchanged from the Middle Ages until today —that of 'the just mean'. Frugality, abstinence and honesty to the point of scruple, deep family affection and a sense of duty, the gentleness of those who ask nothing for themselves, the dignity of self-effacement—these were her attributes, and with them a certain dry shrewdness in her judgements and her comments, which is also peculiarly Tuscan. Kind she was always, but entirely realistic. It was a glimpse of this world and of its attitude to life that I owe to her. It would not be true to say that it has changed the course of my own life or of my behaviour, but its memory has never faded—and sometimes it has made the life of luxury seem a little thin.

Thinness, however, is not the right word to apply to the varied and entertaining world of which echoes floated up the schoolroom stairs at Villa Medici, even in the comparative segregation which (I think rightly) my mother had decreed. Gradually I began to see and hear a little more of what was going on, especially during the visits of my mother's gay, pretty young English cousin, Irene Lawley, only ten years older than myself. She would stay with us for weeks at a time, bringing with her a breath of carefree enjoyment and fun which I found both intoxicating and upsetting. Wearing a gay and somewhat transparent dressing gown, she came to schoolroom breakfast (much to my governess's disapproval) and distracted me from my lessons by playing the guitar; she bought one of the Palio banners at Siena and, with some of her young men, practised its complicated furlings on the lawn; she went out riding (while I gaped from the passage window) with a smart young cavalry officer in a blue cloak; she planned moonlight picnics; she produced a children's play which I had written, and herself took part in what seemed to me an extremely daring comedy about a foreign spy, for the benefit of the Red Cross (this was in 1915). Wherever she went, there was laughter and fun, and also a host of admirers, of whom one, Charles Lister—one of the brilliant young Englishmen who, like Rupert Brooke, lost their lives in the Dardanelles—came to say goodbye to her at Villa Medici. He gave her a pair of love-birds bought at the Fiesole fair, which eventually were handed on to me, and I regret to say, pecked each other to death.

With Irene came her enchanting mother, Constance, Lady Wenlock—whom I called 'Aunt Concon'—one of the Edwardian 'Souls'. The atmosphere that surrounded her, however, had no touch of Edwardian vulgarity, but belonged rather to the eighteenth century: she had the wit of a Madame de Sévigné, the grace of a Madame de Sabran. Incurably romantic, she attracted the confidence of young and old alike, even when in old age she had become so deaf that she had to carry a long ear-trumpet, trimmed with lace to match the colour of her gown; and if one wished to confide a secret to her it was necessary to follow her to a secluded rose-garden. In her clinging pale gowns of fine Indian cashmere, she flitted about the garden like an elegant, frail ghost, as silvery as the olive-trees; dawn and sunset (the only hours that she considered worth portraying in art) found her on a camp-stool before her easel, enhancing the view at her feet with an imaginary classical column or *tempietto*, producing water-colour landscapes in which the cypresses were a little blacker and the sunset rather more iridescent than in reality, and in which a few additional towers or spires adorned the distant hillsides. Later on, after my marriage, she came to stay with us in the Val d'Orcia, and would have liked to paint our *maremmano* oxen, but, since she attributed to them the wildness of the Indian cattle, she dared not trust herself among them. She continued, however, at home and abroad, to rise extremely early, either to paint, or to feed her roses with liquid manure from a little watering-can, curiously incongruous in her delicate hands. "Roses are gross feeders," she would say, pinning a full-blown Crimson Glory in the soft lace fichu of her dress. Her zest for life, her passion for beauty, was never dimmed by age. On the morning of her death, at the age of eighty, she had risen to paint the dawn.

Sometimes, too, my grandparents came to Villa Medici to visit their daughter—Gran enjoying the house and garden and Gabba the walks and drives in the hills—but both of them a little bored by the constant intellectual and artistic talk, and trying to re-assure themselves by repeating, "But of course Sybil always did like this sort of thing!"

They brought England with them—but indeed England was already there. Florentine society at that time was not so much cosmopolitan as made up of singularly disparate elements—an archipelago of little islands that never merged into a continent. The worlds of the various colonies—Russian, French, German, Swiss, American, and English—sometimes overlapped, but seldom fused, and the English colony itself, though the largest and most prosperous, was far from being, in its own eyes, a single unit. "They are, of course," as E. M. Forster's clergyman delicately expressed it, "not all equally . . . some are here for trade, for example." The real gulf, however, lay not between one kind of resident and another, but between the mere tourist and the established Anglo-Florentine, who felt himself to have become as much a part of the city life as any Tuscan. Some of these residents sank roots so deep that when, at the outbreak of the Second World War, the British Consulate attempted to repatriate them, a number of obscure old ladies firmly refused to leave, saying that, after fifty years' residence in Florence, they preferred even the risk of a concentration camp to a return to England, where they no longer had any tie or home.

The English church in Via La Marmora, Maquay's Bank in Via Tornabuoni, Miss Penrose's school (where their children met all the little Florentines whose parents wished them to acquire fluent English), the Anglo-American Stores in Via Cavour, Vieusseux's Lending Library and, for the young people, the Tennis Club at the Cascine—these were their focal points. If they lived in a Florentine *palazzo* it was at once transformed—in spite of its great stone fireplaces and brick or marble floors—into a drawing-room in South Kensington: chintz curtains, framed water-colours, silver rose-bowls and library books, a fragrance of home-made scones and of freshly made tea ("But no Italian will warm the tea-pot properly, my dear"). If they had a villa, though they scrupulously preserved the clipped box and cypress hedges of the formal Italian garden, they yet also introduced a note of home: a Dorothy Perkins rambling among the vines and the wisteria on the pergola, a herbaceous border on the lower terrace, and comfortable wicker chairs upon the lawns. *"Bisogna begonia!"* (the two words pronounced to rhyme with each other) I heard Mrs. Keppel cry, as, without bending her straight Edwardian back, she firmly prodded her alarmed Tuscan gardener with her long parasol, and then marked with it the precise spots in the beds where she wished the flowers to be planted. The next time we called, the begonias were there—as luxuriant and trim as in the beds of Sandringham.

It was these owners of other villas who were to be seen at my mother's Sunday tea-parties, but she also 'got done', on the same day, such visitors as were passing through Florence. ("The Brackenburys? Oh, we'll get them done on Sunday.") The result was a company which seemed odd even to the eyes of a child, but I can set down very little about it. The exceptions are a few people of whom I was genuinely fond: a sweet-natured, blue-eyed young Irishwoman, Nesta de Robeck, who offered to teach me to play the piano and to whom I owe many hours of happiness and a friendship that still endures; my father's friend, Gordon Gardiner, who would tell me long sagas about his life in the African veldt and the Australian bush, who would read aloud *Ticonderoga* and laugh at me for getting honey in my hair; and Patience Cockerell, my godmother, who—uncompromisingly dressed in the grey tweed skirt and amber beads which she wore

in her Sussex cottage ("I have no money and don't want to look
as if I had")—spent most of the first years after my father's death
with us, helping to furnish the villa and to plant the garden,
but regarding my mother's new 'artistic' friends with a somewhat
quizzical eye. "Too clever for us," she and Gordon agreed—and
as it became clear that this, in future, was to be my mother's
world, they both gradually faded from the scene.

Of all the other figures at my mother's parties, none was three-
dimensional for me, though I dutifully handed them the buttered
scones, and took them round the garden. I can set down a list of
a few of them, but I can't bring them to life. There was old Lady
Paget from Bellosguardo, a rather frightening old lady; there was
sometimes Vernon Lee, her grey hair cropped tight above an uncompromising man's collar and tie, on her way back from a visit to
our neighbour Charles Strong, up to whose villa she stumped
once a week, to exchange philosophic shouts (for they were both
deaf) on the nature of the Beautiful and the Good. Sometimes
the poet Herbert Trench came striding over the hills from
Settignano with his lovely daughters—three silent Graces—
though he preferred to come alone, to read aloud his lyrics or the
long drama that he was writing about Napoleon. Carlo Placci
would look in, just back from staying at Duino with Princess von
Thurn and Taxis, saying that Rilke, poor fellow, was very ill
again, or from Paris, where, he said, Clemenceau had told him . . .
or perhaps (for his range was wide) from Hatfield, where Lord
Salisbury . . . To me, of course, these were only names, but I
saw that the grown-ups listened with interest, and thought that
this large-nosed old gentleman must be a very important person.
But then why did Mr. Berenson laugh, when the stories were
repeated to him the next day, and say, "Poor old Placci—no
pudding can boil in Europe without his stirring it!"

There was sometimes a small sprinkling, too, of Florentines:
the mothers of my friends, correctly dressed for calling, or some
more dashing young friends of Irene's. There were dowdy,
distinguished English couples of my grandparents' generation,
who had come up from the Hotel Grande Bretagne or Miss
Peters' *pensione* to see 'what sort of place Sybil has settled in';
there were American friends, mostly active, industrious sightseers
eager for information, with an occasional representative of 'Old

New York'; and there was also sometimes a contingent from Bloomsbury or Chelsea, critical as well as appreciative. "To think," Mrs. Masefield exclaimed, as we paced the terrace, "that all this great wall was built by slave labour!" But the tea and the the little cakes—which I handed round assiduously—were delicious, the garden was full of flowers, and my mother was the most cordial and expert of hostesses, shepherding her unamalgamable flock into small harmonious groups.

"Iris, will you show Mrs. X and Colonel Y the peonies in the border, while I give Lady Z and Signor Placci some more tea—and Irene, I think Marchese D and Conte R might like to see the view from the *West* terrace!"

In the end they all went down the hill again, after sunset, feeling that it had been a pleasant afternoon, if slightly disjointed, and my mother sank exhausted on to the sofa, while I thankfully ran upstairs to the schoolroom and my own story-book. I made up my mind, even then, that if I stayed on in Italy after I was grown-up, it would only be to marry an Italian. I did not wish, I thought, to go on belonging to 'the English colony'.

Of the other 'interesting' people in Florence at that time, I have, unfortunately, little to tell. Those whom I now wish I had known—Norman Douglas and Gordon Craig, and later on D. H. Lawrence and the Huxleys—steered clear of villadom. They ate in cheap *trattorie*, spoke the highly coloured language which the Tuscans called *anglo-becero*, and disappeared for long intervals into unexplored, exciting regions, of which a few echoes reached us through Geoffrey Scott and Cecil Pinsent. Sometimes I drove over with my mother to Poggio Gherardo—one of the villas to which Boccaccio's youths and ladies had fled from the great plague in 1348 and in which some of the tales of the Decameron were told—to find old Mrs. Ross reckoning up her olive crop with an eye as shrewd and vigilant as that of any Tuscan farmer, and perhaps sometimes consenting, if in a good mood, to take us into the cosy clutter of her Victorian sitting-room and tell us about how she had once taken 'a dish of tea' with the Miss Berrys, and had had a portrait made of her by *il Signor* (Watts) or had sat on the knee of Meredith, 'my Poet'. Once or twice, later on, I was allowed to sit in a corner of Charles Loeser's fine music-room, hung with early Cézannes (for he was

one of the first to discover this painter) while the Lener Quartet
was playing, and our host's elf-like little daughter, Matilda,
peeped in through the half-open door. Occasionally we visited
the most beautiful, and certainly in my eyes the most romantic
garden of all, that of the Villa Gamberaia, and I wandered about,
hoping that I might catch a glimpse of the place's owner, Princess
Ghika, a famous beauty who, from the day that she had lost her
looks, had shut herself up in complete retirement with her
English companion, refusing to let anyone see her unveiled face
again. Sometimes, I was told, she would come out of the house
at dawn to bathe in the pools of the water-garden, or would pace
the long cypress avenue at night—but all that I ever saw (and I
wonder if a hopeful imagination was not responsible for even
this) was a glimpse of a veiled figure at an upper window.

Of the most sharply etched, most celebrated figure of all on
the Florentine stage at that time, I also have, at this point, little
more to tell. The famous art critic and collector, Bernard Berenson, often came to see my mother, and fairly often, too, I went
to I Tatti; but of these visits, my recollections are extremely
inhibited. Not that I was not aware that I Tatti was a remarkable
place and that I was fortunate to have been invited there. The
great, austere library, which seemed to me to contain every book
in the world, the terraced gardens sloping down the hill, and the
long series of *fondi d'oro* in every room and passage—all these
would have been fascinating, if only I could have been left by
myself, uninstructed, to wander alone from one great sad-eyed
Madonna to another, making up my own stories about the saints
and monks, the beautiful ladies and strange beasts, the translucent
landscapes in the background, and the knight riding his white
horse up to a castle on the hill. But I was seldom left alone, and
even on those rare occasions I was not wholly reassured. For
many years I felt the house's presiding genius to be the first object
that one encountered on entering: a great Egyptian cat seated on
a trecento *cassone* in the hall—elegant, inscrutable, irresistibly
attractive. It was only when you put out your hand to stroke
it, that you discovered it to be made of bronze.

When I went to the children's parties given by Mrs. Berenson
for her grandchildren imaginative plans were made for us: we
were bidden to trace the little stream at the foot of the garden,

the Mensola, to its source; or to seek for treasure in the music-room. But we stood about unresponsively, beneath the out-stretched arms of Sassetta's St. Francis, mutually suspicious and dumb. In vain did Mrs. Berenson, whose placid Quaker voice and ample frame should surely have been reassuring, urge us to pick up the little flags she had prepared and to prance round the room in a circle, singing.

"If a child performs the *gestures* of happiness," I overheard her saying to a grown-up friend, "it becomes happy!"

Whether this would have been true in other circumstances, I cannot say, but certainly it was a very self-conscious group of children who trailed round the room at I Tatti, singing a faint lugubrious chant.

My own personal inhibition was a very simple one: I feared that at any moment Mr. Berenson himself might come in. He had never, in his frequent visits to the Villa Medici, been anything but kind to me; yet I could not feel at ease with him. The exquisite-ness of his appearance in his pale grey, perfectly-cut suits, with a dark red carnation in his button-hole, the extreme quietness of his voice, the finish of his manner—these, together with all that I had heard from other people, about his destructive remarks and his encyclopaedic knowledge, were, quite simply, too much for me. When he called upon my mother at tea-time, sometimes bringing with him some of his own guests, perhaps Logan Pearsall Smith or Edith Wharton or Robert Trevelyan, I would wait, hidden at the turn of the stairs, until I heard the car drive away. When he took her out driving in the hills, and sometimes suggested that I should come too, I sat in front beside the chauffeur, only hoping that, when we reached the woods, no more would be asked of me than to unpack the picnic-basket and then slip away with my story-book. Yet on occasions such as these B.B. was a much less alarming figure than the suave host of I Tatti. All affectations cast off, he would leap up the hillside with as much speed and intentness of purpose as if he had still been the young art-student who, in 1888, first gazed upon the Italian scene—his awareness still as fresh as it was then, but enriched and sharpened by every day that had since passed. Whether he took us to see a fading fresco in some remote little country church, or merely stood in the aromatic woods of cypress and pine, looking at the serene outline of a distant hill, or, nearer by, at a happily-placed farm with its dovecot and clump of trees ("Look, a Corot," he would say, or "a Perugino"); to be with him was to realise, once for all, what was meant by the art of looking. One day, after taking us to see some frescoes, he told the Indian tale of how the God of Bow and Arrow taught his little boy how to hit a mark. "He took him into a wood and asked him what he saw. The boy said, 'I see a tree.' 'Look again'— 'I see a bird'—'Look again'—'I see its head'—'Again'—'I see its eye'—'Then shoot!' " It was the same, B.B said, in looking. "One moment is enough, if the concentration is absolute."

And then, if one asked him a question (though this, of course, was in later years), "Yes," he would reply, "there are some portraits of Tartar slaves in the fresco by Lorenzetti of *The Massacre of Tana* in the church of San Francesco in Siena," or "You will find San Bernardino's first pulpit, very small and rather worm-eaten, in a little convent-church two miles south of Montalcino." Or "The best book on *that* subject is in German, but there is quite a satisfactory minor monograph in Italian—you can come and look at it tomorrow." For his library, like his mind, was always at the disposal of anyone, however obscure, who really wanted to know.

It is one of my regrets that, in those early years, I did not learn more from him, nor, indeed, derive pleasure from his company. But just as animals reject food which is not fit for them, so children sometimes instinctively draw back from fare for which they are not yet ripe. That complex personality was still, to my dazzled eyes, undecipherable.

What I still find rather difficult to realise, and will perhaps seem incredible to the readers of this chapter, is that the life I have been describing was taking place during the years between 1914 and 1917—in short, during the First World War. But the truth was that in my mother's ivory tower, as was the case in many other villas inhabited by foreigners on the Florentine hills, the war was only a distant rumble, an inconvenient and unpleasant noise offstage. I do not mean, of course, that there was not a great deal of political talk at my mother's table, and still more at I Tatti, though much of it in a tone of civilised and superior detachment which to the naïve and unquestioning patriotism of fourteen, seemed very shocking. Sometimes, in the early morning, I would be woken up by the sound of tramping feet and soldiers' songs and, running down to the terrace below, would see a squad of weary young recruits tramping down the Via Vecchia Fiesolana, and would hear their songs: *Addio, mia bella, addio* or *Bel soldatin, che passi per la via.*

Every week a long letter from my grandfather in England—containing, even though I was not yet thirteen when this correspondence began, very much the same comments on recent war news or English politics as he would have written to a friend of his own age—carried me back into a very different mental climate. He deeply regretted—for, in spite of his fair-mindedness and international legal experience he had remained very much an old-fashioned Englishman at heart—my being in 'a foreign country' at such a time, and was determined to keep me 'in touch', a result which he certainly achieved. The letters do not, naturally, contain much that is not now familiar, but it was all new to me: descriptions of London during the black-out, of Zeppelin raids, of relations and friends leaving for the front—and there are also many references to the courage and endurance, after Italy had come in, of the Italian troops on the Carso ('Napoleon only thought of *crossing* the Alps, not of fighting there') as well as frequent injunctions to me to realise the importance of the times in which I was living. 'Rest assured that there has been nothing, or hardly anything in history, approaching the magnitude of this struggle between vast forces and between right and wrong. On the outcome depends the future of the world, and of that outcome, humanly speaking, you and not we should be the first fruits.'

One of his early letters contained a long description (very uncharacteristic in its show of emotion) of the retreat from Mons of the First British Expeditionary Force, composed entirely of volunteers. 'Hopelessly outnumbered, without sleep or rest and with the discouragement of ordered retreat, they returned, checked and often defeated by overwhelming forces endeavouring fruitlessly to break their unbreakable line and shake their unbreakable courage. By their tremendous fortitude they gave the unprepared French time to organise their defence, saved Paris and paved the way for the battle of the Marne, upsetting the whole of the German plan, which nearly (how nearly) succeeded. This was about 100,000 men against nearly 800,000. I don't believe the world has ever seen the like. In this long-drawn-out campaign it is likely to be forgotten, and I want you to remember it and to tell it to your children in after days.'

A childish essay of mine, written in 1916, 'The World after the War' (of which my mother must have sent him a copy) pleased him very much. 'It was very thoughtful and well-written. *Sincères félicitations*. You ought now to think what the ideal terms of peace should be. If you put that clearly, you will be the only person of my acquaintance who will have done so. I say "ideal" terms, for the ideal is that which in practice is never attained.' Later on, in 1917, he was writing, 'Are you not gratified, my little Anglo-American granddaughter, that America is now with us? It may well be the decisive step.'

After Gallipoli, my mother must have felt, in spite of her Florentine friends, a recurrence of her wish in 1914 to 'do something', for she wrote to the British Red Cross, offering hospitality in her villa as well as in those of a few English and American friends, to a group of convalescent officers from the Dardanelles. They arrived, in batches of twenty, of whom about eight stayed with my mother and the others were farmed out among her friends, each group staying for about three or four weeks. This enterprise gave great satisfaction to my grandfather. 'I think,' he wrote, 'it is a time you will never forget.' For me, the prospect of the arrival of these soldiers was the most exciting event of the war, but it soon turned to disappointment. I do not quite know what my expectations were, but certainly nothing less than the arrival of the Argonauts themselves, with Jason at their head, would have fulfilled them. Instead I saw a number of young men in very low spirits, still suffering from dysentery or gastritis, some of them disappointed at having been sent to Italy instead of being invalided home, and all, as time went on, more than a little bored. My mother gave them excellent advice about the right diet for their intestinal troubles and was, as always, a charming and accomplished hostess, but I was already old enough to realise, with some discomfort, that they did not much enjoy her intellectual and artistic friends, but preferred to sit about on the terrace in the sun, flirting mildly with my pretty French governess or my cousin Irene, while the more dashing ones went down to Florence in the evenings, to gayer and smarter parties, where whisky and champagne were available, and some pretty girls. The one thing they did not want to talk about was the war; and not one of them, to my eyes, looked like a hero. After a few months, when the tragic enterprise of the Dardanelles came to an end, they stopped coming, and Villa Medici again became an isolated oasis.

Then, in 1917, came Caporetto, and my first glimpse of reality. One morning my teacher of natural history, Professor Vaccari— a Venetian by birth—was late for his lesson, and when he arrived, looked sad and harassed.

"I can't stay today," he said. "I've been up all night at the station with the refugees, and I must go back to them at once."

"The refugees?"

It was then that he described to me, for the first time, what has since become common knowledge: what happens to a civilian population in times of defeat, and had just happened, that week, in his own Veneto; the evacuation of the villages after Caporetto, the exodus of bewildered country folk with their children and their cumbersome bundles, on roads already filled to overflowing by retreating troops and bombed by the enemy; the confusion and the fear, the old people and children who could not keep up, the stumbling into ditches, falling into rivers—the face of humanity in flight. Since then, we have all been familiar with this scene, if not through our own eyes, in a hundred news-reels; but then, it was new, and the man who described it was talking about his own neighbours at home.

"Can you ask your mother for some blankets," he said, "and for some warm clothes, boots, food—anything? I'll borrow a car and come back."

It was the first time that—since I had helped to pack my parents' clothes and mine for the Messina earthquake victims— someone had suggested to me that there was something which I might not talk about, but *do*.

When Vaccari came back I had, with the help of my mother's car, made the rounds of her friends: the schoolroom was piled high with blankets and clothing.

"I won't thank you," Vaccari said briskly, "but if *la mamma* will allow it, I'll take you with me."

An hour later I was with him at the station in Florence, wrapping cold, sleepy children in blankets and helping to hand out cups of coffee and milk from the Red Cross canteen, but most of the time standing bewildered in a corner, uncertain what to do next, watching train after train steam in. The families who poured out—dazed with fatigue and bewilderment—were mostly peasants from the villages along the Piave, the older women swathed in black shawls, the younger ones clutching their children, the old men (for only the old were there) wearing a shuttered, blank look, armoured against incomprehensible misfortune. Huddled on the platform in family groups with their bundles, their one thought was to stay together; all preferred to sleep where they were, rather than to be billeted in different houses. One half-crazed woman, whose child had fallen into the Adige while crossing a crowded bridge, wandered from group to group, tugging the sleeve of anyone who seemed to be in authority.

"Have you seen my Bartolo? He was with me on the bridge." And then again, peering up into the next face that passed: "Have you seen my Bartolo?"

I went back to Fiesole, and persuaded my mother to let one of the refugee families move into the upper floor of our gardener's house and, with Doody's help, bought the necessary furniture, cooking utensils and clothes. After a few months, they were able to go home again, to their own farm near Belluno.

After this, life at the Villa Medici was never quite the same again for me, and during the following autumn, when we were staying in a villa which my mother had taken on the saddle between Capri and Anacapri, I had another enlightening glimpse of real life: the terrible epidemic of Spanish influenza which, in the autumn of 1917, swept across Europe, taking a greater toll of lives than any battle. In Capri, where the little white, flat-roofed houses stood so close together that one could stretch from one roof-top to another, the epidemic spread like the plague in the Middle Ages: there was hardly a house in which there was not a victim. It was then that I saw, at work, a man of whom, until then, I had only thought as one of my mother's 'clever' friends, but a more formidable one than most, Dr. Axel Munthe. During the summer we had spent a good deal of time with him, sometimes beneath a pillared pergola of his villa at Anacapri, San Michele—'a strange mixture' as Compton Mackenzie remarked, 'of Scandinavian Gothic and Imperial Rome'—and sometimes in the Saracen tower, Materita, in the middle of an olive grove to which he moved, as tourists began to invade the island, for greater seclusion and privacy. Here I heard the sagas that he told my mother about the influence he wielded over kings and queens (and certainly their portraits and souvenirs were there in plenty); the peace that he had brought to dying men in the war, by hypnotising them into unconsciousness of their pain; the bird sanctuary he hoped to form on the island coast, so that the thousands of quail, arriving in spring from their long flight across the Mediterranean, might not sink to a wretched death on the nets smeared with pitch-lime which were prepared for them. Sitting silent in the background, mesmerised by his talk and yet faintly suspicious of it, watching the glance of his blue eyes (so sharp, in spite of the blindness that was already coming over him) I would wonder whether he was really one of the most remarkable men I had ever met, or merely a teller of tales, with a touch of Cagliostro. But during the epidemic, I saw a very different man. Fearless, resourceful, kind, he strode from house to house with unflagging courage and endurance; he saved innumerable lives, and brought comfort, when there was nothing else to bring. It is thus, striding like an ancient, bearded Viking through the narrow streets of Capri, with women stretching out their hands to him in doorways, imploring his help, that I remember him, no longer merely the protagonist of his own legend, but truly the physician and healer.

By then a new phase of my life was beginning, and when, in 1918, my grandfather wrote to me from London about the rejoicings over the Armistice, my one wish was to get to him and to England as soon as possible.

It was during that same summer that, for the first time, I realised that I was no longer a child, but did not yet belong to the grown-up world—a stage familiar to every adolescent, but intensified by my circumstances. This was the summer after Geoffrey Scott's marriage to my mother, and every week-end, when he came down from the British Embassy in Rome to join us and I would be an unwelcome third in our picnics or evening excursions, I would feel, not jealous, but lonely. Sitting in the prow of the boat, in which we would row out at night to some isolated headland or bay for a picnic, while my mother and Geoffrey talked in low voices in the stern, or after the meal, climbing up over the rocks by myself, I would long, with the passionate rebelliousness and intensity of sixteen, for a life of my own, and friends.

Sometimes, too, other friends of my mother's came to stay: Algar Thorold, suavely and benignly discoursing on Buddhism and presenting me with a little booklet on *The Eightfold Path* which I still possess; and Herbert Trench, who would join us on our moonlight picnics, declaiming lyric verses about feminine fragility and masculine chivalry, while I staggered up the rocky path behind him carrying the picnic-basket, or else after dinner reading aloud to us the blank verse of his magniloquent, interminable drama about Napoleon. Recently, opening a volume of Compton Mackenzie's *Memoirs*, I was much amused to find this incident recorded there from an observer's point of view.

"I read the play to Sybil and Iris last night," said the poet to Compton Mackenzie, "and at the end they were like that." He made a gesture of admiration and wonder, unable for a moment to find words to express it. It was on this occasion that he went on, his voice lowered into a reverential murmur, "You won't misunderstand me, my dear fellow, when I say it is genius."

'The next day Lady Sybil and Iris were lunching with us at Casa Solitaria. "Oh, my dears," said Lady Sybil, "Herbert Trench read his Napoleon play to Iris and me yesterday. It went on for hours and at the end of it we were both of us like that"—but the gesture Lady Sybil made was not of admiration and wonder, but of utter exhaustion.'

It was at the Casa Solitaria, the Mackenzies' enchanting white villa built into the cliff just above the Faraglioni—the rocks on which, according to legend Ulysses heard the Sirens' song—that to my mind the most exciting, if not always comfortable, evenings of the summer were spent, listening spellbound on the curved terrace above the sea to the stories of our host's exploits in Greece, while indoors Renata Borgatti was playing Chopin, or the booming voices of two Russian singers, a baritone and a bass whom Mackenzie had nicknamed Bim and Boom, echoed out over the rocks. Compton Mackenzie has written in his *Memoirs* that he already then foresaw 'a name in literature for me'. If only he had said so to me *then*! Both he and his wife Faith were unfailingly kind, but I felt a very stiff, awkward *backfisch* at their witty, Bohemian parties, and sometimes wished that I were taking part instead (but no-one had asked me) in the gay, unexacting musical entertainment which the boys and girls of my own age were getting up in the little town.

It was in the piazza of Capri, too, that I witnessed my first historical occasion—the proclamation of the Armistice, with all the island bells ringing out, the little square crowded with all the local population and foreign residents, the *sindaco* in his tri-coloured sash, and Compton Mackenzie in British naval uniform addressing the town councillors in Morgano's café in a d'Annunziesque speech in Italian in honour of the *tricolore*, " . . . *rosso col sangue dei combattenti eroi, verde come la terra della nostra Italia irredenta . . .*"

All this took place on November 4, 1918, a week before the proclamation of the Armistice in England. We hastily returned to Florence, to find a letter from my grandfather describing the rejoicings in London and I wrote to him in return that my greatest wish was to get back to him and England as soon as possible.

'I sympathise with you,' he wrote. 'I would not have been away from London then for anything (except direct national service elsewhere), and I do deeply regret that you have missed the national outpouring of heart in the centre of our united Empire . . . for no rejoicing in a foreign world can move the heart like that among our own people.' He characteristically added: 'No generation in history has seen greater days than ours and no-one can I think foresee the problems of the future, whose solution they have rendered necessary. In the midst of rejoicings the nations must pray for sanity'—a prayer which, as we now know, was only partially answered.

In the following spring, I was back again in England with him and Gran and then at Desart, though that visit was inevitably clouded by his deep disappointment over the failure of the Dublin

Convention, and his anxiety for the future of Ireland. But the closeness of my bond with my grandparents was renewed and, though after only a few months I returned to my mother in Italy, my childhood at Fiesole was over.

6

Reading and Learning

... As pines
keep the shape of the wind
even when the wind has fled and is no longer there
so words
guard the shape of man.

GEORGE SEFERIS, *trans. Walter Kaiser*

WHAT DO WE MEAN by being alone? Rumer Godden is of the opinion that, from the day that a child has learned to read, he will never be so again. "When you learn to read," she said to her own daughter, "you will be born again, and it is a pity to be born again so young. As soon as you learn to read, you will not see anything again quite as it is. It will all the time be altered by what you have read, and you will never be quite alone again."

I think that there is something in this, in the sense that we do not look at a landscape again in quite the same way after we have once seen a great painter's rendering of it: the blue hills of the Veneto come to resemble the background to Bellini's Madonnas, the *crete senesi* turn into the landscapes of Sassetta or Sodoma. But I do not agree that it is an argument against teaching a child how to read, or if it is, then we must also exclude all telling of stories. 'The Three Bears' and 'Little Black Sambo', 'The Constant Tin Soldier' and 'The Dog with Eyes as Big as Saucers', have already become our companions long before we can read ourselves; they have already peopled our world. All that is achieved by the final act of reading to itself is to enable a child to summon up that other world at its own will. 'My whole being', wrote Coleridge of his boyhood, 'was, with eyes closed to every object of present sense, to crumple myself up in a sunny corner and read, read, read,—fancying myself into Robinson Crusoe's island, finding it a mountain of plum-cake and eating a room for myself and then eating it into the shapes of tables and chairs.'

It is the extreme concreteness of a child's imagination which enables him, not only to take from each book exactly what he requires—people, or genii, or tables and chairs—but literally to furnish his world with them. I can remember no time when I did not do this, nor can I remember when I learned to read. I only know that it must have been fairly soon, since a letter of my mother's, when I was just four, speaks of my finding it easier to read in Italian than in English, and by six I could also read French. German I spoke from the age of four, but only learned to read it later on. This early teaching did not, unfortunately, make a good linguist of me, but it did leave me with the knowledge that any language will do for telling a story. Struwelpeter and Sophia were as familiar figures of the nursery as Humpty Dumpty, Pinocchio as Alice. It was only a little later on that it began to dawn on me that some things were said better, more naturally, in one language than in another, and indeed that I myself did not say quite the same things and was not the same person, in Italian as in English.

As to reading matter, all I knew was that there were always enough books about: picture-books, story-books, poetry-books; 'difficult' books, out of which the grown-ups read aloud and 'easy' books at my own disposal. Only one person was slightly disapproving, my English grandmother. "As you're doing nothing, Iris—only reading", was the formula, followed by "Come and help me to wind my wool, or to pick the sweet peas." And sometimes she would add, "If you read so much now, there'll be no books left for you when you grow up."

This even then I knew (much as I loved and respected Gran) to be nonsense. Of all the pleasures of life, this is the only one that, at every age, has never failed me. But inevitably, I have paid for it with other limitations. 'I cannot sit and think,' wrote Charles Lamb, 'books think for me.' For many years that was true of me, too—not only did I not think, but I did not look or listen. I heard 'the aziola cry' in Shelley's poem, but was deaf to the little night-owl hooting outside my window; I knew all the flowers that bloomed in Ophelia's garden, but few of those in our own. Above all, the boys and girls whom I found in my books were so vivid to me that those I met in real life seemed by comparison a little tame.

In early childhood, my choice of books was directed by two contrasting, but simultaneous, preferences, one for the remote, the fantastic, the heroic; the other for a world exactly like the one I knew, only a little safer, more harmonious, more rounded. The latter satisfied my need for the reassurance of a set moral frame; the first, for an 'expanding universe'. In very early childhood, indeed, there were a few much-loved books which gratified both tastes at once, which brought the fantastic and the marvellous through the gate at the top of the nursery stairs. Pinocchio was eaten by a whale and saved by *la fata dai capelli turchini*, but his long wooden feet were also solidly planted on familiar ground: he had to go to school, like any other little boy, and Geppetto had to pawn his coat to buy him an ABC. A little later on, I found a similar mingling of the fantastic and the quotidian in Mrs. Molesworth's *The Cuckoo Clock*, and in the stories of Mrs. Burnett—not the odious *Little Lord Fauntleroy* but *The Secret Garden* and *Sara Crewe*. The turbaned Indian servant who stole across the roofs into Sara's attic and transformed it, and the country boy, Dickon, who charmed birds and wild animals and helped Mary to bring the deserted garden to life again, both had a touch of authentic magic; but Sara and Mary were also real children, in whom another little girl could personify herself.

Real children, good and naughty, those were what I sought— they fulfilled my craving for company. No family was too large (not even the one in *The Daisy Chain*), no incident too dramatic, and, besides, I had a strong taste for what was, even then, old-fashioned. I had what most children nowadays would consider a positively morbid liking for stories with a moral. *Leila on the Island, In England and at Home*—an immensely long book of which I can only remember that poor Leila was set, for half an hour every day, to look for a lost needle in the sands of the desert island on which she had been cast—*Holiday House*, with the delightfully naughty Harry and Lucy, who rolled their birthday cake down from the top of Arthur's Seat—these were classics of the Victorian nursery which still delighted me, and which led on to Mrs. Molesworth, Mrs. Ewing, Charlotte Yonge and Louisa M. Alcott.

Do any children still read these books today? With the exception of *Little Women*, which appears to be a hardy perennial, I think not. Yet I still think that they were very good. The world they described was, it is true, a circumscribed one—'little ladies and gentlemen' on one side of the fence, and 'the village children' on the other; strong omniscient Papas who were either country gentlemen, retired naval officers or parsons; and sweet, refined, often delicate Mammas—all living in a landscape of great trees and green meadows, of thatched cottages and spacious houses, in which Nanny, in a large apron, addressed her charges (although whipping them) as Miss and Master, and the kettle was forever boiling on the hob for nursery tea. But if the setting was old-fashioned, the characters were alive, and the moral values both crisp and true—and often expressed with dry humour as well as firmness.

There was another, wholly different world that also beckoned from books, the kingdom of magic and fantasy. It was the same world as that of a child's secret rites and incantations; the line between the paving-stones that you must not tread on, the magic formula that will keep you safe on the dark corner of the stairs. Sometimes a single phrase would take you there—'How many miles to Babylon?' There lived the princess whose dress was '*de la couleur du temps*'; there was the little white cottage in the wood where Goldilocks found three chairs, three little beds and three bowls of porridge, the enchanted garden of Beauty and the Beast, the marble staircase where the Prince came to meet Cinderella and take her by the hand. This was the other country, the country of our dreams.

Gradually Cinderella and Goldilocks vanished, other forms began to beckon: The Lady of Shalott, La Belle Dame Sans Merci, Christabel. And now I no longer wished to travel alone:

> *Kennst Du das Land wo die Zitronen blühn?*
> *Allons, faisons un rêve, montons sur deux palefrois.*

The world of fantasy was fading into the world of romance, and childhood was coming to an end.

It was then that I read increasingly, not only in order to escape into another world but, as I believed, to learn about life itself. Mauriac has justly remarked in his *Mémoires Intérieures* that 'the characters invented by the novelist only awake to life, like recorded music, at our bidding. It is we, the readers, who offer these imaginary creatures time and space within ourselves, in which to unfold and engrave their destiny.' Moreover it is by identifying ourselves with them that we do, in a sense, anticipate experience: we try on the parts of love and hate, of jealousy and desire, like our first grown-up dress. I became in turn Maggie Tulliver and Jane Eyre, Catherine Morland and Natasha: *'elles incarnaient mon destin encore voilé'*. Their shadows are thrown upon the screen of my adolescent years with a vividness denied to most living figures.

During all this time, of course, I was also pursuing my formal education—but with how much less gusto! From my governesses I learned some French and German, though not as much as I could have learned had I liked these ladies better. For one brief, exciting term in 1914, when we were in London, I was allowed to attend Miss Woolf's excellent classes in South Audley Street (though mortified by the contrast between my black velveteen frock from Liberty's and the sensible tweed coats and skirts of the other girls) and was delighted to find myself placed, for literature and history, with the Seniors, three years older than myself. But these classes, too, came to an end and, in spite of my earnest pleas to be allowed to go to an English boarding-school, I returned to Fiesole and to the dull, solitary lessons with my governesses.

* * * * *

At the age of twelve, however, a piece of great good fortune befell me. Bernard Berenson, to whom I shall always be grateful, advised my mother to let me receive a classical education and even supplied her with the name of the brilliant tutor with whom I worked for the next three years, Professor Solone Monti. It was with him that I spent the happiest hours of my girlhood—perhaps the happiest I have ever known.

My first impression as I entered his study was of a haze of smoke, so thick that I could hardly see across the little square room, lined with cheap deal bookshelves, to the desk behind which sat a dark, stocky little man, with dandruff on his collar, and with such thick lenses to his spectacles that they seemed more suited to a windscreen than a human eye.

"Mind those books, *signorina*," was his greeting, as I stumbled over a pile near the door, "they are meant to be read, not trodden on."

I would have liked to ask why, in that case, great piles of them covered the floor, except that, looking about me, it was plain that there was no other place for them to be, every inch of the walls and tables being already filled.

"Wait a minute, the lexicon can go on to the floor too. Now sit here and we will take a journey to Greece and Rome. You know no Latin? And of course no Greek?"

I shook my head.

"And you have not yet read Dante?"

"No."

"And Carducci and Pascoli are just names to you?"

I muttered something about *Valentino vestito di nuovo*.

"Yes, yes, I dare say," impatiently, "but it's the other Pascoli I mean, the great classical scholar. Well, we shall have a long way to travel—and we'll pick a great many flowers on the way." Then suddenly, explosively, taking off his glasses and gazing straight into my round, startled face, "But you *like* poetry, in the languages you know? You have read Keats, Shelley, Milton —perhaps some Goethe—perhaps Corneille? You read poetry for *pleasure?*"

"Yes, oh yes!"

"Then we'll begin. Listen now, *signorina*. All you need to do today is to listen."

And he took up Pascoli's *Epos*—his anthology of Latin epic verse, of which the preface and the notes are still so vividly evocative that (in the words of another great classical scholar, Valgimigli, who had been Pascoli's pupil) 'it was like a fluttering of wings'.

The passage that Monti had chosen was the famous one about the Trojan camp-fires on the plain.

"This is how Pascoli describes the scene—for people like you who cannot yet read Greek:

"*Da una parta la pianura scintillante di fuochi, con un cielo sereno di stelle (i Troiani erano all'aperto, in faccia alla loro grande città, e* *mille fuochi ardevano, e a ogni fuoco erano cinquanta guerrieri, e i cavalli stavano presso i fuochi, stritolando fra i denti l'orzo bianco e la spelta, e attendevano l'aurora); dall'altra il mare, tutto rumori e bisbigli. Giunti alle capanne e alle navi dei Mirmidoni, giunti a quella capanna, udirono un canto. Era Achille, che accompagnandosi sulla cetra predata, cantava le glorie dei guerrieri."**

Monti put the book down.

"No, you needn't try to make an intelligent comment. I saw that you were listening. Now, this is what one of your English poets, Tennyson, made of it:

> "So many a fire between the ships and stream
> Of Xanthus blazed before the towers of Troy,
> A thousand on the plain; and close by each
> Sat fifty in the blaze of burning fire;
> And eating hoary grain and pulse the steeds
> Fixt by their cars, waited the golden dawn."

He closed the book, took off his spectacles and wiped them.

"That is the world you will see if you learn Greek—even if you get no further than Homer. Do you want to go there? Yes?"— for I was speechless—"I see you do. Well, here is a Greek grammar. Learn the alphabet and the declensions for next time, so that we can start reading at once. You know German, don't you? And what a declension is? Well, then, be off with you. Oh, and get a lexicon, too; a small one will do, Homer's vocabulary is very limited—and a Latin dictionary. And here's a Latin grammar; you'd better learn those declensions, too, when you can. We'll start at the beginning on Thursday."

Before I had shut the door behind me, he was immersed in his own book again.

*   *   *   *   *

* Pascoli: Introduction to *Epos*, pp. xvii–xviii.

On one side, the plain shimmering with fires, with a serene, starry sky (the Trojans were in the open, before the great city, and a thousand fires were blazing and by each fire sat fifty warriors, and their horses stood close to the fires, champing the white spelt and oats between their teeth, and waiting for the dawn); on the other side the sea, murmuring and sighing. And when they reached the hut and ships of the Myrmidons, they heard a song. It was Achilles, who as he strummed on the strings of his stolen harp, was extolling his warriors' deeds.

I realise now that Professor Monti was making an experiment. Having acquired a pupil who was not tied by school programmes and exams, he decided to try out on me the Humanist education given in the fifteenth century in Mantua by Vittorino da Feltre to Cecilia Gonzaga and her brothers—one in which Greek and Latin were learned together, as living languages. 'To begin with the best'—that was the precept on which the education of the Renaissance had been based, in the days when poetry was considered the fittest instrument to train the mind. According to Bruno d'Arezzo, who wrote the first treatise of the Renaissance on what a woman's education should be, 'anyone ignorant of, and indifferent to, so valuable an aid to knowledge and so ennobling a source of pleasure as poetry, can by no means be entitled to be called educated'.

Monti agreed with him. If we did not precisely invent the Greek language together, like Benjamin Constant and his tutor, we did start reading the *Iliad* at once, he naturally translating most of the words for me as we went along, and pointing out equivalents or derivatives in Latin or in any modern language I knew, with a complete lack of pedantry or condescension.

"Look, the English rendering here is more satisfactory than the Italian, don't you think?—or do you prefer this German one?" And then we would read the passage over again in Greek, this time with me stumbling through the translation, as best I could, by myself.

"Say it in any language you like, only feel the poetry."

"Now, Virgil," he said, when half the first morning had passed. "We'll start with something easy: *Sicelides Musae*. This is the poem of the Golden Age."

That day we did not get very far. For as we reached, in the second line, *humilesque myricae*, he told me what a tamarisk bush looked like, and took down Pascoli's *Myricae* from his shelf, reading aloud some of its verses.

Then, back to Virgil again. But when, a few lines later, we came to the Child of prophecy—'*Tu modo nascenti puer*'—Monti suddenly realised from my blank look that I had no idea of who that child had been supposed to be during the Middle Ages, nor why, among all the Latin poets, it was Virgil whom Dante had chosen as his guide through the infernal regions—Virgil, who

L

149

*mostrò ciò che potea la lingua nostra.** And then Monti turned to the
first Canto of the *Inferno*, and read aloud:

> *"Tu se' lo mio maestro, e il mio autore;*
> *Tu se' solo colui, da cui io tolsi*
> *Lo bello stile, che m'ha fatto onore."*†

So in a flash the morning passed, and then it was time to go
home and work and work, in an attempt to master the rudi-
ments which would enable me to understand him better next
time.

Monti did not, of course, let me off learning any grammar or
rules; he merely required me to wrestle with them alone, not
wasting our time together on such matters, unless I had a question
to ask, or some point came up which he wished to explain. For
ignorance he always made every allowance; you did not know,
so you asked and were told. But stupidity or laziness were inconceivable. Why, if you suffered from these complaints, had you
come to his little room at all?

I cannot remember the detailed progress of our work. I only
know that for nearly three years, between the ages of twelve and
fifteen, I went to him, when in Florence, three times a week; that
my imagination was entirely filled by the world he conjured up
for me; and that, indeed, I owe to him, not only what he taught
me then, but, in enthusiasm and method of approach, all that I
have learned ever since. During those years, our relationship
remained a curiously impersonal one. I do not remember him
coming to my mother's house, or ever speaking to him of anything unconnected with my studies: but in the time I spent with
him, I was as entirely absorbed in his teaching, as convinced that
this was absolute beauty and truth, as any young disciple at the
feet of his guru.

The path of learning was sometimes made easy, too, and
enlivened by an element of surprise.

"Do you know what Pascoli said to the kettle which wouldn't
boil for his dinner?" Monti suddenly asked one morning,
"*Pentola, pentola, pentola, bolli. Pentola, bolli!*" Then he added,

---

* Who 'showed us what our tongue can do'.

† 'You are my master and creator; from you alone I drew the noble style which
has brought me honour.' *Inferno*, I, 85–88.

Westbrook

A pond in the grounds

Justine and Bayard Cutting at the South Side Club, 1888

My grandmother and Aunt Olivia in 'the electric'

Travel at the beginning of the century:
The W. Bayard Cuttings in Switzerland, 1902

In Pompeii, 1909

The Golden Wedding of my great-grandparents, Bronson Murray
and Ann E. Peyton, celebrated at Westbrook on October 1, 1898.
Olivia Cutting at the head of the table

Desart Court

Lord and Lady Desart, 1904

My father and myself in California, 1904

The *dahabeah* on the Nile near Assuan

My mother and
myself, 1906

Lady Wenlock and her
daughter, Irene, *c.* 1896

The Villa Medici

The *sala degli uccelli* in the Villa Medici

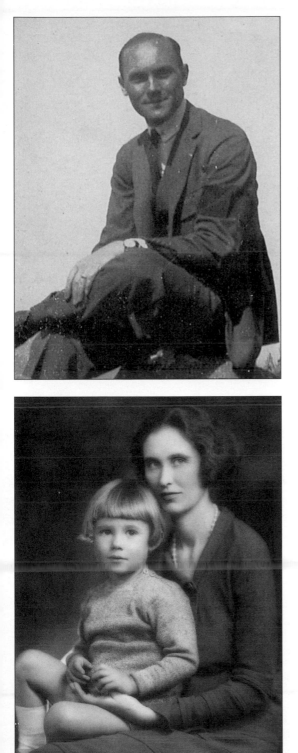

Antonio at the time
of our engagement

Gianni and
myself in 1930

La Foce: boulders in uncultivated land

Threshing

A ruined farmhouse at La Foce

A new farmhouse

La Foce: the house and garden

La Foce: The Castelluccio

La Foce from the valley

In our library in Rome

Antonio at La Foce

The Val d'Orcia and Monte Amiata

La Foce: looking out from the chapel

turning to an equally hungry friend in the doorway, *"Che bell'esametro!"**

Taking a pencil, Monti wrote it down, marking the long syllables and the short—and so, in three minutes, the rhythm of the hexameter was fixed in my mind for ever.

At the end of each lesson he would say, "Now, a surprise!" and would read aloud to me a few perfect lines to carry back in my head during the hour in which the slow, crowded tram toiled up the Fiesole hill. So it was that I encountered for the first time *L'ora che volge il desìo ai naviganti*—and Leopardi's *Le vie dorate e gli orti*, and Pascoli's *L'ultimo viaggio di Ulisse*. Never was there a suggestion in Monti's voice, as he read, that any passage was already familiar to him; he engraved it on the bare tablets of my mind as if for him, too, it were a discovery.

A little later on there was Lesbia's sparrow and Alcman's king-fisher 'with never a care in his heart—the sea-blue bird of spring', and then, in the last year in which I worked with him, Sappho's last apple on the topmost bough, and the great Ode to Aphrodite. It was a morning in May, and even on Monti's dusty desk his wife had put a small vase containing a single dark red rose; as I read, its scent reached me, together with the honeyed words. And I was fifteen—an ungainly, awkward schoolgirl, far more ignorant than any convent-bred child, but dizzy and quivering that morning with questions and unformulated dreams and longings.

"If now she loves thee not, she soon will love . . ."

Something in my stumbling voice made even Monti suddenly glance up from the printed page.

"That will do for today, my dear," he said gently. "Take it home and read it to yourself. *È primavera.*"

As I rode home up the hill under the silver olive-trees, the creaking tram was Aphrodite's chariot, drawn by swallows.

I only remember seeing Monti once outside his study, and that was in the little ruined amphitheatre of Luni—the scene of Marius the Epicurean's 'White Nights'—which lies in the strip of land, set among olive-trees and vines, between Sarzana and the sea. It is one of the most classical, gentlest landscapes in Tuscany and was then very little known, for no road led to it and one came

---

* "What a fine hexameter!" I have since found this story also in an essay on Pascoli by Manara Valgimigli.

upon the ruins quite suddenly at the end of a winding path from a farm. Gnarled fig-trees grew in the crevices of the walls and the centre of the amphitheatre was often piled high with grain, for the farmers used it as a threshing-floor, or, when it had been cleared, danced there on summer nights. I did not know that Monti and his wife often came to stay with friends near the mouth of the river Magra in the summer, and so it seemed nothing short of a miracle when, after bicycling to Luni at the end of a hot summer's day (my mother had taken a villa by the sea nearby) I suddenly heard, as I approached the ruins, a familiar voice and saw, seated on one of the lower steps of the theatre in his rusty black town suit only enlivened by a very old Panama hat, with some peaches on his lap and a paper bag of dry biscuits, dear Monti, talking to his host's two sons. When the greetings were over and we had eaten the biscuits and peaches, we begged him to say some lines to us before going home.

"It's getting late," he demurred, "and I feel lazy." Then he added, "but you are right, children; it is the time and place."

And very slowly, very quietly, leaning back against the stones, with his hat tilted over his eyes to shield him from the setting sun, he recited to us the famous lines in which Virgil grants to the bees something of the divine essence:

> . . . *deum namque ire per omnia,*
> *terrasque tractusque maris caelumque profundum;*
> *hinc pecudes, armenta, viros, genus omne ferarum,*
> *quemque sibi tenuis nascentem arcessere vitas;*
> *scilicet huc reddi deinde ac resoluta referri*
> *omnia, nec morti esse locum, sed viva volare*
> *sideris in numerum atque alto succedere caelo.**

* . . . for a deity
There is pervading the whole earth and all
The expanses of the sea, and heights of heaven:
That from him flocks and herds, men and wild beasts
Of every kind, each at its birth drinks in
The subtle breath of life; and thus all beings
Soon return thither, soon to be dissolved
And so restored; nor for death is there a place;
But, living still, into the ranks of stars
They fly aloft, and find their rest in heaven.
          Georgics IV, 221 30, translated by R. C. Trevelyan

"They fly aloft," he repeated, "and find their rest in heaven."
While he was speaking, the bees were still humming round us
among the mint and thyme, but now the sun was getting low
and they were withdrawing into their hives.

"Look, there's the old Corycian going home."

And, indeed, down the path to the farm an old man was making
his way home, 'like a king', with his basket 'of food unbought'—
some fresh onions and beans, a few peaches and a cucumber—
and an old goat hobbling behind him.

"Buona sera, signoria."

"Buona sera, nonno, vai a cena? Buon appetito!"

For the first time I became aware of poetry as something not
disconnected from life, but incorporated in it, and also realised
how profoundly the classical tradition was still rooted in the
Mediterranean world—transmitted not only in the cadences of
words but in nature itself and in the most familiar objects of
daily use. As I looked around me, there was nothing in sight
that Virgil himself might not have seen: the olive-trees and figs
and vines, the fat-bellied gourd trailing in the grass, the single
clump of lilies beside the farm door, the pungent thyme beneath
our feet, the oxen slowly plodding home, the goat (and Virgil,
too, knew that the damage wrought by goats is even worse than
that of drought or early frost), even the wooden flails leaning
against one of the walls of the amphitheatre, the small curved
sickle with which a bare-armed, dark-skinned girl was cutting a
bundle of grass, and the round bee-hives placed, as the poet
advised, beside a little channel of running water. So, too, many
years later, when first I went to Phaestos, I saw in the underground store-room beneath the summer palace of the Cretan
kings, a wooden scoop with which the oil used to be drawn out
of the great Cretan oil-jars three thousand years before, which
was of exactly the same shape as those that we still use for the
same purpose on our Tuscan farm today.

In Virgil the same word, *arma*, is used for a countryman's tools
and for his arms. Perhaps a poet's words are also not only
instruments, but arms: his means of defending a pattern of beauty,
an established order, as an incantation may preserve a rite. In
Tuscany, more than in any other part of Italy, some of Virgil's
words may still be heard in common speech: a ploughman, when

153

we first came to La Foce, would still sometimes call himself a *bifolco*, and the word reaches us with a patina similar to that of a Roman weapon or an Etruscan vase just turned up by the plough.

But these were, of course, later reflections. Too wise to improve the occasion any further—or perhaps just tired of teaching —Monti lay back dozing until the boys, becoming restless, tried to coax a lizard from his crevice in the stones.

"Come, children, it's late; we must go home."

Had I been able to go on working with Monti for another couple of years, I would perhaps have tried to become a classical scholar or an archaeologist, and my life might have taken a very different course. But in 1917 he suddenly died of Spanish influenza and when, in the following year, we moved to Rome, I was taken on by a teacher who was far too eminent a scholar for me, Professor Nicola Festa, who, having always taught pupils familiar with the conventional school curriculum, did not realise that the English schoolgirl whom he had only accepted because she came from Monti, concealed beneath her enthusiasm such deep wells of ignorance that she sometimes could not follow him at all. It had been Monti's intention, I now realise, to reverse the usual processes of teaching, and—after forming my taste and ear and kindling my enthusiasm—to go back to the necessary spade-work, which would then have seemed worth while. Only now I was like a plant without roots, and very anxious, too, for Monti's sake, to conceal my vast *lacunae* from his old teacher. The hours in which we read Sophocles together thus became desperate feats of ingenuity on my part, trying to understand what Professor Festa plainly considered elementary, and then wrestling at home, between lessons, with grammars and cribs. But, while I was of course impressed by Festa's scholarship and by his dry, penetrating comments, the old fire was not kindled again. I had lost my guru.

7

Growing up and Coming out

ONE OF THE DIFFICULTIES of the painful process called growing up is the absence of a standard of comparison. How is one to measure the importance of what is happening to one when every event is new? How to judge other people and how to assess onself? Are one's emotions shared, in secret, by other girls, or is one, perhaps, unique? Is one's rebelliousness and discontent a sign of unusual wickedness, or as natural as physical growing-pains?

These questions were sharpened, in any case, by shyness, solitude, and the absence of a stable foundation.

As a little girl, the only religious instruction that I remember was given me at Desart by Gran, whose own faith was that of a cheerful, good and unquestioning child. She told us Bible stories, made us learn the Collect by heart, and said we must pay attention in church to the Lessons and the sermon, so as to be able to say, when we got home, what they had been about. On my visits to America, too, I went regularly to the little church near Westbrook at Great River and could not fail to observe that my American grandmother was a religious woman. I think, however, that (taking, as usual, my examples from books rather than from real life) it was the Evangelical heroines of Charlotte Yonge who inspired me to read a chapter of the Gospels every night at bedtime, and, a little later on, a chapter of *The Imitation of Christ* or of St. Augustine's *Confessions*. I was very reticent about all this, but when, soon after my fourteenth birthday, my mother asked me if I would like to be confirmed, I said that I would. I hoped, I think, for a miracle: complete enlightenment and . . . wings.

> The skin and shell of things
>   Though fair
> Are not thy wish nor prayer
> But got by sheer despair
>   Of wings.

The next few months were very disconcerting. The incumbent of the English Church in Florence was an elderly canon with a large hooked nose—an aristocratic nose, he considered—pompous, rhetorical, and insincere. When he glibly held forth about God and love I was overcome with embarrassment; when he said, sinking his portly form on to the ground beside the schoolroom sofa, "Let us kneel for a few moments in prayer," and then, rising carefully, dusted the fine black broadcloth of his trousers, I found it difficult not to laugh. Since, however, there was no-one else whom I could ask, I did try to extract from him an answer to some of the questions that were troubling me. They were very simple ones: I wanted, I desperately wanted, to believe in the divinity of Christ; I wanted to reconcile the world as I knew it to the life of faith and prayer; I wanted to be helped to 'be good'. I received, not a stone, but dust: long, windy dissertations on the Church of England, instructions to learn the Athanasian Creed by heart, an assurance that my besetting sin was pride, explanations with some gusto of the Seventh Commandment, lingering especially on 'impure thoughts' (I had no idea what he was talking about) and finally a promise that, on the day of my Confirmation, grace would assuredly be granted me and I would never again suffer from any doubts. Slowly, painfully, I realised that Canon D was just talking. "And is your dear Mother at home?" he would ask, when our 'little talk' was over—and I gradually realised, as I took him down to the drawing-room, that it was for this that I had been granted the privilege of a 'special private preparation'.

Meanwhile the atmosphere at home was not conducive to piety. Geoffrey Scott—an excellent mimic—added to his repertoire a parody of the canon's drawing-room manner and once, when I had been told to write an essay on 'The Apostolic Succession in the Church of England', offered to do it for me, provided I would promise to hand it over without altering a word. My mother confined herself to cutting the parody short: "Really, Geoffrey, not just now!" Another guest gave a comic description of the Bishop of Gibraltar, whose large diocese included Florence. I laughed, of course, downstairs—and afterwards, in my own room, was overcome by a sense of guilt. But I still hoped that, when the actual day came, everything would be different: grace would be granted me.

When the day came, a cold wet Sunday in March, I had a roaring cold in the head. Dressed in my white dress and veil and thinking only of my fear of sneezing at the moment of receiving the Sacrament, I drove down to the ugly little English church in Via della Marmora. There were only three other candidates: two middle-aged women (one of them a housemaid of another English resident) and a curly-haired little boy, who was going in the following term to Dartmouth. His mother, mine, and Doody formed the rest of the congregation. The Bishop, who belonged to the school of muscular Christianity, delivered to us, I presume, the address which had also served him for boys' schools in Gibraltar and Malta or for crews in the Mediterranean. We were adjured to 'fight the good fight' and 'to play the game'. Behind my veil, shivering, I sneezed and sneezed. I tried in vain to pray. When the great moment came, I tried to hypnotise myself into a state of exaltation; in my heart I knew I was feeling nothing at all.

When we got home, a guest asked, "Well, Iris, do you feel a real Christian now?"

I ran up to my room and burst into tears.

The harm that this episode did me was entirely disproportionate. I had been aware, of course, for some time that many of the people around me were not practising Christians, and that my mother herself only paid lip-service to what she had been taught in her youth out of a sense of seemliness; but it was certainly unfortunate that my first conscious encounter with hypocrisy and snobbishness should have been in a man whom I was prepared to revere as a priest. A simpler or more spontaneously religious child would no doubt have gone on saying her prayers, while looking for other guidance: a more instructed one would hardly have been affected by the canon at all. But there was no-one to guide me. A spring that was just beginning to flow was channelled underground again, for many years.

* * * * *

Then came the process of 'coming out'. Self-consciousness and shyness obscured for me the years between seventeen and nineteen and clouded much of my pleasure. I had, indeed, two good reasons for feeling uncertain of myself: the first, that I was introduced in swift succession into the society of three countries in turn—Italy, England, and America—and had to learn to adapt myself to the various shades of correct behaviour in each; and the other, my very clear realisation that I was not pretty. I had as a child, and indeed still retain, a passion for physical beauty, and knew exactly what looks I would like to have—though the image varied at different ages. As a little girl, my ideal was personified by a large family of Russian sisters who lived in a villa near Florence—all as lissom and slim as ballet dancers, with large almond-shaped eyes, long pigtails and dark little heads as glossy as chestnuts. I looked into my glass and saw a spotty round face with a shapeless nose, too big a mouth, soft, mouse-coloured hair—crimped into unbecoming waves by the damp, tight plaits into which it was put every night—and a plump, shapeless figure. A little later the spots disappeared, but my hair remained mouse-coloured and my figure plump. At fifteen, in the full tide of my classical enthusiasm, I would have liked to resemble one of the mourning maidens on an archaic Greek vase, or, in more cheerful moments, Persephone gathering flowers. I bound a gold fillet round my hair but got no closer to my ideal. At seventeen, having heard the French expression *jolie laide*, I scanned myself anxiously in the glass to see whether I might perhaps be placed in that category. No, I decided, no-one could call me piquante or alluring: I was just plain.

All this was, of course, trivial, but the sense of inferiority engendered was very real—and to this day there is a certain quality of distinction in the looks of some of my friends, a fine-ness of bone and carriage, which I cannot see without a pang of regret, though a passing one. In youth, however, this preoccupa-tion wasted a lot of time: no form of vanity is more disturbing and persistent than that which is based on insecurity. Any echo of faint praise I snatched and treasured far more eagerly than a pretty child. When, at fifteen, having been made up slightly for the first time to play a very small part in a charity performance at the British Embassy, I overheard Geoffrey say to my mother, "At thirty she may be quite attractive," I lived in a glow for weeks.

My other cause for anxiety might have been diminished by a little coaching. The first society into which I was introduced was the highly local and traditional one of old-fashioned Florence. The names of the Florentine families whose decorous parties I attended—the Rucellai, Pazzi, Strozzi, Gondi, Ginori, Frescobaldi, Pandolfini, Guicciardini, Niccolini, Capponi, Ricasoli—had been interwoven into the long tapestry of Florentine history. Some of their houses had been designed by Michelozzo, Alberti or Benedetto da Maiano, or their family chapels frescoed by Ghirlandaio or Filippino Lippi. Their ancestors has been priors under the *Comune*, merchant princes in the Renaissance, or Liberal country gentlemen in the nineteenth century. For centuries they had ruled and administered their city and cultivated their lands, and some of them were still proud to belong to the great charitable Confraternity of the Misericordia, founded in the thirteenth century to succour the sick and the poor and, anonymous in their cowled hoods, would still pace through the city streets at funerals, bearing lighted torches and intoning prayers. It was, according to tradition, Pazzino de' Pazzi who, on his return from a Crusade, brought back from the Holy Sepulchre the flint which still sets alight, from the High Altar of the Duomo, the rocket shaped like a dove which, on Holy Saturday, flies down a wire from the altar to a cart decorated with fireworks.*

It was Capponi who defied the invading troops of Charles VIII of France with the high-sounding phrase, "If you sound your trumpets, we shall toll our bells." It was a Ricasoli who turned Tuscany into the first truly liberal state, on the English model, on the Continent of Europe.

Their estates, never neglected, like those of many great landowners of Southern Italy, but frugally and carefully administered under the master's eye, according to contracts and traditions handed down since the fourteenth century, extended from the rich vineyards of the Chianti to the woods and pastures of the Mugello, from the wheatfields of the Val di Chiana to the wide plains of the Maremma by the sea, where wild buffalo still grazed and there was duck and snipe-shooting in the marshes. Their children were brought up simply and soberly, with strict English nannies and French or German governesses, and spent their long summer holidays, monotonous but untrammelled, on their family

---

* This *festa* is called *Lo Scoppio del Carro*. If the fireworks go off well, it is considered an omen for a good harvest.

estates, varied by perhaps a month at the seaside in a little *villino* at Forte dei Marmi. And when they grew up (with a few exceptions) they married each other and the story began all over again.

It was into this self-contained, local, dignified society that I— a little foreigner chaperoned by someone else's mother—was suddenly plunged, as anxious as any chameleon to suit my colour to my surroundings. The standard of formal good manners for a young girl was high: she was required to be modest and self-effacing, but also self-possessed and alert. Moreover I found that my little Italian friends who, a year before, in their dark blue serge frocks and long black stockings, had been just as awkward and as giggly as I, had suddenly blossomed out, without any period of transition, into graceful, charming young women, who seemed to know by instinct what, on every occasion, they should do and say. I observed, for instance, that they gracefully made their way across the room at a party, asking to be introduced when a married woman came in whom they did not know (with a slight curtsy, if she was an old lady); they would even stop dancing to do this, make their polite greetings, and return unperturbed to their partner. But how could such ease of manner be achieved? Sometimes I pretended blindness when one of these ladies appeared; sometimes, out of an excess of zeal, I asked to be introduced to one whom I already knew, who merely smiled benevolently, saying, "But *cara*, I am Fiammetta's grandmother"; often I stumbled over their feet. (These ladies sat in a formidable row, on chairs of golden or crimson damask, at one end of the room, watching the young people dance.) But the worst occasion was the one on which, in Casa Niccolini, having shyly made my farewells to my hostess in an interval at a tea-dance, I turned and made for the door in such a hurry that—having forgotten how well the floor was polished—I slipped and fell down, but continued to skid at full speed across the ballroom, with such impetus that I was hurled through the door on to the landing outside. As the door swung back a shout of laughter followed me —or did I simply imagine it? I took to my heels and ran down the wide marble staircase. Never, never, I swore to myself, would I go back again!

The only dance that I remember with unalloyed pleasure— since for once I did not fear a lack of partners—was my own, which my mother gave for me at Villa Medici on a moonlit night in June. For the first time I had a ball-dress from a real couturier, with full skirts of varying shades of blue tulle and silver shoes, and my hair was properly done. For a moment, as Doody fastened my dress and I saw my excited face and shining eyes in the glass, I thought, with an exultation surely denied to any recognised beauty, "I really believe I am almost pretty!" The terrace, where supper was laid on little tables, was lit with Japanese lanterns; the fireflies darted among the wheat in the *podere* below; the air was heavy with jasmine and roses, and at midnight fireworks from the West terrace soared like jewelled fountains between us and the valley. It was the night which every young girl dreams of having once in her life—Natasha's first ball—and perhaps all the more glamorous because I was still heart-free and ready to see my Prince André in every partner in turn.

My first English party was a very different matter. It was a week-end at Lord Ilchester's country house Melbury, in Dorset, for a hunt-ball, to which I had been invited because the daughter of the house, Mary Fox-Strangways, had been asked up to Villa Medici the summer before, when she was studying Italian in Florence. Though life has certainly often made me more unhappy, I do not think it has ever given me three days of more unrelieved discomfort. I arrived knowing no-one but Mary—and her only slightly—one day later than the rest of the house-party, when the other guests had already made friends, and was led by my kind but somewhat overwhelming hostess into a drawing-room in which a lot of strange young people were sitting at a round table, playing Animal Grab. Thankful to sink into anonymity, I chose the mouse as my animal and contributed only a few small squeaks. But when, at the game's end, Mary took me upstairs and through a labyrinth of passages to my cold, Victorian bedroom to dress for dinner, and I had to put on the hideous satin dress of electric blue with spangles (suitable for a circus-rider of fifty) which I had injudiciously bought for myself in a small shop near Hanover Square, my first problem arose: how could I find my way down-stairs again? In the far distance a gong was booming, but run as I might in my tight high-heeled slippers down one passage after another, none brought me to any stairs. Breathless and dishevelled, I at last returned to my own room, where Mary had been sent to fetch me. "Let's be quick, Papa's waiting," was all she said; but, as we entered the drawing-room, the whole party was already assembled. I knew that I had begun badly.

The ball itself was not—not quite—as bad as I had feared. There was a disconcerting moment before starting when Mary, charmingly and suitably dressed in white tulle and gardenias and watched by an adoring group of nannies, nursery maids, and house-maids, came down the grand staircase (for it was her first ball) followed by a galaxy of her friends in equally suitable dresses in varying shades of pale blue, yellow, and rose tulle, which I compared with my middle-aged satin.

"How . . . how *gay* you look, my dear child!" said my kind hostess—but I was not deceived.

When, however, we actually reached the ball, the crowd was so great, the scene so novel, that my self-consciousness subsided. All the way in the car I had been absorbed in silent prayer that someone, anyone, would take me in to supper. But almost as soon as we arrived, a tall, fair young guardsman, who had sat next to me at dinner and had told me that he was in my cousin Gerald's regiment, came up and asked me to supper. Has Lady Ilchester told him to do so, or Gerald? I wondered, too deeply grateful for any pride. With my chief anxiety set at rest, I was even able to enjoy the amusing spectacle: the good-looking men, in their pink coats; the hearty, self-assured girls; the general sense of being at a great family party, which increased with Sir Roger de Coverley and the wild gallop at the end. Almost all the young men of our party danced with me and I came home flushed with relief and pleasure, feeling that I was, perhaps, just like other girls after all.

The next day, however, dispelled this belief. No-one had told me that one cannot go to an English country house without a tweed coat and skirt and sensible country shoes, and when I came downstairs in the rather shiny dark blue serge, which was left over from my schoolgirl wardrobe, and black town shoes, I felt like a pekinese in a pack of hounds—only treated with indulgence, because so manifestly belonging to a different species.

"Do let me lend you my brogues," urged Mary with transparent tact, "as you've forgotten yours."

I miserably thanked her and, since they were a size too large, returned from our walk across the turnip-fields with a blister on my heel.

There was a reprieve when my host kindly took half-an-hour in his busy day to show his youngest and most awkward guest the books and treasures of Melbury: in his library and looking at his fine pictures, I was once again in a familiar world. But the only really happy moment of my visit was when, on Monday morning, I climbed into the train that was to take me away.

My first London season, in the following summer, is very vague in my memory—except for the leitmotif of anxiety. My mother reluctantly but dutifully had borrowed from Aunt Constance her charming house in Portland Place, and here we gave a series of dreary little dinner parties, mostly attended by very pink and tongue-tied young men whom I had never seen before and whose only claim to be there was that they, too, had been invited to the same ball. One of them, however, a good-looking, red-haired young man in the Guards,—considered much too 'artistic' by his brother officers—seemed to me delightfully unconventional because, instead of asking me to tea at Gunther's, he took me for a bus-ride to the City to see the Wren churches, and it was a great pleasure to find him again, looking very grand in his dress uniform, at the Buckingham Palace Ball. Like Catherine Morland, I felt that I had 'some acquaintance in Bath'.

Indeed I enjoyed the Court Ball immensely: my conventional long white dress with its train, my absurd headdress with feathers, the snobbish satisfaction of having the privilege of the 'entrée' (because my aunt was then lady-in-waiting), the gaping crowds as we got out of the car, the fine uniforms, the fender-like tiaras of the dowagers and the jewelled turbans of the Indian Princes. And I enjoyed some of the other balls, too—beforehand, if not while they were going on—since an incorrigible strain of hopefulness still whispered before each occasion that tonight would surely be different: tonight would be *the* night!

I got a good deal of pleasure, too, from several other 'features' of the Season: the Trooping the Colour, which we saw from the rooms of a friend of my grandfather's at the Admiralty, with my cousin Gerald suddenly transformed into a symbolic figure, since he happened to be one of the young officers taking part; and also days at Hurlingham, Lords, and Henley—all the occasions, in short, at which I could be a mere spectator. I was even able to hypnotise myself, as I walked round and round Lords in my best pale blue dress with some Etonian friend of my cousin's, or climbed on to one of the coaches for lunch, into not realising how very dull the young men really were, how little I cared about cricket, and how positively glutted I felt with strawberries and cream. Only sometimes a stifled inner voice would whisper, "This is called pleasure, but I am *not* enjoying myself!"

If this description, however, has left the impression that I was already blasé, it has been very misleading. During the long years of the War in Italy I had fallen in love with England—or rather with my idea of England, based chiefly upon my grandfather's letters, my mother's conversation, and a fine medley of the books I had read—from *Six to Sixteen* to *The Most Popular Girl in the Fifth* and, at a later stage, from Jane Austen to Rose Macaulay, from *St. Agnes' Eve* to *The Shropshire Lad*. The world I had built up in my imagination was unlike any country upon land or sea. It was a phantasmagoria of Queen Anne country houses and Oxford colleges and libraries, of village cricket and nursery tea, of hollyhocks in cottage gardens and cathedral spires; of friends, friends, friends with whom I could be at ease, and of a deep swift stream perpetually gliding between green banks, while a young man (his contours still somewhat blurred) read poetry aloud to me. And whenever the real England offered me anything that faintly corresponded to these dreams, I fell in love with it all over again.

I fell in love with Eton on my first Fourth of June—wholly entranced by the beauty of the buildings, of the playing-fields and of the boys' voices at Evensong in College Chapel. I determined to marry an Englishman so as to be able to send my sons to Eton—but unfortunately no candidates were forthcoming.

I spent a long week-end in Rutland with the family of the young man who had taken me to see the Wren churches, and for three days I believed that this was the existence that, for the rest of my life, I would like to lead. I attended the prize-giving of Uppingham School (with my host, a distinguished old General, giving the prizes) and handed the lemonade at the tennis party; I helped my hostess to cut off the dead heads in the herbaceous border and to 'do the flowers' for the dinner-table. I got up very early one morning to pick mushrooms with John before breakfast in the green, lush meadows in the valley, while the grass was still glittering with dew; and, on another day, we bicycled across half the county to rub the brasses of some eighteenth-century tombs in another village. I fell in love with the whole setting: with the little Norman church of grey stone, in which some of my host's ancestors lay with a Crusader's Cross upon their breasts, and the General read the Lesson, as my grandfather had done at Desart (though not so well). I fell in love with my chintz-covered bedroom and its view of gentle meadow land and farm land, with the humming of bees and the scent of mignonette, and perhaps even with my elderly hosts—as rooted, immovable and right in their setting as the grey stones of their church. But I had enough sense to realise that I was not—just not—in love with their charming son, and above all, that he did not care for me. We parted good friends, though I shed a tear or two in the train back to London, not so much for him as for an England to which, I instinctively knew, I would never belong. What I did not, of course, then realise was that, by the time I reached middle-age, that particular England would have ceased to exist.

It was from this society that, after only a short interval at Villa Medici, I sailed in the autumn of 1920 to go through the debutante hoops in yet another setting; that of New York. For four years, during the whole of the war, I had been cut off from my American relations. I had, indeed, been back to see my American grandmother the year before, when I was just seventeen, but this had been merely a short visit, and though it had sufficed to reawaken my affection for her and for Westbrook, it had also made me aware of the rift between her and my mother, which had begun with the latter's decision to bring me up in Italy and had been increased by her determination to return to England as soon as the war was declared in 1914.

I therefore set off for my American debut alone, or rather in the company of the sweet young Irish maid, only a few years older than myself, Alice Walsh, whose life has been intertwined with mine for much of the rest of my life. On the voyage I already felt torn between divided loyalties, and they were put to the test as soon as my trunk was unpacked. After one glance at the clothes it contained—the sage-green woollen dress from

Woollands, the silver brocade evening-dress made out of an
Egyptian shawl, the hand-embroidered but ill-cut linen dress from
the Via della Vigna Nuova—my grandmother, who was herself
the personification of chic and good taste, swept me off to
Bendel's for a complete outfit. Never had I seen such lovely
clothes before! There was a deep rose-coloured taffeta evening
dress with a long, wide-panelled skirt from Lanvin, like a Nattier
painting, which, fifty years later, I can still remember and in
which, I felt, even I would be confident. But was it fair to my
mother to accept so many gifts, which not only replaced, but
plainly by implication condemned, the clothes she had bought
for me? My solution was not a graceful one: I wore the fine
clothes, but (at least in my grandmother's presence) grudgingly
and scarcely saying thank you.

The process of becoming a debutante in New York in 1920
was a truly formidable one. Even for girls who had grown up
together at the same nursery parties, dancing schools and pre-
debutante dances, and whose brothers and cousins had also been
through a similar mill, the pace was grilling, and for a newcomer
like myself the whole routine was misery. The social day would
start with a large debutantes' lunch, entirely feminine, at which—
dressed in our best silk or velvet dresses—twenty or thirty of us
would be given an elaborate meal, the talk consisting almost
entirely of gossip and shrieks of laughter about people I did
not know, or competitive talk about dances and partners. A
stranger like myself could do little but crumble her bread and
eat. Then came a concert or matinee, and, as the evening
approached, a new anxiety: would a white cardboard box be
lying on one's dressing table and would it be from the right
young man? To have a 'corsage' (generally consisting of orchids
or gardenias and costing far more than the giver could afford)
was a sign of success; or rather, not to have one, was so certain
a sign of failure, not only in the eyes of one's friends but of one's
family, that I was told it was not unusual for an unpopular girl
surreptitiously to send one to herself! If two boxes came on the
same day, there was the problem of what to say later on, to the
donor whose gift one did not wear—but this was a dilemma that
seldom offered itself to me. Then came a large dinner-party, at
which I was able to obtain an immediate if fleeting popularity

by dividing my oysters between my two neighbours, and then, two or three balls in succession.

It was then that the real competition began. The 'cutting-in' system seemed to have been especially devised to ensure that a popular girl should increase her popularity, while a 'pill' would be progressively deprived of hope. The men all stood in the 'stag-line' at one end of the room, watching, and one of them would 'cut in' on any girl by tapping her partner on the shoulder. A popular girl would thus often only dance a few steps before she was 'cut in' on again; but a girl who was plain, danced badly, or merely happened to have few acquaintances, would slowly proceed round and round the room with her partner, mercilessly linked together like two figures in Dante's Inferno. The longer her plight lasted, the less likely it was that she would be freed; for it would take a very polite young man or a very faithful old friend to risk being 'stuck' with her for the rest of the evening.

In addition, this was one of the Prohibition years. This did not mean that there was no drinking, but merely that the young 'college boys' who were our partners, instead of having learned to drink wine or good whisky in moderation at their parents' table, now drank, from tepid hip-flasks in their cloakroom, liquor which was often sheer poison and of which a very small amount went straight to their heads. To have upon the stag-line a close friend to whom you could signal for help, if your partner was too obviously overcome or amorous, became extremely useful.

Here, as in London, it was the most formal entertainments that I enjoyed most, since I was then again able to become merely a spectator. My grandfather had been one of the first box-holders at the Metropolitan, and I still remember the glitter of jewels and the exquisite dresses on a gala night, as well as the galaxy of great singers whom I then heard for the first time. Every week, before this occasion, the same social crisis arose. "Have we got any men yet, for Thursday evening?" Music-loving and leisured men who wished to sit through a whole opera were scarce, and were apt to be booked for weeks beforehand by box-holding hostesses; *young* men of this kind were still scarcer, so that I usually sat (to my secret relief) in the front of the box, bolt upright in my best dress and long white gloves, between my grandmother and another lady of her age, attended by two kindly, musical old gentlemen, and felt free to listen to the music in peace. It was thus that I heard Jeritza as Elsa, on the night of her debut in New York, and later on in the *Walküre*; Caruso in *Pagliacci*, on the gala night on which King Albert of Belgium was welcomed to New York in a frenzy of enthusiasm directly after the First World War, and Lucrezia Bori in *Kovancina*; and I was present, too, on the first night after the war, on which Chaliapin returned in the part of Boris Godounov to his adoring public. When, at the end of the performance, he came back to receive his applause and, tearing off his royal cloak and robes, stood in the blouse of a Russian peasant, the Russians in the audience, in a state of delirium, climbed up over the footlights and carried him off the stage; and when, a few minutes later, I was taken behind the scenes by a friend of his, it was to witness a charming scene: the comparatively tiny Lucrezia Bori, unable to reach up to embrace the giant properly, being lifted up by him on to a table, from which she could comfortably throw her arms around his neck.

Looking back on those three years, I am inclined to think that they were a considerable waste of time, for although it is perhaps necessary to learn something of the ways of the world sooner or later, I think I would have been both happier and nicer—because not constricted into a mould which was not my natural one—if I had been allowed to go instead, as I wished, to Oxford. There, working at the subjects I cared about and learning many things which I was later on obliged to acquire without assistance, I would have found my own level. As a debutante in London and New York I was constantly aware of values which I did not share, and yet was not brave enough (or perhaps merely too young) to disregard, and spent my time in striving for prizes I did not really care to win. To prove to myself, as well as to others, that I too could have some beaux, I encouraged young men whom I did not really like very much, and was then both surprised and distressed when they fell in love with me. For fear of being thought a blue-stocking or a prig, I learned to refrain from talking about the things that really interested me, but was extremely bad at talking about anything else. All this was not only a waste of time and energy: just as there are some books which are, in Salvemini's phrase, '*libri fecondatori*', from which new ideas are born, so there are some periods of one's life which hold in them the seeds of growth, and some that do not. In those years I was deflected—by vanity, preoccupation, and lack of self-confidence—from my natural course. I was a less complete person, that is less completely myself, than the unfledged schoolgirl who had read Virgil with Monti.

In the interval, however, I was, in spite of these obstacles, growing up. I began to fall in love, rather often and rather intensely, but was not very clear about what was happening to me, since, in spite of all my precocious reading, I was quite unable to apply what I had found in books to any useful purpose in 'real life'. And then some young men actually fell in love with me. I have sometimes wondered whether any of them realised how much gratitude, as well as ignorance, there was in my response. The one of these young men who surprised me most, and whom I met for the first time when I was still a plumpish schoolgirl of not yet eighteen and he a young man of twenty-eight, tall, dark and reserved, and possessed of more than his fair share of charm—chaperoning his younger sister at a small dance —was my future husband, Antonio Origo. It seemed to me so odd as to be almost incredible that he not only danced with me, but appeared to enjoy talking to me afterwards, and when, a month later, he sent me a picture-postcard of friendly, if formal, greetings, it provided enough food for a whole summer's day-dreams. It was not, however, until two years later that we met again—under very different circumstances, since his father was then dying of cancer and he was nursing him devotedly. After long nights at his father's bedside, he would sometimes walk up the Fiesole hill in the early morning, and we might have a few minutes together, and sometimes, too, we would steal brief walks on country paths where we hoped we would meet no-one we knew. (We did, of course, meet a friend of my mother's one day, but she had the kindness to remain silent.) It was then that we 'reached an understanding', which was sealed by a further meeting in Venice in the autumn, but my mother (who had extracted a promise from me some time before not to become engaged until I was twenty-one) now insisted on a total separation of six months—although she could offer no serious objections except that Antonio was indubitably Italian and a Catholic, and also, she said, too good-looking and too grown-up for me. We kept our promise scrupulously—the only infringement being a little crystal casket of lilies-of-the-valley which Antonio sent me (without a card) on Christmas Day, and which my mother promptly took to her own room, since she still found it inconceivable that anyone should send flowers to me. But on the day when the six months came to an end, a letter was waiting for me, and in the following summer Antonio went briefly to England to meet my English grandparents and then to join me at Westbrook, where our engagement was at last announced.

In deciding to marry Antonio I was not only making—although deeply in love—the personal choice involved in every marriage. I was deliberately choosing life in Italy, rather than in England or America, and, though ignorant of much that I was undertaking, was determined to mould myself to the way of life that my fiancé and I had chosen. Both of us were suffering from a strong reaction against the kind of life for which our parents had prepared us: I against the over-sophisticated, over-intellectual society which had been the background of my youth; Antonio against the world of business for which his education had fitted him, and which was incongruous, not only to his nature and taste, but to the atmosphere he had known in his father's house. Marchese Clemente Origo—Roman by birth, with a Russian mother, Paolina Polyectoff—had cut a brilliant figure in his youth as a smart cavalry officer in the *Genova Cavalleria*, a man as tall and gaunt as Don Quixote and with something of the same *panache*. He bought his horses in Dublin and sent his fine shirts to be laundered in London, but devoted the second half of his life to the arts, becoming a well-known painter and sculptor. He divided the year between Florence and a small house on what was then a wild, lonely stretch of beach and pine-forest at Motrone, on the Versilian coast, with frequent visits to Paris and Venice, to Bayreuth and Munich—wherever, in short, good art, amusing talk and pretty women were to be found. His wife, Rosa Tarsis (previously married to Duke Pompeo Litta), possessed a singularly sweet nature and a charming voice, and their house soon became a centre for many outstanding musicians, painters and writers: Puccini and Catalano, Cannicci and William Storey, Mario Praga and Ugo Ojetti, and above all d'Annunzio, who for many years considered the Origo's house as his own, wrote the best poems of *Alcione* at Motrone; and sent to my mother-in-law the only affectionate, unamorous letters he ever wrote to a pretty woman.

It was in this society that Antonio grew up, but as soon as he was old enough to go to school, his father sent him to Switzerland, to be turned into a successful businessman. For a year, afterwards, he worked in a bank in Brussels and then in the champagne firm of Mumms' in Rheims, but when the First World War broke out he at once joined up. After three years on the Carso and one in the Italian Military Mission in London, he came back to Florence, where we agreed to embark together upon a life entirely new to both of us. Some months before our marriage, we had bought a large, neglected estate, La Foce, in southern Tuscany, hoping to find there not only our home but the work that we both wanted. Antonio had, deep in his bones, the instinctive love of many Italians for the land, and wanted to farm in a region still undeveloped agriculturally, where there would still be much work to do. I had a strong, though uninformed, interest in social work. We both wanted to get away from city life and to lead what we thought of as a pastoral, Virgilian existence.

For some more months our marriage was delayed by my mother's ill-health and mental distress, for her divorce from Geoffrey Scott was just going through, until our family doctor bluntly remarked that if we did not get married at once we never would. So married we were, on March 4, 1924, in the Villa Medici chapel. Only my mother's sister, Lady Joan Verney, and her son Ulick were there to represent the English side of my family and my aunt, Justine Ward, the American side; with Antonio's sister, Carla Franceschi, her in-laws, and a handful of our Florentine friends—and Doody to wave us goodbye as we drove away.

8

Writing

A man will turn over half a library to make one book.

DR. JOHNSON

WHY DOES ONE write at all? After some sixty years spent in this pursuit, I still scarcely know. The first of my writings to be printed was, at the age of ten, a prize-winning essay in *Little Folks*. For this I received ten shillings and sixpence, a copy of *The Christmas Carol*, and a moment of as pure and unalloyed pleasure as has ever come to me out of an envelope. But the essay itself was imitative and flat, like all my other childish works. 'A sedulous ape', I covered a great deal of paper between the ages of ten and seventeen, producing several long romances, many attempts at verse, some translations of Sappho, Leopardi and Pascoli, and a biographical study of the Medici children. These works show much industry, some versatility, and not much talent—a fact which I fully realised myself —and, indeed, I have scarcely more facility now. Some people, it appears, set well-turned, elegant phrases on paper at once, which only require a little subsequent polishing. "*I* think," said my step-father, Percy Lubbock, when I once commented on the exquisitely neat and decorative pages of his manuscript, "*I* think, *before* I write." I do not, alas, resemble him. I have seldom written a sentence which did not have to be altered and trimmed and often entirely recast. Nor have I ever written a book about which I did not ask myself, at some stage, how it was conceivable that anyone should wish to read it. I write because, exacting as it may be to do so, it is still more difficult to refrain, and because —however conscious of one's limitations one may be—there is always at the back of one's mind an irrational hope that this next book will be different: it will be the rounded achievement, the complete fulfilment. It never has been: yet I am still writing.

From the age of twenty-one, however, the year of my

engagement, to that of thirty-five, I never wrote at all. Those were the first years of my marriage, of my son's childhood, and of my attempts to lead, at La Foce, an entirely new kind of life; to identify myself with the work of our farm and with my husband's interests, and to become, if I could, a rather different kind of person. Then, in 1933, after Gianni's death, in an effort to find some impersonal work which would absorb at least a part of my thoughts—I turned back to writing again. It was then that one aspect of my training in youth stood me in good stead.

When I was working with Professor Monti, at the time of the first War, I went to Florence daily on the Fiesole tram, which then took an hour to reach the town. The old trams were falling to pieces, the roof leaked and it was often difficult to get a seat, but since it was the only time in which I could do my homework, I learned my Greek verbs or Latin verses all the same, acquiring a habit which has been of use to me all my life. Far from having a padded room, like Carlyle, I have written in trains and planes, during illnesses, in an air-raid shelter, in a nursery, and among all the ordinary interruptions of domestic life—not always, I admit, without irritation, but at least getting on with the book. And I do not really believe that this has ever done me or my writing any harm.

When I began to write again, I thought that I had better start by trying my hand at biography. I knew that I had neither the creative imagination nor the sharp ear for dialogue which produces good novels; I had long ago given up the hope of becoming a poet. I lacked the historian's training which I might have obtained if—as I had wished at eighteen—my mother had allowed me to go to Oxford, instead of 'coming out'. But for many years I had preferred memoirs and letters to any other form of reading, and I hoped that I might perhaps have a certain aptitude for observing and assembling the different parts of a character and a life until they came together into a pattern, giving a man what Virginia Woolf called 'a kind of shape after his death'.

My first subject I found made to my hand: a life of Leopardi, about whom at that time no study existed in English, except an interesting essay by James Thomson and the scholarly Introduction to the translation of his works by G. L. Bickersteth. Leopardi —apart from being one of the greatest Italian poets—was an almost ideal subject for a biography in the thirties, especially for a generation whose taste had been formed by Strachey and Maurois, by Harold Nicolson and Virginia Woolf. He was young, deformed, lonely, ambitious and embittered; he lived in an old-fashioned, pious family of the *noblesse de province* in a little town of the Marches, and violently rebelled both against the rule of his parents and the restrictions of his environment; he was extremely articulate, setting down his loneliness, his grief, his contempt for his fellow citizens, his longings for friendship and love and his literary aspirations, in what eventually turned into five volumes of letters, as well as in the seven volumes of his day-book, *Lo Zibaldone*. 'In depicting his despair and total disenchantment'—the phrase is his own—'he drew the colours from his own heart.'

Moreover he belonged to a closed society into which English travellers have seldom penetrated (his contemporary, Byron, was perhaps the first to do so, but that was through his mistress) and about which they have consequently felt very curious. 'You must have wondered', wrote Basil de Selincourt in one of the first reviews of my book, 'what went on in the huge rooms of the seemingly unoccupied *palazzi* . . . Here is a book that will put the key of the mystery into your hands.'

It is to these circumstances that I attribute the considerable success—perhaps greater than it deserved—of my first book. Its chief merit, it now seems to me, was the fullness with which I quoted from my subject's letters and notebooks. For while I read those letters myself—sometimes long-winded and self-pitying, but often unendurably poignant—a man had indeed taken shape for me, whom I came to know better than most of my friends and to whom I wished to offer the only tribute that a biographer can pay to his subject—to tell (in so far as is possible) the truth about him.

This has always been one of the cardinal problems of biography: to what extent can or should one tell the truth—and what, indeed, is the truth about any of us? The second question is the more difficult one to answer. 'The world will never know my life', said Carlyle (and the words stand on the first page of his *Life* by his closest friend, Froude) 'even if it should write and read a hundred biographies of me. The main facts of it are known,

and are likely to be known, to myself alone, of all created men.'
Not only are there facts that we do not tell, but some that we
ourselves do not know; at best, some small facet of the truth
occasionally catches the light, and it is that which the biographer
must try to seize. 'For there is', as Virginia Woolf remarked,
'a virtue in truth; it has an almost mystic power. Like radium,
it seems to give off forever and ever grains of energy, atoms of
light.'*

Johnson himself maintained that 'in order to write a man's
life' one must at least 'have eaten and drunk and lived in social
intercourse with him'. But did even Boswell see Johnson's real
life? Would the great Doctor himself have thought that he per-
ceived it? A few days ago I received a letter from Archibald
MacLeish in which he was turning over precisely this question in
his mind. 'We can set down', he wrote, 'a record of happenings
which seem to have a shape or meaning: expectation, achievement, defeat, death; a drama with a beginning, a middle and an
end; a drama often interesting, fascinating, moving; but is that
a life or only a *Life*?'

Perhaps the biographer should be less ambitious; indeed, if he
has not had Boswell's inestimable advantages, but is writing
about a dead man, or one whom he only knew slightly, he will
have to be. He will have to be satisfied if he can catch an occasional
glimpse of a face or sound of a voice. And even to do this, he
will have to accumulate a vast amount of material and then, if
his biography is to be a work of art, to prune and select . . . But
is it possible to choose without bias, to reject without falsifying?

There is a revealing paragraph in *A Writer's Diary*, in which
Virginia Woolf—who was both an artist and a very honest
woman—hints at this process; after six pages of meticulously
exact description of a visit of hers to Mr. and Mrs. Hardy, factual,
detailed, convincing, reproducing scraps of conversation, she
proceeds, the next day, before turning all this into an article, to
ruminate on the nature of art and thought. 'If art is based on
thought, what is the transmuting process? I was telling myself
the story of our visit to the Hardys, and I began to compose it;
that is to say, to dwell on Mrs. Hardy leaning on the table, looking
out, apathetically, vaguely; and so would soon bring everything

* *Granite and Rainbow*, p.149: 'The New Biography'.

into harmony with that as the dominant theme. *But the actual event was different.*

Is 'the actual event' invariably different? I think it is. We can hang mirrors, as Virginia Woolf advised, at every corner—we can look at our subject's face at every angle and in every light. We can discover strange and curious pieces of information: that Dr. Johnson liked to carry an orange-peel in his pocket, that Aristotle had a hot-water bottle made of leather, filled with hot oil, and that Leopardi, during the cold winters in Bologna, spent his day in a bag lined with feathers, from which he emerged looking like Papageno. But never, never, can we see enough. Here is Howell's description of Mark Twain in his old age: 'He was apt to smile into your face with a subtle but amiable perception, and yet with a remote sort of absence: you were all there for him, but he was not all there for you.'

For when indeed—except perhaps for a few brief moments between lovers—is the whole of another human being ever there for us? To Virginia Woolf the central problem of biography was how to weld 'into one seamless whole' the 'granite-like solidity' of truth and the 'rainbow-like intangibility' of personality. The problem was one that fascinated her, not only in literature but in life. "Go on, this is enthralling," she would say, when a friend had brought her an exciting piece of gossip. "I feel as if a buried statue were being dug up, piece by piece." One of her friends once said, that on a cold November evening he came upon her standing in the fog beside an apple-barrow, asking the woman in her deep, quiet, compelling voice: "Tell me, what does it *feel* like to stand in the fog on a dark evening, selling apples?" I cannot vouch for the truth of this story, but certainly it was a question that she liked to ask. I vividly recollect the day on which, not without some misgivings, I took the typescript of my *Allegra* —which had just been accepted by the Hogarth Press—to Tavistock Square. The office was downstairs, but as I was leaving it, Virginia's voice came floating down the stairs: "Bring her up, Leonard, bring her up." And a minute later, we were sitting at a round tea-table, with my hostess pouring out from a large brown tea-pot and asking: "Now do tell me—what does it *feel* like to wake up in the morning on a Tuscan farm?" I am afraid I only gaped at her, quite unable to make an intelligent reply.

But she was right. It is only by discovering what life 'felt like', to our subject—at least in fleeting moments—that we can become aware of him as a *person* at all. And this implies an attempt to see him in every attitude: not merely riding in triumph at the head of his victorious troops, or unveiling a monument in a frock-coat and top hat, but (in so far as possible) in his private, unguarded moments. In this respect, indeed, the aim of classical biography was much nearer to our own than the mediaeval one, which aimed at producing *Lives* of great men chiefly for edification, about subjects who conformed to God's pattern for mankind, while the taste of the seventeenth century again veered back towards the classical attitude. Dryden, in particular, admired Plutarch precisely because he had dared to show his heroes in undress. 'You may behold', he wrote, 'Scipio and Laelius gathering cockle-shells on the shore, Augustus playing at bounding-stones, and Agesilaus riding on a hobby-horse among his children. The pageantry of life is taken away: you see the poor reasonable animal as naked as ever nature made him, are acquainted with his passions and his follies, and find the demi-god, a man.'

Here, surely, is the prelude to modern biography. But with the admission that heroes, too, might be shown as naked and fallible, the problem arose as to whether this picture was likely to dismay or corrupt the reader—and if this danger existed, had the biographer the right to speak?

Pascal maintained that the real danger of describing a hero's vices as well as his virtues was that it would always be the former that would be imitated. 'The example', he said, 'of Alexander's chastity has produced fewer continent men, than those whom his drunkenness has rendered intemperate.' Dr. Johnson, however, when asked if it was right to reveal Addison's miserliness towards his friend Steele, was of precisely the opposite opinion: whatever the interpretation, he said, the facts should be told, for 'if nothing but the bright side of characters should be shown, we should sit in despondency, and think it utterly impossible to imitate them in *anything*.' He believed, in short, in presenting the unadorned facts for a very characteristic reason: 'It keeps mankind from despair.' But in the nineteenth century the suppression of un-edifying or inconvenient facts came into favour again. 'Too long and too idolatrous!' was the comment of Leslie Stephen on one of the three-volume *Victorian Lives,* and 'How delicate', exclaimed Carlyle, 'how decent is English biography, bless its mealy mouth!'

There is, however, one temptation even more insidious than suppression, and that is sheer invention. An excellent instance is the one by Professor Trevor Roper in a somewhat merciless attack on Lytton Strachey: the length of Dr. Arnold's legs. Strachey had formed a very clear picture in his mind of Dr. Arnold: he saw him as a noble, pompous figure, and to introduce just the right additional touch of absurdity, of debunking, it was necessary that his legs should have been too short. Unfortunately, however, as Strachey once admitted to a friend, there is absolutely no evidence to show that Dr. Arnold's legs were shorter in proportion to his body than those of any other man. Now the danger of this kind of invention is that, once discovered, it shakes our capacity to believe anything the narrator has said. 'A story', said Dr. Johnson, 'is a picture, either of an individual, or of life in general; if it be false, it is a picture of nothing.' Even a touch of fantasy may be disproportionately destructive. 'Suppose we believe one half of what he tells', suggested Lord Mansfield to Dr. Johnson, about a common acquaintance whose stories, he said, 'we unhappily found to be very fabulous'. 'Yes', Dr. Johnson replied, 'but we don't know *which* half to believe. By his lying we lose not only all reverence for him, but all comfort in his conversation.'

Strachey himself said that a biographer's equipment consists of three qualities: 'a capacity for absorbing facts, a capacity for stating them, and a point of view'. The definition is a good one, for without a point of view no history can be written, but there is a danger that it may not only shape, but distort the facts. The biographer who puts his wit above his subject will end by writing about one person only—himself. My personal complaint about *Eminent Victorians,* on re-reading it after over thirty years, would not be that it is inaccurate, but that it is thin, and that its thinness springs from condescension. If you wish to see a person you must not start by seeing *through* him.

Moreover, while it is certainly the biographer's business to describe the foibles, passions and idiosyncrasies which make his subject a *person,* his work will be very meagre if these individual traits are not also seen as part of a universal drama—for each man's life is also the story of Everyman. The biographer has, of course, a fixed pattern: he is, as Desmond MacCarthy said, 'an artist upon oath'. But the calls upon his imagination and intuition are hardly less exacting than those of the novelist or dramatist. They too, after all, do not compose their characters out of a void, but out of experience or intuition. Shakespeare himself invented hardly any of his plots, but having accepted a ready-made pattern for his characters' actions was then free to give his whole attention to bring them to life. And so, surely, too, the biographer's true function—the transmission of personality—may also be, within its own pattern, an act of creation.

But there is yet one more snag to guard against: the snares of sheer ignorance, of insufficient acquaintance with the background of one's subject. Behind each biography there should always be a rich treasury of unformulated knowledge, a tapestry that has not been unrolled. (That is, to take only two instances, why David Cecil's *Lord M* and Sandburg's *Abraham Lincoln* are such good books.) We should know more, a great deal more, than what we tell.

I remember only too vividly an occasion on which I gave myself away as lacking precisely this sort of knowledge. It was kindly pointed out to me in a letter by Rebecca West. I had mentioned, as an example of Mrs. Carlyle's touchiness, the disastrous Christmas party at The Grange at which Lady Ashburton presented her, from the Christmas tree, with a silk dress, after which Jane returned to her bedroom in a huff. I thought that she had made a great deal of unnecessary fuss. Rebecca West, however, pointed out my mistake. Her great-aunt, Isabella Campbell, who belonged to the Carlyle circle, had often spoken of the episode, and had considered it 'a most extraordinary thing for Lady Ashburton to have done', as a silk dress was the recognised present for a housekeeper and a friend of the family would have felt bewildered at receiving it. To wear a dress which one had not ordered from the start and had fitted according to one's own measurements was a sign of social inferiority. Plainly, therefore, on this occasion Jane was right to be offended, and I did not know what I was talking about.

In my first book, I tried very hard to avoid mistakes of this kind.

I had lived in Italy since the age of seven, and through both books
and people had tried to make myself familiar with the kind of
provincial society into which the poet was born, and of which
vestiges still remained in some small country towns. I took the
advice of Italian friends and scholars. I steeped myself in
Leopardi's works. I thought about little else. And, of course, I
repeatedly visited Recanati, since I am convinced that, when it
is not possible to follow Dr. Johnson's precept, one can at least
make it one's business to visit the home of the man one wishes to
describe. Nothing that can be learned from papers and books
(even from one's subject's own words) can take the place of a
direct visual image, of the sensation of having lived (even if only
for a few hours or days) in the same physical environment. I
never knew what Leopardi's hours of study were like until I had
actually stood in the icy rooms of his father's great library on a
winter's day, beside the desk at which he wrote and the closed
bookshelf in which, among the writings proscribed by the
Church, his sister Paolina one day sadly locked his own *Operette
Morali*, and felt the thinness of the woollen rugs which, as he
worked on through the night by candlelight, he placed over his
shivering knees and shoulders. I did not fully realise the extent
of his sensation, as a boy, 'of subjection and dependence, and of
not being his own master, indeed of not being a whole person,
but only a part and member of someone else'* until I saw his
bedroom, to which, like his brothers, he only had access through
his mother's own bedroom. I walked about the streets of Recanati,
peering into the courtyards of the shuttered palaces, and felt the
biting blast of the *tramontana* which would sweep the poet's black
cloak off his hunched shoulders, while the street boys jeered,
"*Ecco il gobbetto!*"† I went into the parish church where he made
his First Communion and saw the bench still inscribed, *Gentis
Leopardae*. I went back to Recanati in the summer and walked
about the surrounding countryside, seeing '*le vie dorate e gli orti*'‡
and the grassy banks beside the roads from which his *donzelletta*
cut her bundle of grass. I saw the church steps on which some
old crones still sat at dusk, gossiping about the days of their own

---

* *Poesie e Prose*, II, pp. 5–6: *Pensieri*, II.
† "Here's the little hunchback!"
‡ 'The golden ways and gardens'; *A Silvia*.

youth, and looked across the square towards the window at which he saw Silvia singing at her loom. I climbed the hill from which he gazed at the far horizons of *L'infinito*, and heard, as he had, the wind sighing among the branches. I saw the moon rise above his hills, on a still summer night:

> *Dolce e chiara è la notte e senza vento*
> *E queta sopra i tetti e in mezzo agli orti*
> *Posa la luna e da lontan rivela*
> *Serena ogni montagna.**

And only after seeing all this, and letting it sink into me, did I feel that I could even begin to write. For such journeys are more than a sentimental pilgrimage: they are more akin to the need felt by a man whose sight is dim, to pass his hands over a face.

Nevertheless, eighteen years after the publication of this book, I was dissatisfied with it. Some of its comments—especially on the Leopardi family and the Recanati background—seemed to me both glib and insufficiently informed; and the passages about his writings both thin and second-hand. So I decided to write the book all over again. One excuse, which I proffered in the introduction to this new version (which I called *Leopardi, A Study in Solitude* and which was published in 1953) was that, in the interval, two more volumes of the poet's correspondence had been published, as well as some important Italian critical works and biographies. But the real reason was a different one: that, like a friend whose life one has shared for many years, I felt I had got to know him (and I might have added, his country) a little better.

In the particular case of Leopardi, moreover, I have not been the only biographer who has felt the need to retrace his footsteps. I remember telling the distinguished Leopardian scholar and critic, Giuseppe de Robertis, who was then engaged on the back-breaking task of compiling a subject-index of the *Zibaldone*, that after eighteen years, I was just beginning a second life of the poet. He began to laugh. "I see that you have caught it, too," he said, "*il vizio leopardiano*. This won't be your last book on the subject,"

---

* The night is soft and clear, and no wind blows;
  The quiet moon stands over roofs and orchards
  Revealing from afar each peaceful hill
La sera del dì festa (Translated by John Heath-Stubbs).

he foretold—and indeed he was right, since only two years ago, in collaboration with John Heath-Stubbs, I produced a volume of Leopardi's *Selected Prose and Poetry* (John Heath-Stubbs translating the poetry and I the prose, with biographical notes). Here the main change in the prose section of the book, since its purpose was to serve as an introduction to Leopardi's work in English and American universities, has been that I have only used my own words when they were indispensable, to state a fact, sketch in a background or frame a picture. The rest of the story is told by Leopardi himself.

For more and more, as I have gone on reading and writing about other people, it is the subject's own voice that I want to hear. When a biographer can record what a man actually said, he awakens a degree of conviction denied to any other form of narrative. "I wonder why we hate the past so," says Howell ruminatively to Mark Twain, and when the latter replies, "It's so damned humiliating," we know, without a doubt, that this is precisely what the great man did say. This is the kind of material, the small change of daily life, that I have always found irresistible, and that caused me to write, some time after Leopardi, two books about persons who (in their very different ways) would not otherwise have been my choice: Lord Byron, and the fourteenth-century merchant of Prato, Francesco Datini.

*   *   *   *   *

At this point I have necessarily begun to ask myself: has there really been any connecting link, however tenuous, between the subjects I have chosen? They fall—apart from my little war-diary, which was a straightforward account of personal experience —into two sections: studies of figures of the fourteenth and fifteenth centuries in Italy, and of the nineteenth century both in England and Italy. The mediaeval studies are about a merchant and a saint; the nineteenth-century ones about two great poets; about (on a smaller scale) Byron's little daughter, Allegra, and his Venetian friend, Contessa Marina Benzon—kind, florid, amorous, floating in her gondola down the Venetian canals (with a slice of steaming hot *polenta*, to nibble at now and then, concealed in her ample bosom); about some figures of Victorian England; Mazzini lecturing to Carlyle and Jane in Cheyne Row and being lectured back, Carlyle and Lady Ashburton caught in the meshes of their confused, tormented, innocent friendship and, finally, a figure totally incongruous to the others, that of Marie Lenéru, the French writer and playwright whose extraordinary Journal reveals the triumph—within her own terms—over many years in which she was both deaf and blind.

What, I must again ask myself, was it that drew me towards such different characters and backgrounds? I think that the answer is quite a simple one: I did not choose them because I felt especially drawn to poets, merchants or great ladies, to the disabled, or even to saints, but because of an avid interest in *people*. "*L'historien*," said Marc Bloch, "*ressemble à l'ogre de la fable. Là où il flaire la chair humaine, il sait que là est son gibier*." Yes, that was what I was trying to find. Like E. M. Forster, I believe that 'the true history of the human race is the story of human affections'. The biographer's real business—if it is not too arrogant to say so —is simply this: to bring the dead to life. If he succeeds, it does not matter a rap whether his subject was great or humble, good or bad; and any other information that may come to light in the process is only relevant in so far as it makes the dead man a little more alive. Of course one cannot write a book about Leopardi or Byron without bearing in mind that they were poets; nor about Francesco Datini without referring to trade in the fourteenth century; still less can one write about San Bernardino without mentioning that he was a famous preacher. But unless what comes out of the book is a living person, whom you feel you might meet in the street tomorrow, it will not be a good biography.

The process by which this transmission of personality can be achieved varies, of course, very much. Sometimes a single phrase is enough. "This was a good dinner, to be sure: but it was not a dinner to *ask* a man to"—from whose lips could this remark have issued, but from Dr. Johnson's? "When Poodle Byng comes here"—the comment is on a fellow-guest in a Victorian country-house, and the voice is Sidney Smith's—"all the hedgerows smell like Piccadilly." And here is Carlyle, on his eightieth birthday, when some ladies presented him with a clock: "Eh, what have I got to do with Time?" he said. Sometimes, however, this short-hand will not do. In the case of Francesco Datini, for instance, his personality was so tightly bound up with his possessions and his trade that it was necessary to put together a very detailed mosaic of small facts before a man appeared. And with San Bernardino, whose tool was the use of words, harsh or compassionate, compelling, witty or persuasive, it was necessary to quote a good many of them, to reveal his vision of this world and the next.

I must, however, add a confession: my choice of at least two subjects—Byron and Datini—was not due to a personal liking for either of these two men, nor even to an especial interest in their achievements, but largely to the accident of stumbling upon some irresistibly good material. This is not generally, I think, a good plan: in literature, as in life, one is most perceptive about the people one likes best. (The alternative, as Voltaire showed, is hatred and contempt: '*Écrasez l'infâme!*'). Yet to make use of such material is a very great temptation and the process, once it is found, of rounding it out, of ferreting below ground, of plunging, in short, into an entirely new world, is fascinating. I will not apologise for describing some of my experiences, in the hope that my readers will agree with the statement of the great French historian Marc Bloch: '*Le spectacle de la recherche est rarement ennuyeux. C'est le tout fait qui répand la glace et l'ennui.*'

* * * * *

My first acquaintance with Byron's world (apart from a general acquaintance with his Letters and Poems) was made immediately after my first book about Leopardi, when it occurred to me to find out what had happened to the children of some of the great writers of the nineteenth century, and to inquire whether the forcing-house in which they had lived had stimulated their growth or crippled it. The book was to be called *Poets' Children* and was to be a study of the children of Leigh Hunt ('dirtier and more mischievous than Yahoos', said Byron), of Coleridge, of Byron himself, and of the Brownings' idolised, pampered little Pen, driving in his velvet suit through the streets of Florence in a pony-carriage. This book was never finished. The only story I did write, except for a brief article on Coleridge's son, Hartley, was that of Byron's illegitimate daughter by Claire Clairmont, Allegra, whom he took away from her mother to join him in Venice and then in Ravenna, and whom finally, when he had tired of her, he packed off to a convent-school in the middle of the Romagna marshes, where she died of a low, lingering fever before her fifth birthday. It was then that I became acquainted with a Byron I had not known before: the man who prided himself on having become assimilated, through his love affair with Teresa Guiccioli, into Italian provincial society. 'Now I have *lived* among the Italians,' he wrote, 'not *Florenced* and *Romed* and *Galleried* and *Conversationed* it for a few months, and then home again—but been of their families, and friendships and feuds, and loves and councils, in a part of Italy least known to foreigners; and have been amongst them of all classes, from the Conte to the Contadino.'*

It seemed to me that there must be a good deal more to learn about this aspect of Byron's life, and with some trepidation I set off to Florence to try to persuade Count Carlo Gamba, the great-nephew and heir of Contessa Guiccioli, to allow me to consult the papers of his great-aunt. My fear of meeting with a refusal was not unfounded, since Count Gamba—an old gentleman of much taste, who was both old-fashioned and very deaf—had already refused access to several people, including André Maurois, to the papers of 'poor dear aunt Teresa'. I don't remember how I persuaded him to change his mind, since it is very difficult to be persuasive or reassuring at the top of one's voice, but I suspect that he did so, not because of anything I said, but merely because his niece knew me, and he did not think that I looked too foreign or unreliable. In any case, he accepted my promise that I would, of course, show him anything I proposed to publish, and then, ringing the bell, told his man servant to bring down 'Contessa Teresa's chest'. "It's all at your disposal," he said courteously, indicating, as he lifted the lid of the carved mahogany box, many bundles of letters, tied up in ribbon ("These, I think, are Lord Byron's—but I don't know about the others") and a variety of objects, to which Teresa always referred as Byron's 'relics'. There was the locket containing her hair and hung on a chain of her hair which Byron was wearing when he died and which Augusta Leigh sent back to Teresa; there was another locket containing Byron's own hair which he gave to Teresa when he sailed for Greece. There—carefully wrapped up by Teresa, with an inscription in her writing—were a piece of the wall-hangings in the room in Palazzo Gamba where Byron used to visit her, his

* *Letters and Journals*, V, p. 79. To John Murray, September 23, 1820.

handkerchief and a fragment of one of his shirts and, from Newstead Abbey, a crumbling rose-leaf, the twig of a tree and a small acorn. There was a good deal more hair. And finally the Count drew out a fat little volume bound in purple plush: the copy of Madame de Staël's *Corinne*, which Byron and Teresa often read together, on the fly-leaf of which he wrote one of his most famous love-letters to her* (in English, refusing to translate it for her on her return).

In the book, a number of passages were underlined in the same ink as the letter. 'I had learned to love', one said, 'from the poets, but real love is not like that. There is in the realities of existence something arid, which every effort is vain to alter.' Finally, at the bottom of page ninety-two, there was a footnote in Byron's writing: 'I knew Madame de Staël well—better than she knew Italy, but I little thought that, one day, I should *think* with her *thoughts* . . . She is sometimes right, and often wrong, about Italy and England; but almost always true in delineating the heart.'

Count Gamba showed me these passages, and then replaced the book with the other 'relics' in the mahogany box, while the bundles of letters were transferred into a suitcase for me to take away. Even the most cursory glance at them, as this was happening, showed that there were many letters that were not in Byron's writing: I caught a glimpse of the signatures of Lamartine, of Lady Blessington, of Pietro Gamba and of Teresa herself. Had the letters been listed, I asked the Count, did he realise that they were very valuable?† But he waved my scruples aside: no, no, he did not know exactly what the letters were—perhaps I would tell him when I returned them. But how did he know, I persisted, that I would not lose some of them, or sell them to an American library? Would he not like a list to be made at once, and perhaps witnessed by his lawyer? He replied by telling his servant to put the suitcase in my car.‡ And so, returning to my hotel bedroom, I emptied the whole case on to the bed and spent a fascinating evening. For as I glanced through Byron's love-letters to Teresa

* *L. J.*, IV, p. 50, August 25, 1819 (quoted from Moore).

† The value was even greater than I myself realised. Only recently, at Sotheby's, a letter of Byron's was sold for £500.

‡ Eventually, with the help of Elsa Dallolio, all the papers were sorted, dated (when possible) and properly filed before they were returned to Count Gamba, who presented them to the *Biblioteca Classense* in Ravenna.

(in a style often closely resembling that of an Italian letter-writing manual) and perused the seventeen hundred pages of her own *Vie de Lord Byron en Italie*, I realised that I had indeed come across a new facet of the poet's intricate, complex personality. And, I wondered, might it not be possible to unearth some other local material, which would show him in this Italian world from the angle of his observers, instead of from his own? So I started looking. I received some lively accounts of provincial life in Ravenna in the 1820's, as well as permission to quote from papers in their family archives from Conte and Contessa Pasolini dell'Onda in Ravenna; I consulted the libraries and state archives of Venice, Bologna, Forlì, Florence, and Lucca. Gradually a very curious picture began to take shape. I saw Byron not only through the eyes of the Gamba and Guiccioli families and his other Italian acquaintances, but through those of his fellow-conspirators among the *Carbonari*, and of the Papal, Austrian and Tuscan spies, who dogged his footsteps.*

The process of unearthing all these accounts was very odd. It had (like any form of research) the fascination of a crossword puzzle, but it was also a little like walking in Madame Tussaud's Gallery of Mirrors, in a world in which everything (and Byron himself most of all) was slightly out of focus, every motive misinterpreted, every image magnified or dwindled. I also learned a little more about a much more sympathetic side of Byron's character—the one which, perhaps, in the end earned him a place in Westminster Abbey—'his intensity and strength, his power and passion . . . in resisting the enemies of Freedom'.† These qualities

* There were, for instance, the anecdotes of Conte Francesco Rangone, a literary nobleman and gossip of Ferrara, who wrote a pamphlet entitled, 'Peep at a very cultivated, rich but strange Mylord . . . dear to the Learned and not less so to the Fair.' There was the diary of Cavalier Angelo Mengaldo, a persistent Boswell, who held a swimming-match with Byron down the Grand Canal and even ventured to scold him about his love affairs, 'quoiù mes sermons n'etaient pas de son goût'. There were the reports of a Tuscan spy, Angelo Valtancoli, who, with some difficulty, since he was too much in awe of Milord to draw near to him, kept watch over his movements in Bologna and reported that 'the true object of his residence is still neither his literary pursuits nor his amorous occupations, but the destruction of the Established Government'. And finally there were the accounts of Cavaliere Luigi Torelli of Pisa, known as 'the spy of spies', whose highly exaggerated reports caused the Tuscan Government to banish the Gamba family from Tuscany.

† From William Plomer's address on unveiling the Memorial Tablet to Byron in Westminster Abbey, on May 8, 1969.

found full scope in his association with the Gamba family, since both Teresa's father, Conte Ruggero, and her young brother Pietro ('wild about liberty', wrote Byron) were considered *pecore segnate* (branded sheep) by both the Austrian and Papal governments. It was through them that Byron made the acquaintance of the local *Carbonari* and soon became the head of one of their bands, the *Cacciatori Americani*. He met the conspirators in the pine-forest; he concealed their weapons in his house; he felt himself to have become, at last, a man of action.

Finally, before the book was finished, I was allowed to visit the villa at Settimello, near Pistoia, which had belonged to Teresa (then the widow of the Marquis de Boissy) in which she spent the last seven years of her life, and where she kept her books and Byronic 'relics'. It was strange to take down her books and to find, in the fine, pointed handwriting which she had acquired at S. Chiara, her distressed, indignant comments at the manner in which Byron's friends had treated what she considered the most perfect and unflawed romance. Often she confined herself to exclamation marks or to the words, '*Non!*' or '*Mensonge!*' or even '*Pah!*'—and in Leigh Hunt's *Lord Byron and His Contemporaries*, '*Faux! faux! Hypocrite! Menteur!*' In the margin of Lady Blessington's *Conversations with Lord Byron*, beside the passage describing 'the bad and vulgar taste predominating in all Lord Byron's equipments', Teresa angrily scribbled, '*Mais ce sont des mensonges, pour faire plaisir à Dorset!*' (sic). On the other hand the simple remark, 'Byron's was a fine nature' elicited the comment, 'Oh, true!' and a similar approval was granted to the passage in which Lady Blessington remarked that 'all the malice of his nature lodged itself in his lips and the fingers of his right hand—for there is none, I am persuaded, in his heart'. But it was Moore's *Life* which upset Teresa most. 'The word "Adultery" is *cruel*', she wrote, 'and could at least be sostituted (sic) by another less odious.' Her final comment is on the last page of Moore's book: 'It was a duty in his (Byron's) friends to employ *delicacy* in this task. In what manner they have satisfied it, this work must show sufficiently.'

Poor Teresa! Yet, in setting all this down, I did not feel that I was betraying her great-nephew's trust in me. His original purpose in suppressing the publication of her papers had been to safeguard her reputation—but indeed, when the *whole* story lies before us, it is she who comes out best. Of all Byron's friends, she and her brother Pietro were the only ones who took him entirely seriously, who doggedly, whole-heartedly and against all evidence, believed in him. They believed not only in his poetic genius and his noble aspirations, but in his romantic attitudes, his kindness, his heroism. Pietro died in Greece—two years after the poet himself—for the cause that Byron inspired. And Teresa, her silliness and vanity fallen away from her in old age, wrote that it was her wish that *all* her papers, 'whatever the effect upon my reputation', should be published, for the sake of showing 'Lord Byron's good and kind heart'.

In the case of *The Merchant of Prato*, my researches led me into very different paths. I had written a monograph* about the importation into Florence, after the decimation of the population by the Black Death in 1348, of foreign slaves from the Black Sea, the Balkans, and Africa: and in the course of my researches, I had come across the deed of sale to a merchant of Prato, Francesco di Marco Datini, of a little Tartar slave-girl of ten. In the letter in which he instructed his agent in Genoa to find such a child, he had been very specific. She was to be 'young and rustic, between eight and ten years old, of good stock, strong enough to stand much hard work, and of good health and temper, so that I may bring her up in my own way'. Was the slave-trade, I wondered, one of this merchant's many activities, or was he merely dealing with his own family's servant problem? The latter proved to be the truth. But as I discovered this, I also realised that Datini's papers—his long correspondence with his wife, his partners in Italy and abroad, his factors, his relations and his friends—might provide the material for a family picture of the fourteenth century as detailed and as vivid as that which emerges, for instance, from the *Paston Papers* or from the letters of the *Menasgier de Paris* to his young wife. This indeed proved to be so. Datini's papers—which consisted not only of his 575 voluminous account-books and ledgers (bound in white parchment and headed 'In the name of God and profit') but of nearly 126,000

---

* *The Domestic Enemy: The Eastern Slaves in Tuscany in the XIV & XV Centuries*, published in *Speculum*, vol. XXX, No. 3, July, 1955.

business and private letters—had lain for over three hundred years in sacks in a recess under the stairs of his own house in Prato (occasionally, but not badly, nibbled by worms or mice), and though in 1870 they had been discovered and filed, the use that had been made of them by historians and economists had chiefly emphasised his achievements as a merchant: those relating to his private life had only been very superficially surveyed. As soon as they were transcribed (with the assistance of a skilled archivist, Dr. Gino Corti) I realised that they contained precisely what I had hoped to find: a glimpse of the daily life of a household of the fourteenth century, the relationship of its members to each other, and especially, of Francesco's own dealings with his active, intelligent, argumentative wife. Such a detailed correspondence as theirs was still very rare. Husbands and wives seldom had occasion to write to each other since, if the husband was away, it was probably on a Crusade or trading in foreign ports, where opportunities for letters would be few. But here was a wife living in Prato, to look after her husband's house, while he was busy with his trade in Pisa or Florence; and their letters, together with the washing and the fresh bread and vegetables and fruit from the farm, went up and down between Prato and Florence on muleback once or twice a week. Yes, here was the *chair humaine* that I had been seeking.

To trace the necessary information, however, was often a slow and laborious process. To discover, for instance, the extent of one single item of Margherita's wardrobe it was necessary to examine many pages of washing lists, account-books, and letters merely to be able to write down, at the end of a day's work, the two words 'seven shifts'. Equally, to find out what Francesco ate and drank, I had to consult not only his bills and account-books but his letters to his apothecary and his doctors, who, in later years, forbade him to indulge in too many spices and also, oddly enough (since he suffered from constipation), in much fresh fruit. Among the most illuminating items—for few things reveal a man more clearly than the way he chooses to spend his money—were those which referred to his gifts: very extravagant ones to the rich and great, more modest ones (such as bales of herrings or crates of oranges) to kinsmen and the poor. After the terror, however, brought to Tuscany by the recurrence of the plague in 1400, and as he felt old age drawing near, his alms became much more generous: dowries to poor girls, ransoms for men in prison, gifts to hospices and convents. In the end, he left the whole residue of his large fortune to his Foundation for the poor of Prato, 'for the love of God, so as to return to His Poor what has been granted to me as His gracious gift'.

*   *   *   *   *

Looking back, I do not regret the time spent upon these researches, nor indeed upon any of my biographies, though I do sometimes wish that I had devoted some of my energies instead to writing two books which are still lacking in English: full, up-to-date Lives of Frederick II of Hohenstaufen and of Lorenzo de' Medici—both men who not only saw, but to a large extent provoked, the dawn of a new era. But were I to write these books now, I think they would be somewhat different in tone and treatment from my earlier ones, for a reason which became clear to me, some years ago, after a conversation with George Santayana. During the last months of his life, when he was revising his *Life of Reason*, I asked him whether his opinions had become very different from those he had expressed some forty years before. "No," he gently replied, "I feel I have much the same things to say—but I want to say them in a different tone of voice."

Essentially, this reflects a state of mind not unlike that of Dr. Johnson when, ten days before his death, he asserted that he was 'now ready to call a man a *good* man, on much easier terms than formerly'. With the passing of time, a writer's judgements are likely to become a little gentler and to be expressed in a quieter voice; and of course it is also possible that, in the interval, he may have learned a little more. This is not to say that the works of a person's later years are necessarily better than those of his youth, something may have been lost, as well as gained. But certainly they will be different.

They will be different, too, for other, less subjective reasons. Any writer who has gone on working for many years, is inevitably affected by the changes that have taken place during this time by the *Zeitgeist*, which is something more than a change in literary fashion. He will become aware that his earlier work has become, to a greater or lesser extent, 'dated'. What Virginia Woolf, writing in the 1930's, called 'the new biography'—referring to the works of Lytton Strachey, Harold Nicolson and their followers—has not been so for a long time now. Indeed in recent years there has been a tendency to revert, especially in America, to solid lives in several volumes, less moralistic in tone than their Victorian predecessors, and generally more fully documented, but above all, factual. I think it is, on the whole, a salutary change. There is also a tendency to produce long, detailed records of some single episode, like a presidential election or assassination, or the Cuban crisis—books which to some extent make use of the technique, and convey the feeling of actuality, of a documentary newsreel. And, indeed, some technique of this kind must be evolved today, if only owing to the immense amount of material available to a writer, especially about a public figure. What must Franklin Roosevelt's biographer have felt, surveying the forty *tons* of documents at his disposal? We live in a historically—or at least journalistically—minded age, and I understand that a certain American statesman was in the habit of having even his telephone conversations recorded in large notebooks. Certainly, too, a great change has been brought about by the radio and by television, which can satisfy people's curiosity about their neighbours' lives more directly and dramatically than any written page; every housewife in America could watch Alger Hiss on trial for treason, and follow the progress of the funerals of Jack and Bob Kennedy. And during this very summer, we have all watched, holding our breath, two men taking their first staggering steps upon the moon.

I do not believe, however, that these new outlets for the imagination will necessarily destroy the old. The slow development of character, the processes of thought of the writer and artist, and above all, the relation of human beings to each other —these are things that fortunately cannot be simplified, and will always have to be set down, however imperfectly, in words. Only, perhaps, in slightly different words, and with a different emphasis.

Marie Lenéru, when she was in touch with life again after some years of deafness and blindness, wrote that her desire was 'to write, not as a form of expression, or even for writing's sake, but in order *to be*, to enter more and more completely into one's own thoughts and one's own heart'. It is not necessary to have been deaf or blind to feel like this. But such an intention does imply that an inner change has taken place. If I were to start writing again today, with twenty or even ten years of energy and leisure still before me, I think I would write some quite different books, not in order to meet changes in fashion and approach, but rather in myself. Even when I disagree with what some young writers of today have to say, and do not always like the tone in which they say it, I am more interested in the world to which they belong than in that of my own youth. It is more violent, certainly, and cruder; but perhaps more vital and certainly more socially, religiously and politically involved, an involvement which I respect and from which I cannot now dissociate myself. The books I should like to write now, if any, would be connected with the subjects which most often fill my mind, and which belong, at least in part, to the vision bequeathed to us by the Second Vatican Council. They would probably be concerned with either sociological or religious problems and, even if they dealt with the past, would probably not be as detached as the works of my youth from the swiftly changing world in which we live.

Not that I nourish any illusions that a partial agreement with the ideologies of the younger generation, or at least a vivid awareness that they exist, will necessarily bring me any closer to them. On the contrary, I think that people of my age should have the courage to maintain a certain loyalty to the taste that they have acquired through many years of devotion to one of the arts, and frankly to admit what they do or do not enjoy. One need never again, for instance, listen to an opera by Wagner, if that happens to be one of one's blind spots, nor read the novels of Stendhal, nor the works of Simone de Beauvoir, nor look at a picture by Dali. But, on the other hand, what a subtle delight can be brought by a return to those works of which the flavour still endures or by the sharp tang of pleasure caused by an unknown young author's new book—a pleasure enriched and enhanced by all that one has known before encountering it. Virginia Woolf has somewhere described an evening during which Roger Fry, in a friend's house, was called upon to decide whether a certain picture was or was not by Degas. 'It was a very good picture beyond a doubt; it was signed by Degas—he was inclined to think on the whole that it was by Degas. And yet there was something that puzzled him . . . As if to rest himself, he turned away and took part in a discussion that was going forward in another part of the room . . . Then there was a pause. Suddenly he looked up and said: "No, no, that is not by Degas!" '

I do not know how old Roger Fry was when this little incident occurred, but I would wager that he was not a young man, or at least, that he had already been an art critic for a considerable number of years. For that long process of stepping back to reconsider and compare, perhaps not even wholly consciously, with a hundred other similar objects seen over many years, is precisely one of the great rewards of having analysed and savoured one of the first for a very long time, until the moment comes when one is sure and can say, "No, that is not by Degas", or, on reading a work by a new young author, "Yes, that is a good book."

All this, however, only applies to the critical faculty, to one's assessment of other people's work. What about one's own? Should one go on writing indefinitely—that is, as long as one can listen, read, discriminate and enjoy? This is, of course, a highly personal matter and has little to do with calendar years. But for most writers who are no longer young one obstacle may arise which is both painful and disconcerting. Just as many actors and public speakers form a habit—in order to prevent their speech from becoming lifeless—of singling out in their audience one responsive face and addressing their remarks to it, so a writer is almost always—consciously or unconsciously—writing for *someone*, for a friend or friends who, he knows, have a similar turn of mind, who will understand and like what he says, or will disagree in a manner as stimulating as agreement.

At my age, however, it is almost inevitable that one should sometimes wonder for whom one is writing. It is not only that many friends of one's own generation—the eyes in the audience which one was certain one could catch—have disappeared or are disappearing, but that they have taken with them both reassurance and zest. Yet, when I look at the question detachedly, I know that this is not its crux. One should surely try to go on renewing oneself, both in form and substance, so long as one is capable of thinking and feeling at all and—if one's profession happens to be that of a writer—one should also go on writing, even for a changing and perhaps dwindling audience, as long as one believes that one has anything valid to say. In short, I would give to myself in old age the same advice that I have often given to young writers about to take their first plunge: write only because you *must*, but, if you must, do not let yourself be discouraged by either youth or age. For 'of making many books there is no end'.

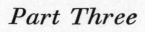

Part Three

9

La Foce

. . . superata tellus
*Sidera donat.**
BOETHIUS

I T WAS on a stormy October afternoon in 1923, forty-seven years ago, that we first saw the Val d'Orcia and the house that was to be our home. We were soon to be married and had spent many weeks looking at estates for sale, in various parts of Tuscany, but as yet we had found nothing that met our wishes.

We knew what we were looking for: a place with enough work to fill our lifetime, but we also hoped that it might be in a setting of some beauty. Privately I thought that we might perhaps find one of the fourteenth- or fifteenth-century villas which were then almost as much a part of the Tuscan landscape as the hills on which they stood or the long cypress avenues which led up to them: villas with an austere façade broken only by a deep loggia, high vaulted rooms of perfect proportions, great stone fireplaces, perhaps a little courtyard with a well, and a garden with a fountain and an overgrown hedge of box. (Many such houses are empty now, and crumbling to decay.) What I had not realised, until we started our search, was that such places were only likely to be found on land that had already been tilled for centuries, with terraced hillsides planted with olive-trees, and vineyards that were already fruitful and trim in the days of the Decameron. To choose such an estate would mean that we would only have to follow the course of established custom, handing over all the hard work to our *fattore*, and casting an occasional paternal eye over what was being done, as it always had been done. This was not what we wanted.

We still had, however, one property upon our list: some 3,500 acres on what we were told was very poor farming-land in the south of the province of Siena, about five miles from a new little

* Earth overcome gives the stars.

watering-place which was just springing up at Chianciano. It was from there that we drove up a stony, winding road, crossed a ford, and then, after skirting some rather unpromising-looking farm buildings, drove yet farther up a hill on a steep track through some oak coppices. From the top, we hoped to obtain a bird's-eye view of the whole estate. The road was nothing more than a rough cart-track up which we thought no car had surely ever been before; and the woods on either side had been cut down or neglected. Up and up we climbed, our spirits sinking. Then suddenly we were at the top. We stood on a bare, windswept upland, with the whole of the Val d'Orcia at our feet.

It is a wide valley, but in those days it offered no green welcome, no promise of fertile fields. The shapeless rambling river-bed held only a trickle of water, across which some mules were picking their way through a desert of stones. Long ridges of low, bare clay hills—the *crete senesi*—ran down towards the valley, dividing the landscape into a number of steep, dried-up little water-sheds. Treeless and shrubless but for some tufts of broom, these corrugated ridges formed a lunar landscape, pale and inhuman; on that autumn evening it had the bleakness of the desert, and its fascination. To the south, the black boulders and square tower of Radicofani stood up against the sky—a formidable barrier, as many armies had found, to an invader. But it was to the west that our eyes were drawn: to the summit of the great extinct volcano which, like Fujiyama, dominated and dwarfed the whole landscape around it, and which appeared, indeed, to have been created on an entirely vaster, more majestic scale—Monte Amiata.

The history of that region went back very far. There had already been Etruscan villages and burial-grounds and health-giving springs there in the fifth century B.C.; the chestnut-woods of Monte Amiata had supplied timber for the Roman galleys during the second Punic war, while, from the eighth to the eleventh century, both Lombards and Carolingians had left their traces in the great Benedictine abbeys of S. Antimo and Abbadia San Salvatore, in the *pieve* of S. Quirico d'Orcia and in innumerable minor Romanesque churches and chapels—some still in use, some half-ruined or used as granaries or storehouses—and the winding road we could just see across the valley still followed almost the same track as one of the most famous mediaeval pilgrims' roads to Rome, the *via francigena*, linking this desolate valley with the whole of Christian Europe. Then came the period of castle-building, of violent and truculent nobles—in particular, the Aldobrandeschi, Counts of Santa Fiora, who boasted that they could sleep in a different castle of their own on each night in the year—and who left as their legacy to the Val d'Orcia the half-ruined towers, fortresses and battlements that we could see on almost every hilltop. And just across the valley—its skyline barely visible from where we stood—lay one of the most perfect Renaissance cities, the creation of that worldly, caustic man of letters, Aeneas Silvius Piccolomini, Pope Pius II, the first man of taste in Italy to enjoy with equal discrimination the works of art and those of nature, who would summon, in the summer heat, his Cardinals to confer with him in the chestnut woods of Monte Amiata, 'under one tree or another, by the sweet murmur of the stream'.

But of all this we knew nothing then, and still less could we foresee that, within our lifetime, those same woods on Monte Amiata, as well as those in which we stood, which for centuries had been a hiding-place for the outlawed and the hunted, would again be a refuge for fugitives: this time for anti-Fascist partisans and for Allied prisoners of war. We only knew at once that this vast, lonely, uncompromising landscape fascinated and compelled us. To live in the shadow of that mysterious mountain, to arrest the erosion of those steep ridges, to turn this bare clay into wheat-fields, to rebuild these farms and see prosperity return to their inhabitants, to restore the greenness of these mutilated woods—that, we were sure, was the life that we wanted.

In the next few days, as we examined the situation more closely, we were brought down to earth again. The estate was then of about 3,500 acres, of which the larger part was then woodland (mostly scrub-oak, although there was one fine beech-wood at the top of the hill) or rather poor grass, while only a small part consisted of good land. Even of this, only a fraction was already planted with vineyards or olive-groves, while much of the arable land also still lay fallow. The buildings were not many: besides the villa itself and the central farm-buildings around it, there were twenty-five outlying farms, some very inaccessible and all in a state of great disrepair and, about a mile away, a small castle called Castelluccio Bifolchi. This was originally the site of one of the Etruscan settlements belonging to the great lucomony of Clusium (as is testified by the fine Etruscan vases found in the necropolis close to the castle, and which now lie in the museum of Chiusi), but the first mention of it in the Middle Ages as a 'fortified place' dates only from the tenth century, and we then hear no more about it until the sixteenth, when it played a small part in the long drawn-out war between Siena and Florence for the possession of the Sienese territory—a war which gradually reduced the Val d'Orcia to the state of desolation and solitude in which we found it. In this war Siena was supported by the troops of Charles V and Florence by those of François I of France, and Pope Clement VII (who was secretly allied with the French) made his way one day by a secondary road from the Val d'Orcia to Montepulciano and, on arriving at the Castelluccio, expressed a wish to lunch there. But the owner of the castle, a staunch Ghibelline, refused him admittance, 'so that the Pope was obliged, with much inconvenience and hunger, to ride on to Montepulciano'.*

This castle, which held within its walls our parish church, dedicated to San Bernardino of Siena, and which owned some 2,150 acres, had once formed a single estate with La Foce; when we first saw it it was still inhabited by an old lady who (even if we had had the money) did not wish to sell. It was not until 1934 that we were able to buy it and thus bring the whole property together again.

As for the villa of La Foce itself, it is believed to have served as a post-house on the road up which Papa Clemente passed, but this is unconfirmed, and the only thing certain is that in 1557 its lands, together with those of the Castelluccio, were handed over to the Sienese hospital of Santa Maria della Scala, as is testified by a shield on the villa and on the older farms, bearing this date, with the stone ladder surmounted by a cross which is the hospital's emblem. The home itself was certainly not the beautiful villa I had hoped for, but merely a medium-sized

* Verdiani Bandi, *I Castelli della Val d'Orcia*, p. 120, quoting the chronicler Malavolti. Subsequently the castle was occupied in turn by the troops of the Emperor and of the French and after the fall of Montalcino passed, like all the rest of this territory, into the hands of Cosimo de' Medici, Grand Duke of Tuscany.

country-house of quite pleasant proportions, adorned by a loggia on the ground floor, with arches of red brick and a façade with windows framed in the same material. Indoors it had no especial character or charm. A steep stone staircase led straight into a dark central room, lit only by red and blue panes of Victorian glass inserted in the doors, and the smaller rooms leading out of it were papered in dingy, faded colours. The doors were of deal or yellow pitch-pine, the floors of unwaxed, half-broken bricks, and there was a general aroma of must, dust, and decay. There was no garden, since the well was only sufficient for drinking-water, and of course no bathroom. There was no electric light, central heating or telephone.

Beneath the house stood deep wine-cellars, with enormous vats of seasoned oak, some of them large enough to hold 2,200 gallons, and a wing connected the villa with the *fattoria* (the house inhabited by the agent or *fattore* and his assistants) while just beyond stood the building in which the olives were pressed and the oil made and stored, the granaries and laundry-shed and wood-shed and, a little further off, the carpenter's shop, the blacksmith's and the stables. The small, dark room which served for a school stood next to our kitchen; the ox-carts which carried the wheat, wine, and grapes from the various scattered farms were unloaded in the yard. Thus villa and *fattoria* formed, according to old Tuscan tradition, a single, closely-connected little world.

When, however, we came to ask the advice of the farming experts of our acquaintance, they were not encouraging. To farm in the Sienese *crete*, they said, was an arduous and heart-breaking enterprise: we would need patience, energy—and capital. The soil-erosion of centuries must first be arrested, and then we would at once have to turn to re-afforestation, road-building, and planting. The woods, as we had already seen, had been ruthlessly cut down, with no attempt to establish a regular rotation; the olive-trees were ill-pruned, the fields ill-ploughed or fallow, the cattle underfed. For thirty years practically nothing had been spent on any farm implements, fertilisers or repairs. In the half-ruined farms the roofs leaked, the stairs were worn away, many windows were boarded up or stuffed with rags, and the poverty-stricken families (often consisting of more than twenty souls) were huddled together in dark, airless little rooms. In one of these, a few months later, we found, in the same bed, an old man dying and a woman giving birth to a child. There was only the single school in the *fattoria*, and in many cases the distances were so great and the tracks so bad in winter, that only a few children could attend regularly. The only two roads—to Chianciano and Montepulciano—converged at our house (which stood on the watershed between the Val d'Orcia and Val di Chiana, and thence derived its name), and also ended there. The more remote farms could only be reached by rough cart-tracks and, if we wished to attempt intensive farming, their number should at least be doubled. We would need government subsidies, and also the collaboration of our neighbours, in a district where few landowners had either capital to invest, or any wish to adopt new-fangled methods, and we would certainly also meet with opposition from the peasants themselves—illiterate, stubborn, suspicious, and rooted, like countrymen all the world over, in their own ways.

We had no lack of warnings. Was it courage, ignorance or mere youth that swept them all away? Five days after our first glimpse of the Val d'Orcia, in November 1923, we had signed the deed of purchase of La Foce. In the following March we were married and, immediately after our honeymoon, we returned to the Val d'Orcia to start our new life.

*   *   *   *   *

How can I recapture the flavour of our first year? After a place has become one's home, one's freshness of vision becomes dimmed; the dust of daily life, of plans and complications and disappointments, slowly and inexorably clogs the wheels. But sometimes, even now, some sudden trick of light or unexpected sound will wipe out the intervening years and take me back to those first months of expectation and hope, when each day brought with it some new small achievement, and when we were awaiting, too, the birth of our first child.

For the first time, in that year, I learned what every country child knows: what it is to live among people whose life is not regulated by artificial dates, but by the procession of the seasons: the early spring ploughing before sowing the Indian corn and clover; the lambs in March and April and then the making of the delicious sheep's-milk cheese, *pecorino*, which is a speciality of this region, partly because the pasture is rich in thyme, called *timo sermillo* or *popolino*. ('*Chi vuol buono il caciolino*', goes a popular saying, '*mandi le pecore al sermolino.*')* Then came the hay-making in May, and in June the harvest and the threshing; the vintage in October, the autumn ploughing and sowing; and finally, to conclude the farmer's year, the gathering of the olives in December, and the making of the oil. The weather became something to be considered, not according to one's own convenience but the farmer's needs: each rain-cloud eagerly watched in April and May as it scudded across the sky and rarely fell, in the hope of a kindly wet day to swell the wheat and give a second crop of fodder for the cattle before the long summer's drought. The nip of late frosts in spring became a menace as great as that of the hot, dry summer wind, or, worse, of the summer hail-storm which would lay low the wheat and destroy the grapes. And in the autumn, after the sowing, our prayers were for soft sweet rain. '*Il gran freddo di gennaio*', said an old proverb, '*il mal tempo di febbraio, il vento di marzo, le dolci acque di aprile, le guazze di maggio, il buon mietere di giugno, il buon battere di luglio, e le tre acque di agosto, con la buona stagione, valgon più che il tron di Salmone.*'†

Some of the farming methods which we saw in those first years became obsolete in Tuscany a long time ago. Then, the reaping was still done by hand and in the wheat-fields, from dawn to sunset, the long rows of reapers moved slowly forwards, chanting rhythmically to follow the rise and fall of the sickle, while behind the binders and gleaners followed, bending low in a gesture as old as Ruth's. The wine and water, with which at intervals the men freshened their parched throats, were kept in leather gourds in a shady ditch, and several times in the day, besides, the women brought down baskets of bread and cheese and home-cured ham (these snacks were called *spuntini*) from the farms, and at midday steaming dishes of *pastasciutta* and meat. A few weeks ago, one of the oldest *contadini* still left at La Foce, a man of ninety—*laudator temporis acti*—was reminiscing with my husband about

---

* 'The man who wants good cheese, will feed his sheep on thyme.'

† 'Great cold in January, bad weather in February, March winds, sweet rain in April, showers in May, good reaping in June, good threshing in July, and the three rains of August—all with good weather—these are worth more than Solomon's throne.'

those days. "We worked from dawn to dusk, and sang as we worked. Now the machines do the work—but who feels like singing?"

An even greater occasion than the reaping, was the threshing —the crowning feast-day of the farmer's year. Threshing, until very recently, had been done by hand with wooden flails on the grass or brick threshing-floor beside each farm, but in our time there was already a threshing-machine worked by steam, and all the neighbouring farmers came to lend a hand and to help in the fine art of building the tall straw ricks, so tightly packed that, later on, slices could be cut out of them, as from a piece of cake. The air was heavy with fine gold dust, shimmering in the sunlight, the wine-flasks were passed from mouth to mouth, the children climbed on to the carts and stacks, and at noon, beside the threshing-floor, there was a banquet. First came soup and smoke-cured hams, then piled-up dishes of spaghetti, then two kinds of meat—one of which was generally a great gander, *l'ocio*, fattened for weeks beforehand—and then platters of sheep's-cheese, made by the *massaia* herself, followed by the *dolce*, and an abundance of red wine. These were occasions I shall never forget—the handsome country girls bearing in the stacks of yellow *pasta* and flask upon flask of wine; the banter and the laughter; the hot sun beating down over the pale valley, now despoiled of its riches; the sense of fulfilment after the long year's toil.

Then came the vintage. The custom of treading the grapes beneath the peasants' bare feet—often pictured by northern writers, perhaps on the evidence of Etruscan frescoes, as a gay Bacchanalian scene—was already then a thing of the past. At that time, the bunches of grapes were brought by ox-cart to the *fattoria* in tall wooden tubs (called *bigonci*) in which they were vigorously squashed with stout wooden poles, and the mixture of stems, pulp and juice was left to ferment in open vats for a couple of weeks, before being put into barrels, to complete the fermentation during the winter. Now, the stems are separated from the grapes by a machine (called a *diraspatrice*), *before* the pressing, and then the juice flows directly into the vats, while for the pale white wine called 'virgin' the grapes are skinned before the fermentation (since it is the skin that gives the red wine its colour).

La Foce

Last, in the farmer's calendar, came the making of the oil. Unlike Greece and Spain, and some parts of southern Italy, where the olives are allowed to ripen until they fall to the ground (thus producing a much fatter and more acid oil) olives in Tuscany are stripped by hand from the boughs as soon as they reach the right degree of ripeness. Then, when the olives have been brought in by ox-cart to the *fattoria* and placed on long flat trays, so as not to press upon each other, the oil-making takes place with feverish speed, going on all day and night. When first we arrived, we found that the olives were being ground by a large circular mill-stone, about two metres in diameter, which was worked by a patient blindfold donkey, walking round and round. The pulp which was left over was then placed into rope baskets and put beneath heavy presses, worked by four strong men pushing at a wooden bar. This produced the first oil, of the finest quality. Then again the whole process was repeated, with a second and stronger press, and the oil was then stored in huge earthenware jars, large enough to contain Ali Baba's thieves, while the pulp (for nothing is wasted on a Tuscan farm) was sold for the ten per cent of oil which it still contained. (During the war, we even used the kernels for fuel.) The men worked day and night, in shifts of eight hours, naked to the waist, glistening with sweat. At night, by the light of oil lamps, the scene—the men's dark glistening torsos, their taut muscles, the big grey millstone, the toiling beast, the smell of sweat and oil—had a primeval, Michelangelesque grandeur. Now, in a white-tiled room, electric presses and separators do the same work in a tenth of the time, with far greater efficiency and less human labour, and clients bring their olives to us to be pressed from all over the district. One can hardly deplore the change; yet it is perhaps at least worth while to record it.

One other sight, too, has already almost disappeared from the Val d'Orcia: the big grey *maremmano* oxen, first brought from the Hungarian steppes to northern Italy, according to tradition, by Attila, and thence to the plains of the Maremma. In our first years in the Val d'Orcia, it was they that were used for ploughing the heavy soil, but then the day came when we bought our first tractor. Never shall I forget escorting it down the valley with a little crowd of admirers, Antonio at their head, to watch it plough

207

its first furrow in a field near the river. Deep, deep went the shining blade into the rich black earth, deeper than a plough had ever sunk before. The children ran behind, laughing and shouting; the pigs followed, thrusting their long black snouts deep into the moist earth. It was an exciting day—but it was, for the oxen (and though we could not then foresee it, for a whole way of life) the beginning of a great change. The first tractor was followed by others, then by a reaper-and-binder and a combine, and after the war, by two bulldozers, to bring under cultivation the parts of the property which still lay fallow. Some oxen continued to be used for ploughing the steeper hillsides, but gradually they were interbred with the finer white oxen from the Val di Chiana, the *chianini*, while after the war Antonio imported, for beef, the brown and white Simmenthal cattle. You may still sometimes meet a pair of *chianini*—'gentle as evening moths'—drawing an ox-cart up a road or driving a plough on a steep hillside; but if you wish to see the grey oxen you must go to those remote hills of the Maremma (and very few are left) where tractors have not yet arrived, or to the few plains by the sea on which they still roam in their pristine freedom or stand on summer days in the deep shade of spreading cork-trees. When all those plains, too, have been handed over to the tractors—and this is swiftly happening—we shall have to go to zoos to find the kings of the Maremma.

I was fascinated in those early days by the survival of some pagan ceremonies and customs, often incorporated, as the Church has sometimes wisely done, into Christian rites. Among the most beautiful ceremonies of the year were the services, after a day of fasting, of the *quattro tempora*, which were held at the beginning of each of the four seasons, and the 'rogation' processions, in which the priest, carrying a crucifix and holy relics, followed by the congregation chanting litanies, walked through the fields, imploring a blessing upon the crops—the women, with black veils upon their heads, joining in the responses, the children straggling in and out and picking wild flowers among the wheat. Both these rites dated back to the days of ancient Rome* and were still being practised

* These 'rogations' were divided into major and minor, the major being held on April 25, the date at which there is a danger of the wheat being invaded by rust; the minor (which corresponded to the Roman *Ambarvalia*) on the three days before

during our first years at La Foce, but they have now come to an end as part of the Church ritual, though I am told that some of the older peasants still hold a brief procession in the fields, and leave a rough wooden cross standing among the ripening wheat.

Other customs, too, linking pagan and Christian piety, were still practised during our first years in the Val d'Orcia, and some of them still survive. On St. Anthony's Day (St. Anthony the Abbot, patron of animals, not his namesake of Padua) the farmers would bring an armful of hay to church to be blessed by the saint, so that for the whole year their beasts might not lack fodder, and a few of the older men still do so today. On Monte Amiata, on the Eve of the Ascension, some women used to put milk on their window-sills which they would drink the next day, in the hope that swallows would come to bless it. This is perhaps somehow connected with the custom still observed on this side of the valley, of not milking any sheep on Ascension Day. And even now, however deeply imbued with Communism a family may be, each one of them will bring a bunch of olive-branches to be blessed by the priest on Palm Sunday.

On Monte Amiata, too, at Abbadia San Salvatore—where chestnuts form a large part of the poor man's diet—a procession used to walk through the streets on St. Mark's Day singing:

> *San Marcu, nostru avvucatu,*
> *fa che nella castagna non c'entri il bacu.*
> *Trippole e lappole, trippole e lappole, ora pro nobis.**

And only a few years ago a peasant of Rocca d'Orcia, after saying the rosary with his family, used to add an Our Father and a Hail Mary to a saint whom you will find in no calendar, called 'San Fisco Fosco', a terrible saint who lived in the middle of the sea and hated the poor, and therefore had to be propitiated.†

Ascension Day, when the wheat is beginning to ripen. Virgil describes them in the *Georgics*, and Cato, in his *De Agricoltura*, quotes the prayer recited by the garlanded peasants. The prayers at the *quattro tempora* were incorporated into the Christian ritual in the third century by St. Calistus.

* 'St. Mark, our advocate, see that no worm enters our chestnuts, and that each kernel bears three nuts; pray for us.'

† This story, with several other local sayings, I owe to an old neighbour of ours, Clemente Bologna, who took a great interest in local customs, and who also, in his lands in the Maremma, had become a friend of the famous brigand Tuburzi.

Some other practices, too, were quite frankly pagan in origin. There are still both witch-doctors and witches in the villages across the valley, and to one of these, a few years ago, two of our workmen took the bristles of some of our swine, which the vet had not been able to cure of swine-fever. The bristles were examined, a 'little powder' was strewn over them, and some herbs were given, to be burnt in their sties—after which the pigs did recover. The same was sometimes done for cattle. There was also a very efficient witch at Campiglia d'Orcia (now dead, but I believe she has a successor) to whom one could take a garment or a hair of anyone suffering from some affliction that the doctor had been unable to heal, and which was presumed to be caused by the evil eye, and she—with the help of some card-reading and some potions—would cure him. Sometimes, however, trouble would be caused by her prescriptions, since two of our tenants' families embarked on a long feud, merely owing to the fact that she had told the daughter of one of them, that one of her neighbours 'wished her ill'. For all such cures, it was pointed out to me, faith was necessary: those who came to mock went away unhealed.

Divining of the future, too, was done by some of our older peasants. One of them, an old man who is still alive, specialised in foretelling, in winter, the weather for each month of the following year, by placing in twelve onion skins, named for each month of the year, little heaps of salt. These he would then carefully examine: the skins in which the salt had remained, represented the months of drought; those in which it had dissolved, those of rain.

The most interesting of our local superstitious practices, however—and probably the oldest, since it presumably had its origins in a very primitive form of nature-worship—was one that I myself have seen, that of the *poccie lattaie* (literally, milk-bearing udders). This took place in a secluded cave on our land, half way up a very steep ravine, surrounded by dry clay cliffs, but in which a hidden spring, oozing down the walls of the cave, had formed something like stalactites, which had the shape of cows' and goats' udders or women's breasts, each gently dripping a few drops of water. Here the farmers would bring their sterile cows and here, too, came nursing mothers who were losing their milk—and always, after they had tasted the water, their wish was granted.

They brought with them, as gifts, seven fruits of the earth: a handful of wheat, barley, corn, rye, vetch, dried peas, and sometimes a saucer of milk.

After nearly half a century, distance has perhaps lent enchantment to these memories, but I must honestly admit that I can also recollect moments of great discouragement. I remember one grey autumn afternoon on which, having ridden on a small grey donkey to visit some remote farms (for there was as yet no road to the valley) I waited alone in a hollow, while Antonio and the *fattore* walked on to another farm. The cone-shaped clay hillocks in the midst of which I sat were so steep, and worn so bare by centuries of erosion, that even now no attempt has been made to grow anything upon them. Seated beside a tuft of broom—the only plant that will grow there—on ground as hard as a bone after the summer's drought, I was entirely surrounded by these desolate hillocks: no tree, no patch of green, no trace of human habitation, except against the sky a half-ruined watch-tower, standing where perhaps an Etruscan tower had stood before it, and then a Lombard, rebuilt in the Middle Ages to play its part in a series of petty wars, and now inhabited only by a half-witted shepherd who sat at its foot, beside his ragged flock. Below me lay the fields beside the river—land potentially fertile, but then fallow, which would be flooded when the rains came by the encroaching river-bed. Against the sky, behind the black rocks of Radicofani, dark clouds were gathering for a storm, and, as the wind reached the valley, it raised little whirlpools of dust. Suddenly an overwhelming wave of longing came over me for the gentle, trim Florentine landscape of my childhood or for green English fields and big trees—and most of all, for a pretty house and garden to come home to in the evening. I felt the landscape around me to be alien, inhuman—built on a scale fit for demi-gods and giants, but not for us. How could we ever succeed in taming it, I asked myself, and bring fertility to this desert? Would our whole life go by in a struggle against insuperable odds?

Perhaps my early discouragement was also partly caused by the fact that our own house was not yet habitable. During our absence on our honeymoon, under the direction of our architect and old friend Cecil Pinsent, some indispensable work had been done. A skylight had been opened in the ceiling of the central room, to let in some light; another room had been lined with bookshelves; all had been cleaned and distempered and some open fireplaces, with chimneypieces of travertine from the local quarries of Rapolano, had been added in the library and dining-room; there was even a bathroom, although, as yet, in the dry season, very little water. But that was all. The cases and crates containing all our furniture and belongings were piled up in the dining-room, unlabelled, so that when we began to look for such necessities as sheets or cooking-pans, we would come instead upon a dinner-set of fine Sèvres or a large group of bronze buffaloes, sculpted by Antonio's father. We settled temporarily in a maid's room upstairs, and set to work. In a few weeks the house was more or less habitable: the red bricks on the floor had been polished and waxed, the furniture was in place (I did not like all of it, but it was what we had), the windows were hung with chintz or linen curtains, the bookshelves were half filled. (This was the only year of my life in which I have had more than enough book-space.) But there was still, of course, no electric light or telephone, and my greatest wish, a garden, was plainly unattainable till we could get some more water, which was far more urgently needed for the farms. We both agreed that any plans for the house and garden must give way, for the present, to the needs of the land and the tenants. Anything that the crops brought in, as well as any gifts from relations, went straight into the land, and I remember that my present to Antonio, on the first anniversary of our wedding-day, was a pair of young oxen which were led under his window, adorned with gilded horns and with silver stars pasted on their flanks. It is sad to have to add that they were such a bad buy that they had to be sold again as soon as possible.

If there was much satisfaction in these efforts, there was also a certain sense of frustration, which was increased (as our advisers had foreseen) by the passive resistance of our *contadini* to any innovation. Our land was worked on the system which had been almost universal in Tuscany for nearly six centuries, the *mezzadria*, —a profit-sharing contract by which the landowner built the farmhouses, kept them in repair, and supplied the capital for the purchase of half the live-stock, seed, fertilisers, machinery, etc., while the tenant—called *mezzadro, colono* or *contadino*—contributed, with the members of his family, the labour. When the crops were harvested, owner and tenant (the date I am writing about is 1924) shared the profits in equal shares. In bad years, however, it was the landowner who bore the losses and lent the tenant what was needed to buy his share of seed, cattle, and fertilisers, the tenant paying back his loan when a better year came.

In larger estates, such as La Foce, which consisted of a number of farms, there was generally a central home-farm, the *fattoria*, usually adjoining the landowner's house, where the estate manager, the *fattore*, lived with his family and assistants, and from which the whole place was run. It was the owner (or his *fattore*) who established the rotations, deciding what was to be grown on each farm, what new livestock or machinery should be purchased, and what repairs were necessary, and it was in the *fattoria* office that the complicated ledgers and account-books were kept, one for each farm, in which the *contadino's* share of all profits and expenses were set down, and also the loans made to him, in bad years, by the central administration. It was in the *fattoria* cellars and granaries that the owner's share of the produce was stored; it was there that the wine and oil were made, that the peasants came to unload their ox-carts, to go over their accounts, and to air their requests and grievances—and only those who have lived in Tuscany can know what a slow, repetitive business this can be. The *fattoria* was, in short, the hub of the life of the estate.

*   *   *   *   *

The origins of the *mezzadria* system are very easy to describe. After the breaking up of the great feudal estates at the end of the twelfth century, most of the impoverished landowners moved to the rising trading cities (Pisa and Siena, Lucca and Florence), exchanging their former castles and lands for a single grim tower in a city street, while their starving serfs, free or half-free, whose fields and houses had been destroyed by an endless succession of petty wars, also fled to the towns, to find work and bread. Many of them joined one of the guilds, and some eventually turned into skilled craftsmen or opened a small shop, or even became notaries or barbers. In a couple of generations they had saved up a small hoard and since, sooner or later, the Tuscan has always been drawn back to the soil, their first instinct was to put it back into the land again. This was not only true of great merchants like the Bardi or Rucellai, but also of small tradesmen and notaries, who, since they could neither afford to pay overseers nor to leave the town themselves, set a labourer—a *colono*—to work the land for them, drawing up a very simple profit-sharing contract, which gradually, during the second half of the *trecento*, came into universal use in Tuscany. The great feudal domain thus turned into a number of small profit-sharing farms or *poderi*, and the serf of feudal days became a *mezzadro* or *colono*. So matters remained for five and a half centuries.

The *mezzadria* contracts—*patti colonici*—that we found in use at La Foce were almost identical with those of the fourteenth century, even down to the specification of the small customary gifts from each tenant to the landowner of a couple of fowls or a brace of pigeons, or so many dozens of eggs, on certain feast-days.

Life on each farm, for obvious practical reasons, was still in the patriarchal tradition. The family had to be large, to provide enough hands to work the land, and its head, the *capoccia*, ruled over his sons and daughters, his sons-in-law and daughters-in-law, with a rule of iron. '*Tristi quelle case*', said a proverb, '*dove la gallina canta e il gallo tace*'.* The *capoccia's* wife, however, the *massaia*, had plenty of power in her hands, too. Together she and her husband assigned the work to each member of the family, chose their sons' brides and, as soon as the grandchildren were old enough to stagger into the woods as small shepherds and swine-herds, sent them off to do their share. This manner of life, too, was to come to an end during our lifetime but it was in full swing when we first arrived.

In theory, the great point of the *mezzadria* was that, though landowner and *mezzadro* might and did differ on many points, their fundamental interests were alike and, indeed, the partnership could only work in so far as this was so. Certainly, in early days, the sacrifices were not all on one side. We read in the *Ricordanze* of Odorigo di Credit, a small Florentine landowner of the four-teenth century, that in order to buy the seed for the next year's wheat he had to pawn his own gown. Moreover there has always been a strong Tuscan tradition with regard to a landlord's responsibilities towards his tenants. 'Aid and counsel them',

* 'Sad is the house, where the hen clucks and the cock is silent.'

wrote a fourteenth-century Florentine, Giovanni Morelli, in his
Ricordi, 'whenever any insult or injury is done to them, and be
not tardy or slothful in doing so.'* Any good landowner of our
own time, too, until a very few years ago, would have felt this
to be his duty; and many of them, if obliged to send away one
of their peasants because his family could no longer work the
land, would have felt pangs of conscience similar to those felt in
1407 by Ser Lapo Mazzei, a notary and small landowner of Prato.
'He is so solicitous', he wrote about his farmer, 'at the plough
and such a fine pruner of vines and so ingenious that I know not
how to make a change . . . and my cowardly or compassionate
soul (I wonder which it is) does not know how to say to Moco:
"Look for another farm." '† A conscientious landowner, too,
always placed the welfare of his fields before his personal interests:
a considerable proportion of each year's profits went back into the
land. If he did this, the tenant, too, profited, and when a hard
year came, there was some margin to fall back upon.

Unfortunately, however, then as now, not all landlords were
conscientious, and the bad aspect of the system, from the first,
was that an idle or self-indulgent landowner, who did not repair
and stock his farms, crippled his peasants, too; while, on the other
hand, lazy or dishonest *contadini* could very swiftly ruin a farm.
This was, I think, the origin of the mutual suspicion and dislike
which, down the centuries, has all too often come to the surface
in the relationship between the *contadino* and his *padrone*. Indeed, in
some ways the relationship had been better—or at least simpler—
in the old feudal days. The feudal lord had often been cruel and had
made hard demands upon his serfs; but for all that, he had been
much more like them than the new city-folk. To the shopkeeper
or lawyer the peasant was merely a dumb brute, who often retorted
with the weapons of the under-dog: sullen resentment and craft.
Many domestic chronicles and books of precepts of the fourteenth
and fifteenth centuries testify to this mutual distrust, in accents
so similar to those which I have heard upon the lips of some of
their descendants today, as to be positively startling. Paolo da
Certaldo, for instance, a Florentine merchant, warned his fellow
townsmen never to visit their lands on feast-days, when their

* Giovanni di Pagolo Morelli, *Ricordi*, p. 230.
† Ser Lapo Mazzei, *Lettere di un notaio a un mercante*, October 27, 1407.

peasants were gathered together on the threshing-floor, 'for they all drink and are heated with wine and have their own arms, and there is no reasoning with them. Each one thinks himself a king and wants to speak, for they spend all the week with no-one to talk to but their beasts. Go rather to their fields when they are at work—and thanks to the plough, hoe or spade, you will find them humble and meek.'*

Another prudent landowner, Giovanni Morelli, gave very similar advice: 'Go round the farm field by field with your peasant, reprove him for work ill-done, estimate the harvest of wheat, wine, barley, oil and fruit, and compare everything with last year's crops . . . Trust him not, keep your eye always upon him, and examine the crops everywhere—in the fields, on the threshing-floor and on the scales. Yield not to him in anything, for he will only think that you were bound to do so . . . And above all, trust none of them.'†

For the other side of the picture we naturally have less evidence, so long as only the rich were literate, but already by the fifteenth century, some of the *colono*'s resentment had come to the surface in the following rhyme:

> *Noi ci stiamo tutto l'anno a lavorare*
> *E lor ci stanno al fresco a meriggiare;*
> *Perchè s'ha da dar loro mezzo ricolto,*
> *Se n'abbiam la fatica tutta noi?‡*

And here are two other sayings, still in popular use, which reflect the feelings of the *mezzadro* only too plainly:

> *Ombra di noce e ombra di padrone*
> *sono due ombre buggerone!§*

and

> *Il bene dei padroni è come il vino del fiasco,*
> *che la sera è buono è la mattina è guasto.‖*

* Paolo di Messer Pace da Certaldo: *Il libro di buoni costumi*, paras. 102–3.
† Giovanni de Pagolo Morelli, *Ricordi* (1393–1421), pp. 235–6.
‡ 'We work all the year round, They rest and doze in the shade—Why should we give them half the crops, When all the toil is ours?' (Quoted by N. Tamassia, *La famiglia italiana nei secoli XV e XVI*.)
§ 'A nut-tree's shade [under which nothing grows] and a master's shadow, Are two buggering shadows.'
‖ 'The Master's affection is like new wine in the flask;
Good for one evening, and sour the next day.'

All this hardly suggests an agreeable or stable human relation-ship, and it has often seemed to me extraordinary that it should have lasted without a break for nearly six centuries. One explana-tion is apparent if one looks at the Tuscan landscape: the system has produced a highly prosperous agriculture. Those terraced hills with their vineyards and olive-groves, those rich wheat-fields and orchards and vegetable-plots, speak for themselves: they show land as intensively cultivated and fertile as any in the world. But this prosperity is the result of centuries of unremitting hard work. Wherever the Tuscan countryman has been allotted a steep, stony patch of hillside, he has laboriously cleared away the tangled roots of ilex or scrub-oak, the bushes of juniper or myrtle, and dug up the heavy soil, the unwieldy stones and boulders; with the stones he has built, on even the steepest hillsides, little walls to support the terraces on which he could plant his olives and his vines. *Selva del mi' nonno, ulivi del mi' babbo e vigna mia,** so the saying runs. In three generations a bare hillside can become a garden.

In addition to this obvious explanation, I think that the dura-tion of the *mezzadria* has a deeper psychological one. Its strength has lain in an unquestioning conviction on both sides (even with a good deal of grumbling) that the system was, on the whole, fair and equitable; it was this conviction that, for six centuries, made it work. A distinguished Tuscan economist of our own time—Jacopo Mazzei, who himself belonged to a family with a long tradition of responsible land-ownership—justly observed some years ago that the point was not the actual fairness or otherwise of the system itself, but 'the conviction of its fairness', which had given it 'a stability and serenity unequalled in history'.† On the day that this conviction began to be shaken, he said, the whole system would break down.

*   *   *   *   *

No such thoughts, however, crossed our mind when first we arrived at La Foce. We set to work, untroubled, within the familiar framework. Everything cried out to be done and, had it been possible, everything at once. Re-reading a paper which my

* 'My grandfather's wood, my father's olive-grove, and my own vineyard'.
† Jacopo Mazzei: *Firenze rurale*, ed. Jolanda de Blasis, p. 643.

husband read to a Florentine agricultural association, *I Georgofili*,
I have found a summary of the work which, on his first arrival,
he considered essential and immediate. Its main points were:

(1) To set up, on each farm, an eight-year rotation.*

(2) To start ditching, draining, and the building of dykes and
dams on the steep clay hills, and of banks in the river-bed in the
valley, so as to be able to cultivate land at present either flooded
or water-logged.

(3) To increase further the arable land by arresting erosion on
the hillsides, and by extirpating rocks and boulders in the fallow
land.

(4) To rebuild and modernise the existing farms, as well as
rebuilding the granaries, cellars, store-rooms and machine-sheds
of the *fattoria*, and to renew the whole machinery for making oil.

(5) To increase the acreage of olive-groves and vineyards.

(6) To build new roads.

(7) To build new farms.

(8) To increase the number, and improve the quality of the
cattle, sheep, and pigs and, for this purpose, to increase the acreage
of alfalfa and clover.

(9) To suspend all cutting down of trees for at least eight years,
and then to establish a regular rotation of twelve years' growth.

(10) To increase facilities for education and medical care.

The programme was a sound one, but its execution was slowed
down not only by lack of experience, but of capital. Every penny
we had, had been spent on the purchase of the estate, so that all
that was left to work with was the allowance of $5,000 a year
given me by Grandmamma. On this we started.

I still felt myself, however, very much a stranger in this new
world and was not very good at fitting into it. The solid, tradition-
bound group of people living in the *fattoria*—the *fattore* and his
wife and children, his three assistants and the *fattoressa* (who
was never, according to custom, the *fattore's* wife, but a woman
who cooked and did the baking and the housekeeping and looked

---

* The sowing, in the first year, of barley and oats interspersed with lupins and
alfalfa; in the second and third years, of only lupins and alfalfa; in the fourth, of
wheat. In the fifth the soil was to lie fallow, while in the sixth we would sow white
and red clover, in the seventh clover only; in the eighth, wheat again.

after the barn-yard) so deeply rooted in the customs laid down centuries ago, so certain that nothing could or should be changed —made me feel as shy and foreign as the peasant-women who, on certain feast-days, came from their farms on foot or by ox-cart, to place in my hands a couple of squawking fowls, a brace of pigeons or a dozen eggs—and often, too, a flow of grievances, tales of all the family illnesses, or requests for advice and help. But what advice could I give them, when I knew so little myself? Nothing that I had learned at Villa Medici or I Tatti was of any use to me now; I doubt whether any young married woman has started upon her new life more ill-equipped for the particular job she had to do. I did not even know, though Antonio told me that it was my business to concern myself with the *fattoria* linen-cupboard and the barn-yard, that the sheets, to be durable, should be made of a mixture of cotton and hemp, however scratchy, and that a part of our wool should be laid aside each year, after washing and bleaching, to make new mattresses; I could not distinguish a Leghorn hen from a Rhode Island Red. Nor did I succeed, for a long time, in being as easily cordial as Antonio with everyone we met, nor realise the fine hierarchical distinctions between the *fattore* and his assistants, the keepers and the foreman, the *contadini* and the day-labourers. I learned day by day, but never fast enough, always hampered by self-consciousness and shyness, seeming most aloof when I most wished to be friendly. I would walk or ride with Antonio from farm to farm and, while he was busy in the fields or stables, would go into the house and try to make friends with the women and children. It was uphill work. The women were polite—and wary. They offered me fresh raw eggs to drink, or a little glass of sweet home-made liqueur; they showed me the sheep-cheese that they had made, their furniture and their children. But I did not know the right questions to ask; I felt it an impertinence to comment on the way they kept their house, as Antonio said was expected of me; I could not tell one cheese from another; I had no idea whether the baby had measles or chicken-pox, and on the only occasion on which I attempted to give an injection to an old woman with asthma, I broke the syringe. I did better with the children and, when the new schools were opened, I spent a lot of time there— playing with the children during recess, looking at their copy-books, providing them with a small library, admiring their little vegetable- or wheat-plots and giving prizes at the end of the school year—and through the children I gradually got to know the women a little better. It was always a very one-sided relationship though, and hampered by the whole framework of the *fattoria* between us. If a woman came to ask for her sink to be repaired or for her child to be taken to hospital it had to be referred to the *fattore*, and sometimes I found that incautious promises I had made had not been carried out. I think, now, that one of the fundamental evils of the *mezzadria* system was the presence and influence of these middlemen—tougher with the *contadini* than any landowner, because conscious of being only one step above them, and often shielding the *padrone* from what they thought it was inconvenient or undesirable for him to know. In our particular case, Antonio was fortunate, particularly in later years, in being surrounded by a group of loyal and devoted collaborators, who have become his close friends, but I still think that the system was a bad one, though perhaps an inevitable consequence of the whole structure of the *mezzadria*. Always, too, I was distressed by a sense of injustice, by the worn, tired faces of women only a little older than myself, and by the contrast—though certainly at that time we did not live in great luxury—between their life and my own. It is now one of my greatest regrets that inexperience, shyness, and my own other interests so often led me to take the path of least resistance and to leave things as they were.

Antonio, however—simpler, warmer and tougher, and living in a world which he took for granted—went steadily ahead, and it was our good fortune that this was just the period in which the new laws passed by the Fascist government to reclaim the undeveloped regions of Italy were coming into action. The programme—that of the *bonifica agraria*—included the enforced development, which sometimes led to confiscation, of many large estates in the South, *i latifondi*, neglected by absentee landlords (who used sometimes to forbid their wretched labourers even to put up any dwelling-place more permanent than a reed hut, for fear that they might acquire 'squatter's rights'); the financing of public works on a large scale to stop land erosion; the encouragement of drainage and irrigation; the building of new roads and schools and, subsequently, large State subsidies or loans at low

rates of interest to enable active landowners to intensify production and improve the standard of life of their tenants. This 'battle
of the wheat'—which was also accompanied by a good deal of
rhetoric, since it formed part of the policy of 'autarchy' which was
Mussolini's retort to sanctions—began with the draining of the
Pontine Marshes, the cultivation of the plains of the Tuscan
Maremma (in which small plots were assigned to war veterans,
i combattenti, in the manner of ancient Rome) and a campaign
against malaria in Sardinia.*

In some regions, such as ours, where confiscation was unnecessary, landowners' associations—*consorzi di bonifica*—were formed,
assisted by State subsidies; and it was after Antonio had succeeded
in forming (in spite of the opposition of some of his neighbours)
one of these *consorzi* in the Val d'Orcia that we came to work with
some men who represented what was best in the Fascist regime:
the main initiator of the *leggi di bonifica*, Professor Arrigo Serpieri
(a man of outstanding ability and charm) as well as some able
technical experts, who were inspired by an uncritical acceptance
of the Fascist slogans, but also by a deep enthusiasm for their
work. In the Val d'Orcia, the *consorzio* was founded in 1930 and
Antonio remained its president and moving spirit for over thirty
years. An office was opened at Montepulciano, an efficient
engineer was engaged, plans were drawn up for government
approval, which included work in areas all over the valley from
S. Quirico to Radicofani. The state contributions varied from
20% to 100%, according to their nature, while the landowners
contributed to the rest in proportion to their acreage and
goodwill.†

One of the most urgent tasks was to arrest the erosion on the
steep clay hills, and for this purpose Antonio built some twenty-
five dams of stone or earth in creeks or gullies as reinforcements

---

¹ In some areas, the results of the *bonifica agraria* were wholly good. In others,
where each family was assigned far too small a plot of land, and far too flimsily-
built a house, it soon became evident that the farmers could hardly extract a bare
living from the land assigned to them. Many attacks, some justified, were consequently made upon these projects, yet—looking back upon them fifty years later—
I think it can hardly be denied that the basic work was valuable. Not only through
drainage, irrigation, and the extirpation of malaria was all this land turned into farm-
land, but the work, however imperfectly done, did imply a social advance.

† The state subsidies were highest for re-afforestation and the prevention of land
erosion.

against the danger of landslides. Simultaneously, by the building of groynes in the river-bed (consisting of broad walls of masonry jutting out into the stream) the course of the Orcia was controlled, to prevent it from flooding the surrounding fields; and water from the hills above was channelled towards the fallow valley-land and allowed to lie there for four or five years, so that a rich stratum of top-soil gradually raised its level, bringing under cultivation some 150 more acres. Artesian wells were also sunk, under the guidance of water-diviners whose forked willow-twigs often enabled them to forecast not only where water was to be found but at what depth and in what quantity. (This is a much more common gift than is generally believed, and I was delighted to find that I, too, could feel the willow-twig quivering in my hands, as we passed over a water-course.)

An equally urgent problem was that of re-afforestation. Here the government's Department of Forestry gave us both technical advice and help; two large nurseries of young plants were started, and some 545 acres of hillsides or of ravines were planted with seedlings or young trees (mostly oak, pine and cypress). Now most of these areas are covered by green woods.

Then came the roads. When we first arrived, the only good road ended at our house, and many of the more remote farms could only be reached by rough tracks, almost impassable in bad weather. (I vividly remember, in our first year, the local doctor —an old man—attempting to reach a child stricken with diphtheria in the ox-cart which had been sent to fetch him, sitting bolt upright in his dark town suit on a kitchen chair, while the oxen ploughed on in the deep mud and the distracted father urged them on.) First the old roads were improved or prolonged, and then—on the additional land obtained by the purchase of the *Castelluccio*—new ones had to be built to link up the isolated farms.

It is difficult to convey the excitement of this whole enterprise, but perhaps the photographs reproduced here may give some idea of it. Here soil was being turned up that had lain fallow for centuries and, before putting hand to the plough, it was necessary to extirpate and remove enormous boulders, as well as the roots of old trees, and to hold the land up with steep gullies by the building of some more small dykes and dams. This was the work of many months, but when we saw a stretch of new road lying before us, and the tractor could at last begin to turn over the great clods of untilled, shining dark earth, we felt some of the deep satisfaction and fulfilment that must have been felt, far more intensely, by pioneers in new countries, when they saw a desert beginning to turn into a land of promise. By 1940, that is, just before the war, some fifteen miles of new roads had been built on our land, as well as the twenty-five miles of main roads built in the same district by the *consorzio di bonifica*—each shaded by poplars in the valley or by pines or cypresses higher up— and every farmer was able to bring his produce to market, each child to go to school.

Next, the farm-houses. I have already described their state on our arrival. Some had to be torn down and entirely rebuilt, others to be repaired, enlarged, provided with modern stables, pig-styes, silos and dung-heaps built on a concrete foundation; wells were sunk or roof-cisterns built for drinking water and ponds made for watering sheep and cattle. Soon, too, modern cooking-stoves stood beside the old hearths with their enormous chimneys, beneath which *il nonno* used to sit to warm his bones on a winter evening, sometimes beside a broody hen in a basket; a bathroom was installed as well as a modern lavatory and, gradually, each farm was also provided with electric light, and then acquired a radio or television set. The first and most important change, however, was in the actual acreage of the land of each farm, which (after we had increased their number from 25 to 57), came to be of between 75 and 100 acres, instead of over 200, thus rendering intensive cultivation possible. A large part of the newly-cultivated land was sown with wheat, maize and various types of clover, some 6,200 young olive-trees were planted, the vineyards were increased to cover about 200 acres, and the quality of the wine, both white and red, was greatly improved.

The need for schools was also very urgent since, when we first arrived, eighty per cent of the population could neither read nor write. We had at once organised some evening-classes for adults and moved the school-children into a better room, but now the *consorzio* built three new schools, one at La Foce and two in the valley. These were run at first along the progressive lines of the country schools around Rome in the *agro romano*, each school having its own experimental field and garden, so that the children's lessons bore a close relation to their future life on the land. Later on, however, they were taken over by the State, and are now like any other school. The children's pride in their new schoolrooms was delightful to witness. I remember that, when the one at La Foce was opened (its walls painted in gay colours and adorned with pictures and maps) we found the pupils, of their own accord, taking off their muddy boots before coming in, so as not to sully the shining floors. (We then provided them with warm slippers to wear indoors.) We also built three small nursery-schools with playgrounds, two in villages across the valley, where many of the women went out to work all day, and one at La Foce, which later turned into the Home for children bombed out of their homes in Genoa and Turin, the *Casa dei Bambini* described in *War in Val d'Orcia*.

The schools were followed by a men's club with a bowling-green and a general shop beside it and, in 1933, in memory of our son Gianni—who had died the year before—we built what we had come to feel was one of the most urgent needs of the region: a small dispensary or *ambulatorio*, with an operating-room, a steriliser, four beds for emergency cases, a small stock of infant foods and indispensable medicines, and a flat upstairs for a resident district nurse. The panel doctor from Chianciano (five miles away) came twice a week, and soon his waiting-room was crowded. The nurse also supervised the school-children's health, but perhaps the most useful of her tasks was her visits to the farms—often forestalling, by timely advice, the outbreak of an epidemic—giving injections, sometimes (but not often) opening windows, persuading young mothers to move their babies from the centre of their double beds into small wicker cribs or baskets, and often, when the midwife or doctor arrived too late, helping a difficult delivery or bringing what relief she could to a death-bed. The *ambulatorio* beds, too, were often filled—by accident cases, expectant mothers, or convalescent children—and, in addition, the nurse held elementary courses in hygiene for girls and young mothers. Later on, during the war (but this, of course, we did not then foresee) the *ambulatorio* also fulfilled another purpose: a wounded partisan had a bullet extracted there, another with tuberculosis was nursed during the last weeks of his life and, when an epidemic of virus pneumonia broke out among the partisans hidden in the hill-farms, Signorina Guidetti went secretly at night to nurse them.

By the time that all these buildings were completed, in 1934, we had been at La Foce for ten years: it had become our home. During those years our financial position had been suddenly changed by the death of a distant American cousin, whom I had never seen and of whom I had only heard as an eccentric elderly miser, who, having gone to live abroad 'to disoblige his family', had spent his last years in a yacht off the coast of the Isle of Wight, amusing himself (so the legend said) by throwing red-hot coppers into the boat of such solicitous relations as attempted to visit him. He did, however, go to London twice a year to visit his broker—and to some purpose, since the sum which was eventually divided among his surviving cousins was extremely substantial, and enabled us to carry out all the work I have described above much more speedily and thoroughly than would otherwise have been possible.

I shall, however, always be glad that this money did not come to us at once, and that we were obliged, in the first years of our marriage, to count every penny and make some personal sacrifice. Not only did this save us from many mistakes, but it gave a certain basic reality to our efforts. We felt this even at the time— indeed, on the evening on which the news of our change of fortune reached us, Antonio and I were walking up and down the pergola at the end of the day's work, discussing whether or not his birthday present to me should be a handsome but expensive umbrella which we had seen in a Florentine shop. I pointed out that it would be a great extravagance, since I would certainly lose it; he retorted that I might learn to be more careful—the discussion being only brought to an end by the cable's arrival. When we had read it and had assimilated its contents, it was with real regret in his voice that Antonio said: 'I don't suppose we shall ever argue about buying an umbrella again!'

*   *   *   *   *

Meanwhile—for I have now reached the years between 1935 and 1940—the clouds were gathering all over Europe, and even in our secluded life at La Foce it became impossible not to observe, read, listen and speculate. I read *Mein Kampf*; I read (as well as hearing) Mussolini's speeches; I read Rauschning's *Hitler Speaks** (at that time a very enlightening book to me) and, later on, Fromm's *Escape from Freedom*.† I began at last to read the daily papers and to join the wide captive audience, all the world over, listening to confused, discordant voices coming out of a little box. Not enough has been said, I think, in accounts of our times (since one is always apt to disregard what has come to be taken for granted) about the psychological changes brought about in uninformed civilians by the mere existence of the radio. Never before in history had so many ears been battered by so many voices. Gradually, as I sat before our radio in the library at La Foce, trying to reconcile their messages and sift the small kernel of truth, these voices became for me the true echo of our times. Previously, non-combatants had been, for the most part, only aware of what the Press of their own country told them, or what they saw with their own eyes. Now, we were all constantly exposed to these confusing, overwhelming waves, from friends and enemies alike. Far more than the whistle and crash of falling shells later on, or the dull roar of bomber formations overhead, this cacophony represents my personal nightmare of the years before and during the war. Hitler's voice with its hysterical screams and the roars of applause that greeted them; Dollfuss's voice, shortly before his assassination, followed by the promise of his personal friend Mussolini, to support the independence of Austria‡ and then, two years later, at the time of the *Anschluss*, that same friend's exclamation: "What obligations have we towards Austria? None!"§ Anthony Eden's voice, urging the League of Nations, if Italy invaded Abyssinia, to a policy of sanctions, and Mussolini's retort, *"L'Italia farà da sè!"*‖ A voice from France, announcing the murder of the Rosselli brothers. Churchill's voice, declaring that "it is not only Czechoslovakia which is menaced, but also the freedom of the democracy of all nations"—and, only a few weeks later, Neville Chamberlain proclaiming "Peace with honour . . . peace in our time."¶ Starace's voice, announcing the decision of the Fascist Grand Council to leave the League of

* *Hitler Speaks*, a record of political conversations with Hitler in 1933 and 34, by Hermann Rauschning (author of *Germany's Revolution of Destruction*), London, 1939.

† *Escape from Freedom* by Erich Fromm, New York, 1941.

‡ Milan, November 1, 1936.

§ March 6, 1938.　　　　　‖ May 7, 1936.　　　　　¶ Sept. 30, 1938.

Nations. The voices of soldiers and children, singing the songs of the time:

> *Dell'Italia nei confini*
> *Son rinati gli Italiani*
> *Li ha rifatti Mussolini*
> *Per la guerra di domani*

and

> *Duce, Duce, chi non saprà morir?**

It is difficult to convey the cumulative impact of these voices, as we sat alone in the library of our isolated country-house day after day, and the increasing sense that they brought of inevitable, imminent catastrophe, of the Juggernaut approach of war.

During those years I was still paying frequent visits to England, and there I naturally met, both some ardent supporters of the pacifist movement, in particular its leader, Max Plowman, a man of such transparent goodness and good faith as almost—but not entirely—to convert me to his views, and the writers and journalists who had volunteered to fight in Spain against Franco, and had returned with varying degrees of disillusionment. (I still think George Orwell's *War in Catalonia* the best account of that confused and disturbing time.) I also, through Lilian Bowes Lyon and some Quaker friends, was able to share the efforts of some people who, already then, were devoting their energies to enabling a few Jewish scholars, old people and children, to make their escape from Germany before it was too late. In particular, there was a little school in Kent—largely run by means of Quaker contributions—in which Jewish refugee children from Germany (and soon also from Austria and Czechoslovakia) were brought up in a new-found security and serenity, as citizens of the United Europe of the future.† Some of them, I remember, gave a highly spirited performance of *The Magic Flute* in the Chapter House of Canterbury Cathedral.

A good many of these children—especially those living as

---

* 'Within the frontiers of Italy, the Italians are born anew, Mussolini has created them for the war of tomorrow' and 'Duce, Duce, who will not know how to die?'

† This was New Herrlingen School, at Bunce Court, Faversham, in Kent, of which the creator was Miss Anne Essinger.

guests in well-meaning but wholly alien, ultra-British families—
were almost ill with homesickness and, among the older ones,
with anxiety for their parents and their brothers and sisters who
had not come with them. I have never been able to forget the
description given to me by one of the Quaker workers in Germany of the agony of mind of the parents obliged to make a
choice, when they were told (as was sometimes necessary) that
only one child from each family could go. Should it be the most
brilliant or the most vulnerable? the one most fitted, or least
likely, to survive? Which, if it were one's own child, would one
choose?

The passage from the world of friends concerned with such
activities and ideas, and the atmosphere still prevailing in Italy
became, whenever I came home, increasingly confusing and distressing. I have a disproportionately vivid memory of a telephone
conversation with a woman whom I scarcely knew. She and I
had been asked to send a nominal invitation to an old Czecho-
slovak professor and his wife, which would enable them to get
a transit visa through Italy and thus escape from Prague and
rejoin their sons in England. "I suppose you've done nothing
about this preposterous request?" she asked. "Did you have a
telegram, too?" I said I had. "I can't think what came over the
woman! She's my husband's cousin, not mine; I don't know her
and never want to. Why, she might have got *us* into trouble!"
I said that I thought that was hardly likely, and that it really was
a hard case: the professor and his wife were old and ill, longing
to join their sons, their only chance, but that, in any case, she
need take no further trouble over it. "Trouble! I should think
not, indeed! I sent back a pretty firm wire. I have no sympathy
with such people. Why didn't they get out months ago, when
their sons ran away? And I don't believe they're really Catholics:
the name doesn't sound like it!" An unpleasant undertone in
her voice made me cautious. "Well, anyway, *I* won't lift a
finger to help such people. Those are the cases that get taken
up by interfering, hysterical Englishwomen, like that woman who
says she's a friend of yours." I said that Lilian Bowes Lyon was
one of my greatest friends, and rang off. But a few minutes later
the telephone rang again; this time the woman's voice was sharp
with curiosity. "You didn't say what *you* are doing about it!

Now remember, this isn't a neutral country. You've no right to risk getting your husband into trouble. Why, it's the sort of thing one would hardly do for a member of one's own family!" Swallowing my anger—which was the sharper for being mixed with a mean little twinge of uneasiness—I hedged, and then, having rung off, sat on the edge of my bed, trembling. The ugly trivial conversation seemed to have a disproportionate importance: it seemed to symbolise all the cowardly, self-protective, arrogant cruelty of the world—our world.

In August, 1939, I drove up with Antonio to Switzerland, for what proved to be our last trip abroad for six years, in order to attend the concerts conducted by Bruno Walter and Toscanini in Lucerne. The day of our arrival was over-shadowed by a typical tragedy of our times. Bruno Walter's daughter, who had married a young Bavarian Nazi some years before, had moved to Switzerland after the intensification of the Jewish persecution, and was visited there occasionally by her husband. Gradually they had drifted apart, but on the preceding day, he had flown down to Zürich to meet her, and to make a last effort to persuade her to return to Germany with him. When she refused (her sister was in a concentration camp, and many others of her relations and friends were dead or imprisoned) he shot her with his revolver, and then himself.

On that evening the concert was conducted, in Bruno Walter's stead, by Toscanini, and the programme concluded with *Götterdämmerung*. The audience filed out in a grim, sad silence, and when we got back to the hotel the late evening news announced the Non-Aggression Pact between Germany and Russia. We all realised its implications.

The next morning, the hotel emptied swiftly—the guests leaving hurriedly for their respective countries. I put through a last telephone call to England, then climbed into the car and drove off with Antonio towards the Italian frontier. My diary brings back very vividly my feelings on that day as, after driving up the green, trim little Swiss valleys and lunching on *truite au bleu* at Martigny, we climbed up the Simplon pass and crossed the frontier. There, sitting beside the customs office, we watched an Italian car which had driven up a few minutes before, being turned back and sent home again.

"No more Italians jaunting abroad now!" said the *carabiniere* with a friendly grin, as he handed back our passports. "Come in, and stay in!"

The pole of the barrier swung slowly back behind us. I realised that I had made my choice.

But even after this, it was curiously difficult to persuade the Italian man-in-the-street that war, real war, was coming. "You'll see," said a taxi-driver, "the Duce will stop at the last moment. He has never made a mistake yet." We spent a few days in Florence, hanging about waiting for news, and hearing nothing but wild rumours—that an Italian division had been sent from Bologna to Nüremberg—why Nüremberg? That the Duce had had a stroke—that the mysterious passenger that landed in England was Mussolini himself, no, Beck, no, Grandi. There was not even the faintest pretence of martial ardour. 'It is,' as a young officer of our acquaintance wrote to his mother, 'a nonchalant and cold vigil.'

When we got home, we found that two of the *fattoria* employees had been called up, and several of the farmers' sons. They were all very upset, but still did not realise that it was anything worse than Abyssinia or Spain. "We've had enough of this," was the refrain, "*ora basta*. We only ask to be left alone." We walked from farm to farm on a still, lovely summer's evening; the grapes ripening, the oxen ploughing. Still blindly they believed: 'It won't come to a real war: the Duce will get us out of it somehow.'

Two days later we went round the farms again. Everywhere the older people came hurrying out to meet us, everywhere the same question: "What do you say, *sor padrone*? Will there be war?" From each family, by now, at least one man had been called up: "My Cecco went yesterday; Assunta's Beppe had his card this morning. *Madonnina bona*, what's going to happen? Who's going to work the farm?"

On September 3, Antonio and I drove up to visit some friends in a village in the Apennines, and in the villages on the way we saw little groups of recruits and women in tears. Then, as we reached our friends' house, one of the sons came down to meet us: "Chamberlain's speech is just over. War is declared." An hour later the speech was repeated, and all the evening we sat beside the radio, listening to one country after another: Europe moving towards war. I found myself remembering, as many people of my generation must have remembered in England, Grey's famous phrase in 1914, 'The lamps are going out all over Europe.' When would they be lit again?

After the invasion of Poland—overcome by an almost unbearable sense of frustration at my own inaction and uselessness—I went to Rome to see whether there was any organisation whatever in which I could do some form of war work. But I found all doors securely closed. 'The country's delicate position—the Vatican's delicate position . . .' I did meet the head of the Polish Institute in Rome, who had been in his youth one of Pilsudski's legionaries, a tragic and embittered figure, but there was nothing I could do in Italy to help his compatriots, and when an American Relief Mission—headed by Senator Walcott, who had worked with President Hoover on a similar mission some twenty years before—came to the American Embassy in Rome, on their way to Warsaw, I implored the Ambassador* to ask them to take me with them in any capacity whatsoever. In the same week I discovered that, after seven years of childlessness, I was pregnant. Reluctantly, and feeling more and more useless and cut off, I went back to La Foce.

During the next months—until on June 10, 1940, German pressure caused Italy, too, to enter the war—I found much comfort in seeing, at Montepulciano, the small group of anti-Fascists who gathered together in the house of our friend and neighbour, Margherita Bracci. Her husband was an old friend and brotherofficer of my husband's, and Margherita herself—the daughter of the historian and writer, Francesco Papafava—belonged to an old Paduan family which had always preserved a fine tradition of Liberal thought and feeling. Many of their friends, in the early years of Fascism, had been imprisoned or sent into exile, while most of those who were still in Italy had retired from public life or (often at great personal sacrifice) had resigned from their jobs, and were living in a closed, semi-conspiratorial circle, seeing only the small group of people who shared their opinions and hopes, often embittered and factious, but firmly clinging to their principles and determined to come to no compromise with any aspect

---

* The American Ambassador in Rome, William Phillips, had been my father's closest friend and was my godfather.

of the regime they hated and despised, and which, they were convinced, would lead their country to destruction.

It was with these friends, and with a few others like them in Rome, that I could speak most freely; and yet I remember sometimes coming away from an evening in their company, during which the conversation had the heightened intensity peculiar to minorities under authoritarian governments, with a sense of discouragement. 'One feels,' I wrote after one of these occasions, 'yes, these are enlightened, high-principled, courageous people, but they are not, as yet, of any *importance*. It is not through them that any change will come.'

I think now that I was mistaken. If I felt a certain sense of unreality in these conversations, it was of course not because this handful of people was not yet able to change the course of events: it was rather because many of them, in their allegiance to an already old-fashioned form of Liberalism, did not see the Fascism they rejected as the glorification of the bourgeosie which it had already become, but rather naïvely took it at its own face value as a true revolutionary movement, and were also still cut off from the other new political trends in the country which, after the Liberation, swiftly took on a definite shape. All the same, the conversations that then seemed to me unrealistic or sterile were a token that all over Italy there were still men and women whom Fascism had not numbed into conformity. It was they who kept alive the clandestine anti-Fascist press, who kept in touch with foreign books and (when possible) foreign friends, and who fostered the increasing pressure of public opinion which paved the way for the fall of Fascism. Some of them, later on, played an active part in the Resistance movement, others exerted an influence in Court circles at the time of the first negotiations with the Allies, and yet others—when Mussolini had formed the 'Republic of Salò' in the north—made their way to the south and joined the Allied forces or formed part of the temporary government in the south or the Committees of Liberation in their respective cities. But I now think that their most important action was in those early, unrewarding years, when many of them lay in prison in Lipari or were confined to remote mountain villages, but still kept alive an incorruptible, unswerving vision of freedom.

Meanwhile, day by day, it was becoming clearer that Italy's

La Foce

entry into the conflict could not be delayed much longer. After the Brenner meeting between Hitler and Mussolini, the invasion of Norway and that of Belgium and Holland, Italy's solidarity with the Axis was no longer a matter of choice. I succeeded, with some difficulty, in obtaining visas for Switzerland for my mother and step-father, and was entrusted with the valuables and belongings of some other English people who were leaving or who feared to be sent to concentration camps. On June 7, 1940, the first outer sign of war reached the Val d'Orcia: a formation of 35 Allied bombers flew over us, heading south. On the 10th, we woke to the news that the Germans were within 40 miles of Paris. At midday an order came from the Fascio of Chianciano to summon all our farmers at five that evening to listen to a speech by the Duce. We installed our radio in the loggia in front of the house, which gives on to the garden, and they all slowly filed in. By five o'clock we were all there: Antonio and myself and Schwester Marie Blaser, the children's Swiss nurse, Flavia and Gogo della Gherardesca, who were staying with us, the *fattore* and all his employees, the schoolteachers, the household, and about eighty *contadini* and workmen. "*Attenzione!*" brayed the loud-speaker, "*Attenzione!*" I looked at the listening faces, grave, expectant, anxious. "At six o'clock the Duce will speak to the assembled Italian people from the balcony of Palazzo Venezia." Then the *Marcia Reale*, and the Fascist song, *Giovinezza*. Nearly an hour more to wait. The tense faces relaxed, the crowd broke up into little groups. The older men stood under the ilex tree, talking in low voices; some settled down on the loggia steps: some had brought a loaf of bread or a flask of wine and passed it round; one group sat in a circle on the gravel, playing cards. Antonio and the keepers talked about the young partridges and the twin calves born that morning. I joined the school-teachers, to discuss how many evacuated children we could put up, if necessary, in the schools. I went indoors again: a bowl of delphiniums and lupins took me back for a moment to an English garden. A whiff of jasmine blew in through the window. It was all curiously unreal. Then again: "*Attenzione, attenzione!*" The men got to their feet, coming closer. We heard the shouts of the crowd in Piazza Venezia, the cheering and the bands and then (presumably because the scene was also being relayed to a German

233

station) a harsh, guttural voice speaking German. At the foreign, unpopular sound the men's faces became blank and faintly hostile. Antonio made a joke (I couldn't hear what) and they all laughed. Then deafening cheers from the radio, presumably as Mussolini appeared on the balcony—and then his unmistakable voice: *"Combattenti di terra, di mare, dell'aria*, Blackshirts of the Revolution and of the Legions, men and women of Italy, of the Empire and of Albania, listen. An hour marked by destiny is crossing our country's sky: the hour of an irrevocable decision. The Italian declaration of war has already been handed to the ambassadors of Great Britain and France . . . People of Italy, hasten to arms and show your tenacity, your courage and your valour."

I glanced again at the listening faces. They wore the closed, blank look that is the last defence of those who cannot argue or oppose. Impossible to tell how much they had taken in or what they felt—except that it was not enthusiasm. The speech went on, touching the same old themes: Italy's imprisonment in the Mediterranean, sanctions, the war of the poor against the rich, of the young against the decadent. Mussolini affirmed, too, that Italy had done "all that was possible to avert the storm". But somehow none of it carried. The speaker's voice was loud, strained; the applause, even from Piazza Venezia, sounded forced, very different from that which had greeted last year's speeches about Abyssinia or even at the time of Munich. Then at last it was over; there was a silence. Antonio said, *"Saluto al Re! Viva l'Italia!"* The men reacted automatically, limply. We heard their feet crunching on the gravel as they left, in silence, and we went back into the house and stood looking at each other. "Well, it's come," said Antonio. "I'm going out to look at the wheat." But who will be there for the harvest?

It was really only then, I think, that I fully faced the problem of divided loyalties which confronts every woman whose marriage has placed her in a country at war with her own. (In my case, within two months, the countries of both my parents.) As to behaviour, of course, the matter is very simple: she should obey the laws of her husband's country and keep quiet. But in feelings and principles? In a land which was itself swayed by so many different currents of opinion, was it indeed necessary to identify oneself with the majority? I decided that, for the time being, all that was demanded of me was to try to keep as steady as possible, to close my ears to alarming rumours and my heart to nostalgia and dismay. 'If England is invaded tomorrow', I wrote then, 'I shall certainly not know how much of what I hear is true. All that I can try to do is to foster within myself something that is not merely fear, resentment or bewilderment. Perhaps it might be useful to try to clear my mind by setting down, as truthfully and simply as I can, the tiny facet of the world's events which I myself, in the months ahead, shall encounter at first hand. It will not be, I know, an unprejudiced account; and my prejudices will probably have many causes that I cannot at present even foresee; but at least it may help me to preserve a thread of serenity and hope.'

This was the starting-point of a detailed diary which I kept during the next few months (until my work in Rome left me no free time), and then began again in 1943–44, when the war came to La Foce, and of which the latter part was published later on, entitled *War in Val d'Orcia*.

It was the first months that were the hardest. A few weeks after Italy's entry into the war, having been seized by premature labour pains, I went down to our nearest station, Chiusi, to catch the first train to Rome. The trains were all, of course, overflowing with troops, but the kind owner of the station bar, an old friend, tried to reassure me by pointing out that the next one passing through still had a dining-car: "If necessary, the baby can be born there." I was not much attracted by this prospect, but agreed that it would be preferable to standing in the passage. My baby, however, was so considerate as to delay its arrival, and when at last we reached Rome, we were whisked off, in almost embarrassing comfort and splendour, in the American Embassy's car to the beautiful house and solicitous care of my godfather who, though his wife and staff had already gone home, was still waiting for orders from Washington to leave himself. I ended, indeed, by considerably overstaying my welcome, since the baby delayed for three more weeks, and the Ambassador was obliged to leave before I had moved to the nursing-home in which, on August 1, my daughter Benedetta was born.

It was a strange period of waiting, knowing that one was about to bring a new life into such a very unstable world. The Roman summer, with the streets half-empty and the black-out at night, was more beautiful than I had ever seen it, and we would dine out at night under the ilex trees of the Villa Taverna, shimmering with fireflies, sometimes hearing the sirens and distant bursts of gunfire of the, as yet, most unalarming air-raids, and wondering each evening what the next day would bring. On July 8 the return of seven hundred Italians from London, headed by the Italian Ambassador Bastianini, in the *Monarch of Bermuda* (a ship described by the travellers as both filthy and ill-equipped) gave rise to a fresh wave of anti-English feeling. At a lunch party a few days later I heard, in impotent exasperation and disbelief, Bastianini describing the decadence and softness which had overtaken the English people (as exemplified by *il weekend inglese*). They had lost, he declared, any capacity for patriotism and self-sacrifice (this had been Ribbentrop's mistake, too) and would never be able to stand up against a German attack. "*Non vi sono più rimaste che le qualità che non rendono.*"* "But surely they still have some courage?" one guest enquired. "*Anche il coraggio, da sola, è una qualità che non rende.*"† At the end our hostess rose, saying brightly, "Yes, you must be right, England is done for."

Had I trusted myself to speak, I could have supplied at least one small piece of evidence that did not point in the same direction. In the preceding weeks, when it was becoming plain that the invasion was a real danger and the radio had said that some English children were being sent away from danger areas to stay with friends in America, I asked my relations there whether they, too, would find a temporary home for some children of close English friends. They at once sent the warmest of invitations; but when I transmitted it, the parents, in each case, refused. 'It is not a reasoned refusal, perhaps,' wrote one father, 'but the feeling that we can't leave this country even vicariously proceeds out of some mysterious depths and is beyond the reach of reason. Though there are cogent reasons for removing children from any sort of danger of coming into contact with war, it must also be admitted that we think we are going to win.' And in a later letter he added, 'I know you entirely understand that our refusal has nothing to do with the very happy life that I know they would

* "The only qualities left to them are those that don't pay."
† "Even courage, by itself, is a quality that doesn't pay."

lead there, and I think it would be selfish merely to fear separation. It comes nearer, perhaps, to being an act of faith.'

A good many other people, I think, felt as he did, and, as the
menace of invasion receded and the long years of war dragged on,
I do not think there was one parent who regretted his choice;
while I have often seen, after the return of the children who *did*
go—happy as they were with their American hosts and deeply
as they remained devoted to them—that they yet felt as if they had
somehow been cheated of something more important than even
security or happiness.

During my week in the nursing-home I listened to the news of
the Battle of Britain on the little radio concealed under my
pillow, and read and re-read the last letters from England which
still reached me. ('We have been', wrote my aunt from London,
'like Brunnhilde, in a circle of fire, but nothing to upset one.')
Then I went back to La Foce and, within a few months, was so
fortunate as to find, in spite of my Anglo-American origins and
my non-adherence to the Fascist party, a job in the Prisoners of
War office of the Italian Red Cross in Rome, where I worked for
the next two years.

This office, which came to perform a large and important role,
operated within an extremely cumbersome and complicated framework. Its President was an old Italian general, Generale Clerici;
its Secretary-General was Elsa Dallolio, the founder of the Italian
Branch of the International Social Service, whose work was
amalgamated with that for prisoners of war; and its staff consisted,
on the one hand, of Red Cross military personnel, rightly considered unfit for active service, and on the other of an awkward
mixture of civilian volunteers and regular employees. The volunteers, of whom I was one, were well-meaning, untrained, and very
unevenly efficient; the professional secretaries and typists knew
their jobs but (with a few notable exceptions) kept strictly to their
regular office hours; the military staff had no knowledge of any
language but their own, and were unaccustomed to any form of
office work. That this strange amalgam of human beings should
have managed to do any work at all; that, roughly speaking, the
organisation of the camps of the Allied prisoners of war in Italy
did work; that the men received their mail and their parcels and
that, on the other hand, news of the Italian troops in Allied

hands did reach their families, was a tribute to the devoted work of the heads of the various sections, and of a few people who worked immediately with them, particularly of Conte Umberto Morra, the head of the section for Allied p.o.w's who was also the Italian representative on the Commission of the International Red Cross which inspected the Allied prisoners' camps in Italy, and of Elsa Dallolio herself. Umberto's tact and humour were as useful in these tasks as his thorough knowledge of the English language and of the English character, while it was Elsa who, without ever moving from the big table weighed down with files in her little office, somehow managed to keep the whole creaking machinery in constant motion, with the minimum of friction, strain or fuss. Permanently overworked, harassed by a hundred major and minor problems, torn by an intense personal compassion for the human suffering involved, she yet managed to preserve an atmosphere of quiet, humorous serenity, which steadied everyone who saw her; and whenever there was a disagreeable or painful task to be done, it was she—at an inner cost which she kept to herself—who took it on. What she said to the weeping, hysterical women who, after days or weeks of waiting, were at last called up to her office to receive some news—sometimes the worst, sometimes merely the announcement that they must go on waiting—I have never known. But day after day, I have seen them come out again, sometimes weeping still, but no longer despairing.

The building in which we worked—a sequestrated school—was ill-furnished, unheated, and very unsuited to its new purpose. The working hours were from 8 a.m. to 2 p.m., but most of the heads of sections and some of the volunteers would come back again for the afternoon, to sort and censor the mail, and to go on deciphering and translating the interminable lists of Italian dead, wounded or missing which would arrive after any major Allied advance, such as that in North Africa. I can still see the wide entrance halls packed with the silent, anxious mob of wives and mothers, waiting for the news that we were feverishly deciphering upstairs. Names and birthplaces dictated by illiterate Sardinian or Calabrian peasant-boys to overworked Allied officials with only a slight knowledge of Italian, or none, often arrived in so incomprehensible a form that we had to ask for them to be repeated.

And when, on the same list, some thirty Luigi Rossis (the Italian equivalent of John Smith) appeared—some dead, some missing and some captured—it was not until the most careful checking of their birthplaces, dates of birth and parents' names, that any news whatever could be given out.

At one time, I was working in the section for the Italian dead and wounded in which, in addition to the lists, our main task was the reading and translating of the hospital chaplains' letters which accompanied the meagre little parcels of personal effects returned with his identity disk to a dead soldier's family: the children's photographs, the wedding group, the first Communion medal; sometimes a creased letter to '*mio amato sposo*' or '*mio caro papà*'; a postcard of his home town, a rosary, a good-luck charm. The chaplains' letters were then translated and the little parcel was sent off, with a brief letter of condolence, to the soldier's family. Never could I get accustomed to writing those stereotyped letters; never could I teach myself not to imagine the faces of those who would read them.

I worked in this office (with brief week-ends at La Foce, when possible) for nearly two years until, in the autumn of 1942, I was again pregnant and had to go back to La Foce. There, to my surprise, I found plenty to do, but I do not propose to describe this period in any detail here, since I have already done so in *War in Val d'Orcia*.

When I got home, I realised that there was scarcely a farm on the place which had not got some of its men fighting, in Africa, Russia or Greece, or else interned in some remote prisoners' camp. Their wives and mothers hurried to meet me, asking why those who had been sent to Russia had never written, or those stranded in Greece and deported to Germany were always asking for food. What could I tell them? I helped them to fill in the postcard forms for their replies, or the requests for news through the International Red Cross in Geneva and to address their pathetic parcels of home-baked biscuits, cheese and ham, well knowing how unlikely it was that any answer would come back. I tried to give an encouraging answer to their question, "But when will it all come to an end?" Then we settled down, like many others, to listen to the radio, to surmise, and to wait.

One good thing that this period brought about was unforeseen: a closer relationship with our tenants and our neighbours. The men of the Val d'Orcia had paid lip-service to Fascism in so far as its laws were favourable to agriculture; and when, in spite of their conviction that the Duce would somehow keep them out of the war, they discovered that they, too, were to be involved, their surprise was very soon coloured by an indignation which turned into a more positive, active resentment, embracing both the Fascists and the Germans, and producing a kind of local solidarity, a drawing together to meet common dangers and common needs.

After the fall of Mussolini in 1943, the country people enjoyed a few hours of hope for peace, but it soon became clear that the Fascists had only left us in the hands of harder and tougher masters, the Germans. It was then that at La Foce (as, I expect, in many other country places) we drew together into a tight little community, like a small rural society in time of war in the Middle Ages. For food we were almost entirely self-supporting (not only for ourselves, but for the twenty-three refugee children from Turin and Genoa who had come to live in the *Casa dei Bambini*); for fuel we used, besides the small rations of lignite, our own wood and the kernels of our olives. We made our own soap, spun our own wool, and occasionally, in secret, killed a calf and had its hide tanned for leather. We ran our car, until the Germans took it away, on charcoal from our woods. Then, after the armistice of September 8, when the Val d'Orcia was suddenly filled with liberated Allied prisoners of war who were trying to avoid the Germans and rejoin their own armies, as well as with Italian soldiers from disbanded regiments who were making their way back to their own homes, innumerable problems brought us all still closer together. It was the inhabitants in the more remote farms (our house was too close to the main road and too frequently inspected by the Germans, to be a safe hiding-place) who housed and fed the Allied prisoners on the run, with a courage and generosity beyond all praise. When, later on, groups of partisans, including some Allied prisoners of war, came to live in our woods and in some of the farms up the hill, they were joined by local young men who wished to avoid being called up to fight on the German side. It was our ox carts which took up wheat and wine to them; it was the local cobbler who (without asking any questions) re-soled the boots of the Allied soldiers on their way south; it was one of our foremen who, when the Germans came in a lorry to capture some Allied ex-prisoners working in a field, gave them the pre-arranged signal to scatter and escape; it was the partisans living in one of our farms on the edge of a beech-wood at the top of the hill who, when a threatening article in a local paper pointed me out by name as a person who should be deported to Germany, suggested that I should go into hiding with them. For several months, I slept with a small suitcase beside my bed, ready to start, and a back-door open towards the woods.

So, at last, the old barriers of tradition and class were broken down, and we were held together by the same difficulties, fears, expectations and hopes. 'Together', as I then wrote in my diary 'we planned how to hide the oil, the hams and the cheeses, so that the Germans should not find them; together we found shelter for the fugitives who knocked at our door—whether Italians, Allies or Jews, soldiers or civilians—together we watched the first bombs fall on the bridges of the Val d'Orcia, and listened hopefully for the rumours of landings in Tuscany which never came.' And together—when the Germans had turned us out of the cellar which had become our air-raid shelter and had obliged us to walk to Montepulciano with all the refugee children and our own, as well as three new-born babies—we came home, after the Allies' arrival, to bury the corpses in the woods and farms, to reap the harvest, to remove the mines still concealed in the woods and fields and in our own front garden, and to rebuild the shattered farms.

It was on that day that we found in our front hall, which lay open, like the rest of the house, to the winds and, still worse, to the flies, a welcome and moving surprise which at the time, perhaps because it seemed too personal, I did not write about in my diary. We had expected, when we left, to find our house destroyed by shell-fire, but instead found no more serious damage than a few large holes in the roof, the cutting-off of water and of light (this lasted for many months), the removal or destruction of any window-pane or door, a few bullet-holes in books and pictures, and an all-pervading stench of excrement and refuse.

But on the hall-table, intact but for a few mud-stains, lay a copy
of the book which, after the death of our son Gianni, I had
written as a private record of his short life, illustrated by many
photographs, and of which a few copies had been printed for
relations and close friends. On the flyleaf a pencilled note told
me that this book had been found in the woods (left there by the
Moroccan troops with the Fifth Army, the Goums, who had
ransacked everything they could lay hands on) by an English
soldier, who 'realising that it must be of great sentimental value'
had obtained permission to walk back many miles with it, so that
we might find it when we came home. This piece of imaginative
kindness, at such a moment, was so consoling as to outweigh
every other loss. If, by any chance, this page should ever meet the
eyes of this friend, I should like it to take him my belated, but
undimmed, gratitude.

On the day of our return, Antonio, by request of the *Comitato
di Liberazione* (a committee set up in most Italian cities by members of the Resistance before the arrival of the Allies, as a pro-
visional local government), became the Mayor of Chianciano and,
in collaboration with the representatives of the Allied Military
Government, dealt with the local problems there: the refugees
from the south who clamoured to be sent home at once, the lack
of light, water, sugar, salt, soap, medical supplies, Diesel oil,
petrol transportation. Of our own farmhouses, two were a heap
of ruins, and in many others only one or two rooms had still
got a roof. In one of them thirteen people were sleeping in two
beds; in another the whole family slept on the stable floor. All
had lost their dearly-prized furniture, their linen, their blankets,
their clothes, and above all their cooking-pots, since the Goums
had looted everything that the Germans had not already taken
away. Everywhere the most urgent problem, as soon as the harvest
was in, was to get a roof on to at least part of each farm before
the winter, and this was achieved. The other most urgent problem
was health, since, owing to the number of unburied corpses,
both of men and beasts, and the multitude of flies, an epidemic
of gastro-enteritis and dysentery had broken out, especially among
the children. There was little water and no light (this lasted for
the whole following winter) and the woods and fields were still
strewn with mines. Yet our prevailing feeling was one of gratitude

and hope. 'Destruction and death have visited us,' I wrote on the last page of my diary, 'but now, there is hope in the air.'

*   *   *   *   *

Many questions have since been asked me about those years— some of which I have been able to answer, at least to myself. One of them is, was I much afraid? The answer is no, except for one single moment of panic. This is odd, for I have generally been quite easily frightened. As a child, I had all the usual childish fears; of strangers, of other children, of the unfamiliar and of the dark: when expecting my first baby, I incurred the contempt of Antonio's family doctor (a bluff, kindly man who expected me to be overjoyed) by my ill-concealed dread of labour pains, which eventually I found much less bad than I had expected; after my uncle's death in an air-crash, I was for several years terrified of flying. But during the last months before our liberation, we were really too busy, and too much interested, to be afraid. This was partly owing to the continuousness and variety of the demands upon our resourcefulness. Twenty-three refugee children, in the last months, moved into our own house and had to be fed, clothed, instructed and amused; hiding-places and food had to be found, not only for partisans and escaped p.o.w's but also for Jews who had fled from the larger cities; German officers who came to sequestrate cars, tyres, horses and houses, etc. had to be dealt with (this was Antonio's job, sometimes at the same moment as I was giving a map, a compass or a pair of socks to a fugitive Allied soldier on the other side of the house, or up the hill). Later on, as the Front came closer, we moved down to the cottage hospital, from the farmhouse where he had been in hiding, a young partisan who was so obviously dying that we felt the risk of his discovery by the Germans to be a secondary considera-tion. And in the last weeks, after the food situation in Rome had become serious, there was a constant stream of people who had got lifts on army lorries to beg in the country for a little flour, oil or a sack of potatoes for hungry children or sick relatives in town. There were appeals for help from the families of men who had been taken as hostages by the Germans, or who had been condemned to be shot because their villages had sheltered or helped the partisans, or from refugee families from south of

243

Images and Shadows

Rome, or from mothers whose sons had been taken off to Germany for *Arbeitsdienst*. Our problems then, as I wrote in my diary at the time, 'arose from a continual necessity to weigh in the balance not courage and cowardice, or right and wrong, but conflicting duties and responsibilities equally urgent . . . Moreover these were problems which, since the local situation was often fluctuating according to changes in the military situation and the arrival of different officials, could never be solved once for all: every day each incident had to be met on its own merits. At the end of each day prudence inquired, "Have I done too much?" and enthusiasm or compassion, "Might I not, perhaps, have done more?" '

With regard to my own children, I was not unduly anxious, having a blind confidence that (if Antonio or I should be shot or deported) Schwester Marie would somehow see them through. But I did have, in connection with the younger one, Donata, one instant of blind panic. This was when, after having been turned out of our cellar and having trudged through the mined woods, with all the children and some old people, towards Montepulciano, we came to some open fields which were being shelled, and Antonio, who was carrying Donata (aged eighteen months) on his shoulders, walked ahead, to a part of the field which seemed to me to be more exposed. I ran across to him, blind with fear, saying furiously, "What are you doing with that child? Give her back to me!" He merely smiled indulgently, saying, "We're just as safe here as anywhere else," and walked on, while I recovered my senses. Except in hospitals, before operations, I have never been afraid since.

I have also been asked what, after twenty-five years, is my most vivid and painful memory of that time. This is a more complicated question to answer, but I think that my predominant memory of the war years, for myself and others, can be summed up in a single word: parting. Bombs, shell-fire, mines, the unpleasantness, after Mussolini's fall, of being in an 'Occupied' country, the long periods of waiting, the sense of isolation—all these have left no painful mark: they were just immediate, and sometimes exciting, problems. But the parting of people who love each other and are separated, whether endured oneself or witnessed in others— mothers and sons, husbands and wives, lovers, friends—without

244

news or only with uncertain news, with alternating fears and hopes, this belongs to the category of pain that is never wiped out, that leaves a permanent scar. '*Ayez pitié de ceux qui s'aimaient et ont été séparés*'—this was the first supplication in the prayer composed by the Abbé Perreyve and which Madame Jean de Marmol, who died in a German concentration camp, used to recite every evening with her fellow-prisoners. '*Ayez pitié.*'

These were the memories that began to haunt me, as soon as the need for immediate action came to an end and the Allied armies moved on towards Florence. By then news from English relations and friends was beginning to reach me, through Allied officers passing through Tuscany, but we were still cut off from all news of friends in Northern Italy, and when I went for the first time after our liberation to Florence (in an Allied jeep) I found my mother's house at Fiesole, Villa Medici, very thoroughly equipped with booby-traps before the Germans had left it, while our own smaller house in the garden was still in flames. (I fell through a charred hole from the first floor on to a stone floor on the one below, but mercifully did not break my neck, and was given first aid by the young Irish officer in charge of the mine-detecting squad.)

After this, I began to work with the American Red Cross, taking medicine and clothing to villages just behind the lines, to be distributed (not without much friction) by the local Committees of Liberation. The need indeed was very great: I remember one village above Arezzo, suspected of having helped the partisans, in which no male creature between the ages of seven and seventy had been left alive: they had all been lined up one Sunday morning in the little piazza after Sunday Mass and shot. In the following year I drove up to Bologna, immediately behind the Allied troops, with the President of the Italian Red Cross, Umberto Zanotti Bianco, to act as his interpreter in the task of reorganising the local Red Cross. We found hospitals without doctors or nurses—the Fascist ones having fled and the anti-Fascist ones not yet returned. In Bologna I found, to my infinite relief, Elsa Dallolio and her seventy-year-old father, still alive. They had been forced to leave their country-house, between the main road and the main railway of the Gothic Line, before it was totally destroyed by shells.

In those months I was forced to become aware of what, in the wave of euphoria immediately after our liberation, I had not foreseen: the mutual misunderstandings (sometimes comic but often painful) between the liberators and the liberated, in which the members of all the countries concerned demonstrated their less endearing qualities, the swift end of the temporary mutual solidarity and union produced by times of crisis, and the rise of party struggle and class hatred, the disappointments and resentments which follow upon excessive hopes. One of the ugliest features of this period—the working off of individual grudges on political pretexts—was much less evident in a country district like ours than in the towns, and we were also entirely spared such bloodshed as took place immediately after the liberation in, for instance, Bologna, where the A.M.G. was able to do little to control the mock trials and summary executions of former Fascist officials and sympathisers by Communist partisans. In the country, on the other hand, it was particularly easy to foment social discontent, since it is not difficult to inculcate new hopes in times in which any change seems possible. And once changes began, they came, all over the country, with great speed. Even while rebuilding and re-planting were still going on, Communist cells were being formed at La Foce, under the direction of the provincial Communist centre in Siena, and very soon almost all our farmers were converted to the new doctrine which promised that, if they obeyed orders, they would swiftly come to own the land upon which they worked. The first step was, as elsewhere, the formation of a commission of their representatives, *le commissioni interne*, to represent in each *fattoria* the farmers' point of view and their requirements, of which the most immediate was the increase of the proportion of wheat allotted to the *contadino* from the traditional 50% to first 53% and then 57%. This was opposed by landowners' associations all over the country on the grounds that it would not leave a sufficient margin to keep up and improve the estates—in short, that the *mezzadria* would no longer work. I do not propose to dwell at length on the rights and wrongs of this controversy, which raged for three or four years; it is no longer relevant; what is certain is that Mazzei's forecast, that the *mezzadria* would break down on the day on which 'the conviction of its fairness' ceased, now proved to be true. Strikes were organised at the most crucial moments of the farmer's year, especially during the harvest; tenants who had received notice refused to leave; and ill-feeling ran so high for several years that, if we met two or three of our *contadini* together, they would refuse even to greet us. We had become 'the Enemies of the People', the abusers of the poor. The church was no longer attended, and in the school the children's essays stated, a little puzzled, that now all the *padroni* had become 'bad'. Even the women, when they wished to consult me about their children's health or schooling (for this they still did) would do so furtively, without telling their husbands or meeting mine. It was a painful, distressing period, in which all the evils—economic and social— that had been latent in the whole system of the *mezzadria* for so many centuries, came to the surface.

Often I wondered whether the root of all this dissension did not lie (as I had instinctively felt, when I first came here in my youth) in a failure in direct human communication: whether it would not have been possible, casting off the barriers of our respective inheritances of custom and class, to speak to each other more openly and simply, as we had done during the war, airing our respective grievances and opinions. But the habit of this should have been established long before; the old mutual reserve and mistrust had already sunk far too deep and were now deliberately fomented by those who wished to break up the old order. Now, when any new controversial question arose, it was merely the mouthpieces of two opposing orders, of two contrasting ways of life, who addressed each other: it was too late for individual understanding or compromise.

Moreover, though the actual question of the farmers' percentage was eventually settled by law, the real forces at work were far more deep-seated and complex. Plans were brought forward by the Left Wing of the government for the expropriation of all large estates, which were to be converted into small holdings, purchasable by the men who lived and worked upon them—*la terra ai contadini* was the slogan—but the scheme did not take into account that in the regions where large private properties had been most neglected, a great deal of preliminary basic work (draining, re-afforestation, road-building, etc.) would have to be done, whether by the State or with private capital, before such holdings could produce even a bare living for their new owners, and eventually—with the exception of the remarkable work done by the *Cassa del Mezzogiorno* in the South—these projects, for purely economic reasons, became a dead letter. For it was becoming evident that the new trend in Italian agriculture was only one aspect of far more complex changes, not only in Italy, but in the whole economic system of the Western world. The industrial boom in the North, as well as the increasing discontent in the country (partly caused by the absence of any government measures to protect the farmer by stabilising the cost of staple food-stuffs) all contributed to an exodus from the country to the city, only comparable with that which took place in the eleventh and twelfth centuries. The old patriarchal life, for good or ill, was over. No young man could find a bride to take back to his father's farm, since what girl would submit herself to the absolute rule of her mother-in-law, or cut herself for ever from the new, free life that the television had shown her? Above all, who was willing to give up independence? So one farm after another came to stand empty. Their inhabitants, in our region, did not often move (like the peasants of the South or of Sicily) to the large industrial cities of the North, but rather to Chianciano, the prosperous little water-ing-place nearby—where their savings sufficed to put up a small concrete house and open another *pensione* for summer visitors —or else to the towns with small factories in the Val di Chiana. Now, as I write (and the whole process has not taken more than ten years), only six out of our fifty-seven farms are still inhabited by their old tenants and are run *a mezzadria*; a few are lived in by skilled workmen, who can use the new machines: the others are slowly falling to pieces.

As far as the actual farming of the land was concerned, how-ever, Antonio, with great resilience, swiftly readjusted to the new conditions, and at once started to reorganise the estate on an entirely different basis, making use of much more machinery and, necessarily, of much less labour. The property has been divided into three parts, of which he only attempts to cultivate the one containing the best land. Here three artificial lakes have been built, with a total capacity of 460 thousand cubic metres, and with this water more than seven hundred additional acres of land are irrigated. The fodder thus acquired has enabled him greatly to increase the stock of cattle, from which both the grey *marem-mano* and the white *chianino* have been eliminated, giving place to the red and white *Simmenthal*, grown only for beef, not ploughing or dairy-farming. These are no longer scattered in various farms, as they used to be, but collected in three large farms with stabling in open sheds—some four hundred head in all, with four bulls. The pigs, too, have been increased, though their price, like that of beef, is of course dependent upon the fluctuations of the Common Market. In addition to the new machinery that has been purchased, tractors are hired from small local firms. The vine-yards and olive-groves have been increased, and the quality of the wine and oil greatly improved. Of the rest of the property, about a third is woodland; the rest is used for grazing or lies fallow.

But meanwhile, inexorably and steadily, the population continues to decrease. The Foce school, which once had ninety pupils, now has fifteen; the church is nearly empty. On Monte Amiata some villages consist entirely of old people and small children (who will join their parents, they hope, as soon as these have got good new jobs in town). It is possible that, within a generation, the woods will again spread down towards the Orcia, as they did ten centuries ago—and already, just across the valley, a large colony of Sardinian shepherds are grazing their sheep on what used to be cultivated fields.

> *Le vostre cose tutte hanno lor morte*
> *Sì come voi . . .* *

Sometimes, looking back upon all these changes and on the destruction or reversal of so many things that we have spent our lives in building up, we have been tempted to wonder whether all that time and energy was wasted, whether it has all been a mistake. I do not really think so. Paternalism has now practically become a dirty word, but I doubt whether, in the Val d'Orcia of 1925, a modicum of prosperity could have been restored without the employment of some private capital and the enthusiasm and direction of a few enlightened landowners. While the *consorzio di*

---

* 'All your possessions will meet their death,
  Even as you will . . .'
  DANTE: *Inferno*, XVI, 20.

bonifica was active, all the basic work that I have described *was* carried out: the erosion arrested, the woods re-planted, the roads, schools and houses built. Production did increase. The valley's inhabitants did gradually come to lead, as we had hoped, a less hard and poverty-stricken life. Workmen, who used to trudge many miles on foot before and after their day's work, were able to buy bicycles, then Vespas and motor-bicycles, and now mostly have their own cars. Buses took the children, when their first five years of local schooling were over, to secondary schools in Chianciano or Montepulciano. Every farm had its radio or television, every girl could buy some pretty clothes. If all this led to a further step—the desire for independence and city life—this was surely an inevitable and logical consequence, one aspect of a general evolution. We are not yet detached enough to appraise it, nor to see clearly where it will lead.

From a purely agricultural point of view, besides, the situation is even more complex. We cannot yet tell what part agriculture will play in the new industrialised Italy, nor indeed in the general economy of Europe. We may hope that, whatever form it may take, some of the basic work done in the last forty-five years, and recently brought up-to-date by mechanisation, will not have been wholly wasted, but we can be sure that, whatever developments there may be, they will take place within a new, perhaps a better, social pattern.

As for ourselves, we have been singularly fortunate. For forty-six years we have had the work we wanted, in the value of which we believed, and in a setting which has become more and more dear to us. And if we cannot foresee the future—what right have we to expect to do so, in this rapidly changing world?

*   *   *   *   *

Two other aspects of our personal life at La Foce have not yet been described: the making of a garden, which began as soon as we had any water, and the foundation of a permanent children's home in what used to be the nursery-school. During the war, as I have said, we used this for refugee children from Genoa and Turin and, when we had returned them all to their families, safe and sound, we felt that we should like to keep the home going for a similar purpose. Like every other country through which the War had passed, Italy at that time had a large number of orphaned, abandoned, illegitimate or under-nourished children—and it was for these, or for the children of refugees in concentration camps, that the home was then used. My intention was to keep it small enough to be as much like a family and as little like an institution as possible, and for this reason I have never accepted more than twenty children—both boys and girls, between the ages of four and twelve. But I soon realised that whatever we might do to make it homelike and welcoming, the greatest need of most of the children was for parents of their own. Many of them came from broken homes; some from sanatoria for tuberculosis (clinically cured but in need of a long time of convalescence) others from large, impersonal institutions where they had never had quite enough of anything: space, food, toys, instruction or love. (Some of the smaller ones, when first they arrived, shrank away from a kiss, expecting instead a blow.) Many showed the obvious symptoms of insecurity and instability that are the fruits of 'institutionalisation': nightmares, bed-wetting, backwardness, fits of temper or of fear; all had a deep craving for affection. Some took several years to become normal children again; others, under the wise guidance of the home's directress, Signorina Vera Berrettini (who was already in charge of the home during the war) recovered with remarkable speed. As soon as they were ready, I tried to find adoptive homes for them—at first in the U.S.A., through the International Social Service, with which I had already worked for several years, and recently, owing to a change in Italian adoption laws and also in the attitude to adoption in this country, in Italy. This, indeed, has now become the chief purpose of the *Casa dei Bambini*, which has now existed for twenty-six years.

Of the children who are not adopted, the boys go on to boarding schools when they are over twelve and, later on, are prepared for some profession or trade, but return here for their holidays and consider this their home—and often come back at Christmas and Easter, long after they are grown up, sometimes bringing with them their fiancées or their wives. Some have branched out into the world: one, after a successful career in the hotel business, is now helping to run some galleries of modern art; one is a prosperous business-man in America; two are working in the Fiat works in Turin; others have become accountants or clerks or, according to their ability, have learned various trades. One—half Chinese by origin—cannot bear any job in which he is not entirely independent, and so runs (very successfully) merry-go-rounds at fairs, but comes back to La Foce every year, to celebrate his birthday. "Where else would I celebrate it?" he says. Only one—the son of an alcoholic, sub-normal father—has failed to keep a job or make a life for himself. Of the girls, two have had their weddings at La Foce, others have become teachers or trained in the hotel-school at Chianciano, or have got other jobs in Florence. The greater part have married, and sometimes bring their babies to La Foce. But the happiest stories are those of the children who, while they were still quite small, found adoptive families of their own. Looking back, I remember— among many others—Pietro, a little half-blind foundling from southern Italy, who, at the age of five, could not even talk, and who is now the happy, independent fourteenth son of a large American family. I remember Jean, who came to us from Tunisia, unable to speak any language but French, and who is now also happily adopted in America; Paolo, a little boy of seven, whom the large institution in which he lived had described as 'a-social and un-adoptable', and who, after two years at La Foce, is now settled and happy with Italian parents in northern Italy. I remember Andrea, the son of an alcoholic mother who arrived here so frightened and dazed that he could hardly speak, and who is now completely reassured and secure after being adopted into a warm, extrovert, cheerful large Florentine family. I remember Giovanni, a bigger boy, so emotionally crippled by his mother's total rejection of him that for years he refused to consider attaching himself to any other family, but who has now found one in which he is taking the place of their own only son, killed in an accident. This long procession of children, renewing itself as surely as the succession of each year's crops, has perhaps been the most rewarding of all the gifts that La Foce has brought us.

One other enduring pleasure, throughout the years, has been the making of our garden. In the year after our marriage, my American grandmother—somewhat startled to find herself, in mid-summer, in a house in which there was so little water, even in the baby's bathroom—presented us with the wonderful gift of a pipe-line which, leading from a spring in the beech-wood at the top of our hill (some six miles away) brought us our first abundant water-supply. It then became possible to plan, not only new bathrooms, but a kitchen-garden and flower-garden, which gradually grew, year by year, in proportion to our means and to the water available. First, at the back of the house, I made a small enclosed Italian garden: a stone fountain with two dolphins and a small lawn around it, and a few flower-beds edged with box. A couple of years later, we made another larger terrace, passing through two pillars of travertine with ornamental vases into a less formal flower-garden, with wide borders of flowering shrubs, herbaceous plants and annuals, big lemon-pots on stone bases, a shady bower of wisteria and banksia roses, and a paved terrace with a balustrade, looking down over the valley, on which we would dine on summer nights when, just before the harvest, the whole garden would be alight with fireflies and the air heavy with nicotiana and jasmine. On the walls, in the spring, grow great clumps of aubretia and alyssum and, later on, rhyncospernum and climbing roses, and the grass is edged with daffodils and irises. Some steps—for the whole garden is on a fairly steep hillside— lead up to an avenue of cypresses and a rose-garden, while a wide pergola winds round the hillside towards the woods. Finally, just before the war, we made another enclosed formal garden— designed, like the first, by our friend and architect Cecil Pinsent, with hedges of cypress and box and big trees of magnolia grandi-flora, while the rest of the hill above has been gradually trans-formed into a half-wild garden with Japanese fruit-trees and Judas-trees, forsythia, philadelphus, pomegranates and single roses, long hedges of lavender and banks fragrant with thyme, mint and assynth, and great clumps of broom. Gradually, by experiment and failure, I learned what would or would not stand the cold winters and the hot, dry summer winds. I gave up any attempt, in my borders, at growing delphiniums, lupins or phlox, as well as many other herbaceous plants; and I learned, too, to put our lemon-trees, plumbago and jasmine under shelter before the winter. But roses flourish in the heavy clay soil, and so do peonies and lilies, while the dry hillside is where lavender thrives —a blue sea in June, buzzing with the bees whose honey is flavoured with its pungent taste, which also, in the winter, not only scents our linen but kindles our fires. Every year, the garden grows more beautiful; even the war brought no greater destruction than the shelling of a few cypress trees. The woods were already carpeted, according to the season, with wild violets, crocuses, cyclamen, anemone *alpina*, and autumn colchicum, and among these I also managed to naturalise some other kinds of anemones, daffodils and a few scillas. But bluebells I have failed with, and the exquisite scarlet and gold tulips which grow in the fields round San Quirico, just across the valley, still stubbornly refuse to flower here.

A path through the woods leads to a little chapel of travertine, with a churchyard round it, which we built in 1933, when our only son Gianni died, and here he is buried. At the time of his death in Fiesole—since the greater part of the eight happy years of his childhood had been spent at La Foce, and every inch of the house and garden, every field and tree, seemed full of his presence —I felt that I could not bear to come back. But we did return, almost at once, and I have always been glad that we did so. We have, of course, never ceased to miss our son—perhaps even more bitterly in old age than in youth. We have had many ups and downs and have made many mistakes. We have had periods of discouragement, in which we wondered if we had not taken on a task beyond our strength. There have even been moments in which, driving up the old winding road from Rome and catching a first glimpse of the grim towers of Radicofani, we have felt as if we hated the whole place and everything connected with it. But I do not think that either of us has seriously wished that we had chosen to live somewhere else, nor to lead another sort of life. The fascination of the Val d'Orcia held—and still holds.

Now we are both growing old and La Foce is too cold for us in winter. But it is still our home; we live there when we can. Antonio still takes an active part in managing the farm, and I still enjoy the children and the garden.

A friend, who has stayed with us in recent years, once wrote to me: 'I sometimes think that your garden is like an allegory of life itself: one passes from the warm, sheltered house into the formal garden, with its fountain and flowers and intricate box hedges, then coasts the hillside under the pergola of vines. The view opens out on to tilled fields, the flowers become rarer; one

254

passes into the path through the woods. Here it is darker; the wind stirs in the branches. A few steps more, walking uphill in the shade, and one has reached the still chapel, with those four stone walls around it.'

Up that path, when the time comes, we both hope to go.

Epilogue

"I don't know where to go."
"Neither do I. Let's go together."
IGNAZIO SILONE

THE PATTERN is set now—though not all set down—and I am looking back upon my life. What do I see? For every life is not only a string of events: it is also a myth.

First of all, perhaps, one should ask: is it possible to see one's own life? "What the devil then am I?" cried Carlyle at the age of eighty, as he was drying his old bones after his bath. "After all these eighty years I know nothing at all about it."

To 'see' one's life (though the end is lacking—and perhaps that is why it is so difficult: perhaps, when the end has come, the pieces may fall into place and form a pattern) one should surely try to look back upon it with as much detachment as if it were someone else's. Humboldt, I think, was saying something of this kind when he spoke of history as 'a landscape of clouds'. 'The man who is within it, can see nothing. It is only by looking at it from some way off, that he can perceive how clear and various it is.' It is the experience of the traveller whose plane has broken through a bank of clouds and who looks down upon a vast, billowy sea, constantly changing its shape, forming new valleys and new peaks.

A friend of mine whom I asked if he could look back as detachedly as this upon his life replied that he had succeeded in doing so in regard to every part of it except the immediate past. He vividly remembered both what he saw and felt up to a few years ago, but could no longer identify himself with his own past emotions, any more than if they had belonged to a character in a novel or a play: "The stage setting is still there, but the lights have gone out."

I do not think that I could say quite the same, at least not yet, though it would be true of many parts of my life. The child riding her donkey on the Nubian sands; the schoolgirl reading the *Iliad* with Monti; the self-conscious débutante in the English country-house—they are me and they are no longer me. 'We are like the relict garment of a Saint,' said Keats, 'the same and not the same:

256

for the careful Monks patch it and patch it: till there's not a thread of the original garment left, and still they show it for St. Anthony's shirt.'

Yet there is something that remains. If I think back, I can sometimes recapture certain intense moments of feeling: the hour beside the Nile when I saw that my father's tent had been taken up and suddenly knew that he was dead; the evening on which I read, on the terrace of the Villa Medici, the letter from Antonio which, after six months of separation, renewed our engagement and determined the course of our life; the night, forty-four years ago, on which, immediately after Gianni's birth, I heard the Florentine bells ring out and saw the sky lit up with fireworks for St. John's Eve, and felt happiness sweep over me. Proust, who cultivated the art of memory as perhaps no-one else has ever done, would say that these recollections have always been part of me. He wrote in *Du Coté de Chez Swann* that in later life he was able again to hear certain sounds which 'in reality had never stopped', the sobs which had shaken him at a certain moment of his childhood. 'It is only because life is now growing silent about me', he wrote, 'that I hear them afresh, like convent bells which one might believe were not rung nowadays, because during the day they are drowned by the city hubbub, but which may be heard clearly enough in the stillness of the evening.'

If Proust is right, I am carrying within me (in spite of all the changes that have taken place) the *whole* of my life, from the day when 'the arable field of events' first lay before me, until the moment in which the typewriter is tapping out these words. And certainly it is also true that some of the memories I can now summon up have a greater intensity than the events themselves seemed to possess at the time, or rather—since memory has a filter of its own, sometimes surprising in what it suppresses or retains, but always significant—some of them stand out in disproportionate clarity to the rest.

Bernard Berenson once said in his old age that if he were a beggarman on a street corner, he would stretch out his hand to every passer-by, begging for 'more time, more time!' I do not agree with him. I should like, of course—for I enjoy living—to have a few more years (provided all my faculties remained) in which to watch my grandchildren growing up, to see a little more of the world and of the overwhelming changes that are taking place in it and, above all, to see a little more clearly into myself. But the time I would really beg for, at any street corner, would be *time in the past*, time in which to comfort, to complete and to repair—time wasted before I knew how quickly it would slip by.

Most of us, however well we may know that remorse is fruitless, carry in our memories some heavy burdens, and perhaps at least one so poignant that we can hardly bear to look back on it: a weight of sadness and regret, a knowledge that we have failed even those who needed us most—especially those, since with other people one is not upon that plane at all. Nor is it of much consolation to realise that almost everyone, while life is actually going on, is constantly being distracted by irrelevances. Just as, in travel, one may miss seeing the sunset because one cannot find the ticket-office or is afraid of missing the train, so in even the closest human relationships a vast amount of time and of affection is drained away in minor misunderstandings, missed opportunities, and failures in consideration or understanding. It is only in memory that the true essence remains.

The question then arises: how much of these memories can be conveyed? How much can or should one tell? 'I believe,' said Keats, 'in the holiness of the heart's affections.' But what is holy is also *private*: as soon as it is told, some of its essence may be distilled, diminished, perhaps lost for ever. Yet one should, I think, at least refrain from suppressing—unless this implies the violation of someone else's privacy—what has given, in some period of the past, the greatest meaning to being alive at all, and now that this book is drawing to an end I realise that to have confined myself merely to a passing mention of Gianni, of Elsa Dallolio, and of one or two other friends, is so large an omission as to falsify the whole picture. One of the reasons why I have refrained until now has been because I was afraid of saying either too little or too much, and I still fear this now. Yet I found no difficulty in writing about my father. I think that this was partly because I was less than eight years old when he died, so that my memories of him, though poignant, are still a child's, and I can call them up with a certain detachment. But with Gianni and Elsa I have never achieved this, nor do I wish for it. I remember Elsa once saying, in connection with the waves of longing for Gianni which would sometimes come over me many years after his death, that I should not fight against them, since they were what was left to me of him, his living presence within me. "Otherwise all that is left is memory, which becomes static, a composition of lines and planes, like the rows of graves in a churchyard." But how can one recapture, except for those who knew him, the essence of a child? I can say: he was generous, gay, sweet-natured, apprehensive, gentle, and above all, loving—but what are all these, but a list of words? A child's life is movement: if you arrest the movement, choose one quality and pin it down, you give the solidity of a grown-up person's character; the fluidity, the ever-growing, quick-changing life is gone. He was not a particularly imaginative child, in the sense of living in a world of his own or of making up many 'pretending' games; all his imagination seemed to go into his intuition about other people's feelings, and a consequent gentle considerateness and almost fierce loyalty. He had, too, a quality not unusual in sensitive children, but very difficult to define: a certain spiritual *integrity*, an instinctive rejection of whatever was insincere, gushing or slightly silly. His greatest security was with his gentle, serene, old English Nanny; his greatest friend, Ugo, the gardener's little boy at La Foce; but he also had friends everywhere else, both among children and grown-ups. I used to like to watch him sitting on the lawn at Westbrook with his great-uncle Bronson, both apparently equally absorbed in serious conversation, or walking with Charlie Meade, looking up and saying: "Do you know, Charlie?" in a rather confidential grown-up voice.

Many people who wrote to me after his death used the same word—'radiance'—and indeed I can think of no better one. But it cannot bring back the love of life which would shine in his face as he burst into my room in the mornings, or which echoed in his voice, as he snuggled down in his pillow at bedtime, saying, "More fun tomorrow." Of his long-drawn-out, terrible illness (he died of tubercular meningitis)—during which he himself asked me what death was—I cannot bear and do not wish to write. A few months after his death, some American friends, who had stayed with us in the country with their children a couple of years before, asked me if I would like to see a film they had taken at La Foce. I agreed, not realising what I would see—and then, as we sat in the darkened room, could not believe my eyes: there was

Gianni running down the wood path towards me, running and laughing. It is so that I wish to remember him.

* * * * *

It is still more difficult, in a very different way, to write about my friendship with Elsa. For twenty-five years, whenever I was in Rome, we saw each other almost daily. We worked together during the war in the Prisoners of War Office of the Italian Red Cross—and sometimes, in the evenings, I would join her in her own house with a briefcase of papers, on which we continued to work before the little brick stove in her bedroom, eating our meagre rations, until it was time for me to return home late at night through the darkened, silent city. Later on, after two years of separation, during which she was living in her country house, which was completely destroyed by bombing, on the northern side of the Gothic Line, and I on the southern, neither of us knowing whether we should see each other again—I arrived in Bologna with the President of the Italian Red Cross, only two days after the Allied troops, to bring her and her ninety-year-old father, General Dallolio, back to Rome again. She was with me when both my daughters were born. She stayed with us, until her health no longer allowed it, at Lerici and La Foce, meeting Antonio there upon common ground, since she, too, was a countrywoman at heart. She helped me with every line of my books. I was with her when she died. She is buried in the churchyard at La Foce. These are the bare facts: they do not reveal the quality of the friendship. Differing in age, in nationality, in upbringing, in our circle of friends, we found, in Montaigne's words, a friendship 'in which we could no longer find the seam that had joined us together'. Possibly one thread in the bond between us was the fact that I found with her the relationship that I had always wished and failed to have with my mother, and that to her I was, as well as a friend, the daughter she had never had. But this is an over-simplification, and also suggests an inequality which was certainly not there. Friendship—any close friendship—is so *various*, made up of so many strands: companionship, the sharing of laughter, grief and anxiety, and then common work and common tastes— in people, books, art, manners, and above all, in values. In addition there is, or can be, between friends of the same sex, a great feeling of relaxation: less danger of emotional complications, nothing to suppress or conceal, but comfort, trust, security, and delight—and an exchange that makes no demands. One can afford to be—perhaps it is only in such company that one ever becomes—fully oneself. *'Lui seul jouissait de ma vraie image, et l'emporta.'*

Not only did we work together during the war, but when it was over, Elsa was the first reader and critic of all my books. I am naturally, in my writing, both impulsive and inaccurate. 'Three years later', I would specify (when in point of fact it was five), and many pages would be scattered with incomplete quotations and inaccurate references or dates. All these she firmly set right—but her help came to a great deal more than this. Though she never published a line of her own, she possessed what Leopardi called *'le grand goût, le goût véritable'*, a touchstone for many of her friends, both in art and life. For it was always for other people that she worked, never for herself. Many widely different people relied upon her judgement, her unfailing recognition of what was or was not first-rate—among others, Marguerite Caetani, the founder of the international review, *Botteghe Oscure*, who seldom reached a decision without seeking her advice, especially about new young authors. Incurably averse to any form of limelight and solitary both by temperament and circumstances, she yet possessed, to the day of her death, *'l'esprit jeune'*, and it was this which drew to her high, shadowy, book-lined room a great many young writers from different countries. They might come the first time a little doubtfully, fearing to find a dull old lady: and then they came back again. For she had another quality, almost unique in the present day: she was always there. She found, too, a great deal of entertainment and interest in these contacts: people and books, these were what she liked best, and by this channel both came to her. In later years, too, many visitors began to tire her, but always her mind remained equally alert and inquiring, though the actual effort of concentration became a burden. Sometimes, then, I would still try to make plans for her—gradually dwindling, as time went on. First they would be for a very small country house in Tuscany, not too far away from ours, to take the place, at least in part, of her own house near Bologna, entirely destroyed during the war; then merely for a small balcony outside her room, on which she could sit out, and grow some flowers—plumbago, jasmine, petunias, and a rose saved from her own old garden—or an occasional drive on a country road or to some Roman sight she wished to see again. For she possessed, both for the beauty of the Italian landscape and for its works of art, the unfading, discriminating passion that is generally only granted to those who have in them also a drop of foreign blood. "I can never understand how one can get *accustomed* to Italy," she once said to me: "for me it is always a fresh surprise, which catches at my heart."

La progettista, she would call me, as I turned up with another plan, and joined me in pretending that it might take shape. But slowly, inexorably, the horizon drew in. I still brought her occasional glimpses of the outer world, so long as they amused her: new books, picture-catalogues, stories about common friends or distant journeys (though these she thought rather unnecessary). What she liked to hear best was news of what was happening at La Foce, in the country life she most missed. "Go on," she would say, "tell me a story *che mi faccia compagnia*." Then, very gradually, even this became too much, too remote from the journey for which she was preparing. I learned fully to accept what I had known, but fought against, for a long time: that the changes that any of us can bring into a friend's life, however close the bond, are very much more limited than one had believed in youth, that there is only a very restricted field in which we can help each other. Physical pain, acute anxiety, the accumulated burden of the past, these are matters that the most devoted affection may assuage but cannot change or heal. And yet, is this wholly true? In the long run—the very long run—of any deep relationship, who is the giver and who the receiver? In what scales can affection be weighed, and its transmuting power? How far may the ripples in the pool extend, even after the people directly concerned have ceased to exist? One cannot answer these questions: one can only wonder.

All I know is that for many years, up to the last day of her life, to me as to her other close friends, Elsa gave a far rarer gift than any that we brought her: she gave us peace. I have never quite understood—I still do not—how this happened. There she would be, sitting by her window in her dimly-lit, book-lined room, full of papers, pictures and small objects, with a brown rug over her legs and a pen in her hand, sometimes correcting someone else's proofs—almost always in discomfort, often in pain—and one would come in with a long list of worries, irritations and anxieties, or else of hopes and plans. She would listen and—or so it seemed at the time—hardly interrupt at all, except with an occasional smile or dry comment. But as one came away, one suddenly realised that all the anxieties and uncertainties had fallen into their right place, assumed their true proportions. We had meant to cheer her up and comfort her; we went away comforted.

I should like to say something, too, about some of my other friendships with people of many different nationalities and ages, and belonging to very different social worlds. They have been men and women, old and young, writers, scholars and musicians, lawyers, diplomats and travellers, teachers and social workers, or just—without any label—people with whom I feel secure and at home. But—since I have never belonged anywhere to an enclosed and harmonious social circle—they have seldom felt equally at home with each other. They have had widely different backgrounds and tastes and have often disliked each other. On the whole, these friendships have brought me a more constant and steady happiness than any other factor in my life, and many of them still endure. But the only one that has been upon a plane similar to Elsa's has been in England, and has been not only with one person but with a whole family—I would almost say, with a house: Pen y Lan, the country house in Wales of my mother's cousin Charlie Meade, and his wife, Aileen.

I first entered Pen y Lan forty-five years ago, on my first visit to England after my marriage and, until Charlie and Aileen moved to live in London a few years ago, it never occurred to me to go to England without staying with them—always assured of the same unfailing, warm, relaxed welcome. The doors and the French windows into the garden were always open—metaphorically and literally—with children and dogs wandering in and out, and the scent of cherry-pie, pinks and roses mingled with that of the wood-fire and the old leather bindings in the library. One came in, stood for a moment in the hall with its white columns and curved, broad staircase, looked down over the valley—and was enfolded by peace. Aileen might be in the garden, pricking out seedlings, Charlie at his typewriter, writing about the Himalayas (or perhaps not writing much, but travelling back there in his memory, with his clear blue eyes lit up as by a celestial vision); one of the three enchanting little girls—Coney, Pin and Flavia— would be picking raspberries or strumming upon the piano, another catching and saddling her pony, and the youngest dabbling her toes in the garden pool. But as the car drew up, there they would all be around one, and one had come home. Occasionally too, Charlie's Swiss Alpine guide and close friend, Pierre Blanc, would be staying there, and there would be endless talk between them about old climbs in the Alps or the Himalayas—"Bumbling", said Aileen—and when suppertime came, "*Ah, la bonne soupe!*" Pierre would cry. "*Ça rafraîchit les intestins, ca ramollit les boyaux!*" A very few years later, Charlie's son, Simon, was born—and it is now he who lives at Pen y Lan with his wife and children, so that the house we all loved is still alive.

Yet in any case, I think, it would still be alive for all of us— since it was, like Heaven, not a place but a state. I still do not quite know how to account for that condition of security and bliss, which innumerable other guests have felt quite as strongly as I. Perhaps it was partly, as at Westbrook and Desart, the emanation of a singularly happy marriage (though of course I am not pretending that its owners,like the rest of us, did not have their share, in the course of the years, of anxiety and grief), partly the gentle beauty of the lie of the land: the steep green hill behind the house, the little stream beside it, where cyclamen from La Foce swiftly took root and spread, and the wide valley below, with its poplars beside the river and (I always seem to have been there in summer) the fragrance of new-mown hay. Partly that the food was so delicious, that we all laughed so much, that everyone was free to do as he pleased—to 'help' (or more often hinder) in the garden, to climb the hill, to wander in the valley, or to sit in the broad library window-seat piled with books, old and new.

> I remember a house where all were good
> To me, God knows, deserving no such thing:
> Comforting smell breathed at very entering
> Fetched fresh, as I suppose, from some sweet wood.

And, in addition to all this, I could talk to Aileen, in particular, as I have never been able to talk to anyone else but Elsa: a com-

pletely free, unselfconscious exchange—I think on both sides—
which has now lasted for over forty-five years.

Now the old life at Pen y Lan has naturally to some extent
changed, but a very odd thing has happened. Charlie and Aileen
have moved, partly for reasons connected with their health, to a
flat in Onslow Square, in London, taking with them only a few
pieces of their furniture and some pictures. Yet, in some
strange way, it is still Pen y Lan that one finds in that small square
sitting-room. Their children feel this, too, and—apart from their
devoted affection to their parents—come back, when they can,
almost daily to find it—not of course the space and the beauty,
the glowing fragrant garden and the wide valley— yet something
that evokes and includes all these.

As for myself, who now only go to England once or twice a
year, I have only to come in by the door—greeted by the deafening
barks of the small wire-haired dachshund, Tiger—to feel the
years slip away and know that I am again secure. The brilliant
window-boxes of the first years, containing in miniature the same
exquisite mixture of colours as in the flower-beds around the pool
at Pen y Lan, or in the posies on the visitor's dressing-table, are
now no longer kept up, but there are still patterns of brocade
hanging over the back of at least one of the shabby armchairs—
and still, as at Pen y Lan, one thinks it likely that, at one's next
visit, the chair will still be uncovered. Aileen's welcome is still as
warm, even if she cannot now clearly see one's face, or read the
books which used to pile up on her bed; and Charlie's expression
still has the same kindness and selflessness; there is still the same
sense of harmony. And here too, as at Pen y Lan, the daughters
and their children and grandchildren wander in and out—one
bringing a basket of country apples or a great tub of flowers,
another setting to work in the kitchen, and yet another just sitting
down to gossip and giggle. Then another old friend comes in and
reads aloud an absurd headline in the evening paper, or a poem
from an old common-place book—and soon everyone is laughing,
though I cannot quite remember why. What is it that makes it all
so comfortable, so warm? Plainly it can only be something in the
essential character of our hosts, that has overcome misfortune,
straitened means and the passage of time. I think one can only
call it goodness.

Do the walls of a house sometimes become imbued with the nature of its inhabitants? I think so—and indeed, why should it not be so? Many people would agree that there are certain places whose walls are impregnated by centuries of faith and prayer: I am thinking in particular of some little fishing-village churches in Britanny, and of the crypt of San Michele Archangelo on the Gargano, where, throughout the Middle Ages, pilgrims and Crusaders would come to pray before setting off for the Holy Land. And so, too, I believe that, on a more modest scale, the walls of some private houses may also be coloured either by good or evil: in short, by the character of those who live there.

With friends such as these, long ago, all assessments, criticisms or doubts have become irrelevant: one can cast off all unnecessary garments. And perhaps the easy, friendly talk that is then possible is indeed, as Virginia Woolf once suggested, a preparation for a final retreat. 'Do you suppose', she wrote, 'that we are now coming like the homing rooks back to the top of our trees and that all this cawing is the beginning of settling in for the night?'

*   *   *   *   *

And now we are back where we started. If life is indeed 'a perpetual allegory', if what we seek in it is awareness, understanding, then the small stream of events I have set down here has only been a means—a means to what? I seem to have been diverted a long way from my original inquiry, but perhaps it has not really been so very far, since it has only been through my affections that I have been able to perceive, however imperfectly, some faint 'intimations of immortality', a foretaste, perhaps, granted to the short-sighted of another, transcendental love.

Looking back at the first thirty years of my life, two events have an outstanding significance: my father's death, when I was seven and a half, and Gianni's, when he was the same age that I was then. And both of these events are significant for the same reason—that neither of them was an ending. I do not mean of course that there was not the pain of *parting*—but that separation did not prevent my father's personality from pervading my childhood, as Gianni's has pervaded the rest of my life. Since then, a few years ago, there has been the death of Elsa, the closest companion of my middle age, and the same has been true about her. I am not

266

speaking now about an orthodox belief in 'another life'—nor am I entering upon the complex question of the survival of personality. All that I can affirm is what I know of my own experience: that though I have never ceased to miss my father, child and friend, I have also never lost them. They have been to me, at all times, as real as the people I see every day, and it is this, I think, that has conditioned my whole attitude both to death and to human affections.

It is very easy, on this subject, to become sentimental or woolly, or to say more than one really means. I think I am only trying to say something very simple: that my own personal experience has given me a very vivid sense of the continuity of love, even after death, and that it has also left me believing in the truth of Burke's remark that society—or I should prefer to say, life itself—is 'a partnership not only between those who are living, but between those who are living, those who are dead, and those who are to be born'. Not only are we not alone, but we are not living only in a bare and chilly now. We are irrevocably bound to the past—and no less irrevocably, though the picture is less clear to us, to the future. It is this feeling that has made death seem to me not less painful, never that—for there is no greater grief than that of parting—but not, perhaps, so very important, and has caused affection, in its various forms, to be the guiding thread of my life.

At the time of Gianni's death, I received a letter from George Santayana (who in his later years to some extent returned, at least in feeling, to his Spanish, Catholic origins) which expresses, far better than I ever could, my feelings upon this subject.

. . . We have no claim to any of our possessions. We have no claim to exist; and, as we have to die in the end, so we must resign ourselves to die piecemeal, which really happens when we lose somebody or something that was closely intertwined with our existence. It is like a physical wound; we may survive, but maimed and broken in that direction; dead there.

Not that we can, or ever do at heart, renounce our affections. Never that. We cannot exercise our full nature all at once in every direction; but the parts that are relatively in abeyance, their centre lying perhaps in the past or the future, belong to us inalienably. We should not be ourselves if we cancelled them.

I don't know how literally you may believe in another world, or whether the idea means very much to you. As you know, I am not myself a believer in the ordinary sense, yet my *feeling* on this subject is like that of believers, and not at all like that of my fellow-materialists. The reason is that I disagree utterly with that modern philosophy which regards *experience* as fundamental. Experience is a mere whiff or rumble, produced by enormously complex and ill-deciphered causes of experience; and in the other direction, experience is a mere peephole through which glimpses come down to us of eternal things. These are the only things that, in so far as we are spiritual beings, we can find or can love at all. All our affections, when clear and pure and not claims to possession, transport us to another world; and the loss of contact, here or there, with those eternal beings is merely like closing a book which we keep at hand for another occasion.*

About more orthodox beliefs, I am very hesitant to write, for fear of saying a little more or less than I mean or than is true. I have spent a good deal of my life in various forms of wishful thinking—trying to persuade myself, in one way or another, that things were a little better than they really were: my feelings or convictions deeper, and situations pleasanter or clearer, than was in fact the case—and I think it is time to stop. For this is what Plato called 'the true lie', the lie in the soul, 'hated by gods and men', of which the lie in words is 'only a kind of imitation and shadowy image'.

Yet it is also true that all my life (though not steadily, but rather in fitful waves) I have been seeking a meaning, a framework, a goal—I should say, more simply, God. '*Tu ne me chercherais pas si tu ne m'avais trouvé,*' was Pascal's reply—but is this not too easy a way out for a fitful purpose and a vacillating mind? I remember a passage in Julian Green's *Journal*: '*Je lis les mystiques comme on lit les récits des voyageurs qui reviennent de pays lointains ou l'on sait bien que l'on n'ira jamais. On voudrait visiter la Chine, mais quel voyage! Et pourtant je crois que jusqu'à la fin de mes jours je conserverai ce déraisonnable espoir.*'

* Published in *The Letters of George Santayana*, ed. Daniel Cory, London: Constable & Co.; New York: Charles Scribner's Sons.

Epilogue

That 'unreasonable hope' is always latent: one should perhaps open the door to it more often. Someone to whom I once spoke about these matters suggested that instead of nourishing a sense of guilt for what one cannot comprehend or fully accept, it would be better to start by dwelling upon what one honestly can believe. I think the advice is good, and have tried to ask myself that question.

I have seen and believe in goodness: the indefinable quality which is immediately and unhesitatingly recognised by the most different kinds of men: the simple goodness of an old nurse or the mother of a large family; the more complex and costly goodness of a priest, a doctor or a teacher. When such people are also believers, their beliefs are apt to be *catching*—or so I myself, at least, have found. It is the Eastern principle of the *guru* and his disciples: goodness and faith conveyed (or perhaps evil and disbelief dispelled) by an actual, living presence.

The outstanding instance in our lifetime has been that of Pope John XXIII. I do not think that anyone—believer or agnostic—who was present in St. Peter's Square during the Mass said for him as he lay dying could fail to have a sense of what was meant by 'the communion of the faithful', or to receive a dim apprehension of his own vision of 'one flock and one shepherd', of the love of mankind as a whole. And if, since then, the realisation of this dream has been full of complexities, and many minds have been disturbed and confused by conflicts, upheavals and innovations, the vision still endures.

I believe in the dependence of people upon each other. I believe in the light and warmth of human affection, and in the disinterested acts of kindness and compassion of complete strangers. I agree with Simone Weil that 'charity and faith, though distinct, are inseparable'—and I share her conviction 'whoever is capable of a movement of pure compassion (which incidentally is very rare) towards an unhappy man, possesses, implicitly but truly, faith and the love of God'.

I believe, not theoretically, but from direct personal experience, that very few of the things that happen to us are purposeless or accidental (and this includes suffering and grief—even that of others), and that sometimes one catches a glimpse of the link between these happenings. I believe—even when I am myself being blind and deaf, or even indifferent—in the existence of a mystery.

Beyond this, I still do not know—nor do I feel inclined to examine here—how far I can go. Yet I derive comfort, at times, from a passage in one of Dom John Chapman's letters. 'There is worry and anxiety and trouble and bewilderment, and there is also an unfelt, yet real acquiescence in being anxious, troubled and bewildered, and a consciousness that the *real* self is at peace, while the anxiety and worry are unreal. It is like a peaceful lake, whose surface reflects all sorts of changes, because it is calm.'

A still lake, ruffled only upon the surface: a world of clouds, through which it is possible to break to the light—are these indeed metaphors more true than I can yet fully perceive?

> Man is one world, and hath
> Another to attend him.

Index

Index

273

Index

Index

Index

United States, 3, 20 99

Vaccari, Professor, 136–37
Val di Chiana, 204, 208, 248
Val d'Orcia, 127, 199; history of, 200–201; farming in, 204–208; customs in, 208–11; war comes to, 233–34, post-war changes in, 249
Valentino, Italian chauffeur, 97
Valtancoli, Angelo, 187n.
Verleth, Judith, 15–16
Verney, Desmond, 58, 69
Verney, Major-General Gerald, 58, 68, 162, 163
Verney, Lady Joan, 18, 51, 69, 171
Verney, Joy (Hon. Mrs. G. Hamilton Russell), 58
Verney, Lt-Colonel Ulick, 58, 170
Vevey, 108
Vittos, Dr., 117
Voltaire, F.-M. Arouet de, 184

Wagner, Richard, 193
Walcott, Senator, 231
Walpole, Horace, 114, 115
Walsh, Alice, 165

Walter, Bruno, 229
Ward, George, 30, 31
Washington, 31, 32
Weibel, Fraulein, 119, 120–21
Weil, Simone, 269
Wenlock, Constance, Lady, 126–27
West, Rebecca, 179
Westbrook, 18–20, 20n., 28, 34, 36–37, 39
Wharton, Edith, 14, 21, 23–25, 30–31, 80–81, 95, 132
White, Stanford, 23
Wilde, Oscar, 68
Winthrop, Egerton, 23
Woolf, Miss, 102, 146
Woolf, Leonard, 176
Woolf, Virginia, 173, 174, 175, 176, 192, 193, 266
Wortley Montagu, Lady Mary, 96

Yeats, William Butler, 23, 55, 56
Yonge, Charlotte, 144, 155
Yucatan, 3

Zanotti Bianco, Senatore Umberto, 245

278